Advance Praise for

SIR LEWIS

"*Sir Lewis* is an engrossing, deeply detailed portrait of a powerful role model that transcends sport. This book is timeless, illuminating, and necessary."
—Mirin Fader, author of *New York Times* bestseller *Giannis* and *Dream*

"A thought-provoking contribution to the literature of race, sports, and society, Michael Sawyer's riveting narrative brings fuller context to the rise of Lewis Hamilton as the first Black, winningest race car driver, and worldwide tastemaker. This is a must read."
—Tamara Payne, Pulitzer Prize and National Book Award–winning author of *The Dead Are Arising*

"Gripping storytelling. An insightful examination of race and class. Sawyer takes us on a journey of Lewis Hamilton's career as a race driver, human, and humanitarian, one that is passionate, humorous, sympathetic, and critical. Ultimately, we come away as fans and, more importantly, better versions of ourselves. This book is a reminder that sports still have so much to teach us about ourselves and our world and that, in our current moment, there are sports icons among us who not only can inspire us but hold a mirror up for us to see who we are and how we must change. This is a book that I will read again and again to be entertained and challenged."
—Myisha Cherry, author of *The Case for Rage*

"With *Sir Lewis*, Michael E. Sawyer has given us one of the most probative books on Formula One since Tom Rubython's *The Life of Senna*. In a manner very much akin to what C. L. R. James did for the great Trinidadian cricketer Sir Leari Constantine in *Beyond a Boundary*, Sawyer takes us beyond the body to the bones of Lewis Hamilton's career. Through a deeply engaged, knowledgeable study of Hamilton's impact on the art and technology of Formula One racing, we discover how that impact reflects profound global socio-political transformation."

—R. A. Judy, author of *Sentient Flesh* and winner of the Truman Capote Award for Literary Criticism

SIR LEWIS

MICHAEL E. SAWYER

LEGACY
LIT

New York   Boston

Legacy Lit
Hachette Book Group
1290 Avenue of the Americas
New York, NY 10104
LegacyLitBooks.com
@LegacyLitBooks

First Edition: March 2025

Legacy Lit is an imprint of Grand Central Publishing. The Legacy Lit name and logo are registered trademarks of Hachette Book Group, Inc.

The publisher is not responsible for websites (or their content) that are not owned by the publisher.

The Hachette Speakers Bureau provides a wide range of authors for speaking events. To find out more, go to hachettespeakersbureau.com or email HachetteSpeakers@hbgusa.com.

Legacy Lit books may be purchased in bulk for business, educational, or promotional use. For information, please contact your local bookseller or the Hachette Book Group Special Markets Department at special.markets@hbgusa.com.

Library of Congress Cataloging-in-Publication Data
Names: Sawyer, Michael E., author.
Title: Sir Lewis / Michael E. Sawyer.
Description: First edition. | New York, NY : Legacy Lit, [2025] | Includes bibliographical references.
Identifiers: LCCN 2024044026 | ISBN 9781538769744 (hardcover) | ISBN 9781538769768 (ebook)
Subjects: LCSH: Hamilton, Lewis, 1985– | Automobile racing drivers—Great Britain—Biography. | Automobile racing—Great Britain—History. | Grand Prix racing—Great Britain—History.
Classification: LCC GV1032.H33 S28 2025 | DDC 796.72092—dc23/eng/20240923
LC record available at https://lccn.loc.gov/2024044026

ISBN: 9781538769744 (hardcover), 9781538769768 (ebook)

Printed in the United States of America

LSC-C

Printing 1, 2024

This book is dedicated to my parents, Theresa and Ernest Sawyer,
who taught me to love sports and, more importantly,
to understand that heroes are not defined by wins and losses.

For all the kids out there, who dream the impossible . . .

Lewis Hamilton

CONTENTS

INTRODUCTION

Met Gala
Metropolitan Museum of Art
New York, New York
September 13, 2021

Lewis Hamilton entered the Met Gala in a custom-made suit, looking none the worse for almost being killed on a legendary racetrack on a beautiful fall day in Italy. It may seem strange to open a book about a Formula One race car driver from Great Britain with an event in New York City that has become the fashion world's equivalent of the Oscars. Like all of these types of events, the Met Gala is a "who's who" of celebrities, fashion industry elites, and global socialites. They convene annually to pose for the cameras and see who wears what from whom. In 2021, the event had been moved from its usual time on the first Monday in May to the thirteenth of September because of the COVID-19 pandemic, which had canceled the event in 2020. The 2021 soiree was necessarily smaller than usual, featuring sanitary precautions that didn't necessarily lend themselves to fashion, but the world had adapted, and the show had to go on.

Lewis Hamilton was there. The fact that he had been in Italy the day before probably didn't make him unique among a guest list for whom the limitations of commercial flight schedules are not a concern. The fact that he was working on Sunday likely set him apart from some, but driven people often work weekends. The fact that his job on that particular

Sunday was driving an open-wheel race car at an average speed of 200 miles per hour in Monza put him in a class with only twenty other people in the world. But Lewis Hamilton was the only one at the Metropolitan Museum of Art who was almost killed at work the day before.

The 2021 Formula One Heineken Grand Prix Premio d'Italia was held at the Autodromo Nazionale Monza. Just uttering "Monza" in a group of F1 fans is enough to get them to reminisce about their favorite race or the incredible speeds cars record on that famed circuit. In 2023, a Formula One car was clocked at 223.1 miles per hour at the end of the main straight at Monza, a record for this type of vehicle. Just to offer some perspective, at 220 miles per hour, the 95 miles from Manhattan to Philadelphia on the aptly named Interstate 95 South would take you a searing twenty-six minutes, give or take a few seconds.

Hamilton was in the midst of a season that had major implications for the sport as a whole. Lewis won his seventh world title in 2020 and came into the 2021 season with the intent of becoming the only driver to have won eight world driver's titles. His closest rival, Max Verstappen, a Dutch wunderkind competing for Red Bull Racing, was fighting for his first title, and after a win at his home race the previous week, came to Monza with a three-point lead over Lewis. A series of botched pit stops for the two top competitors 22 or so laps into the 53-lap event caused Lewis and Max to find themselves next to each other on the track. As the drivers hurtled side-by-side toward turn two at Monza, things got ugly. Max refused to back out of the turn, though Lewis was clearly leading the way into what is called the "racing line," the route that allows drivers to take turns as quickly as possible before reaching the limits of grip. Max went over a curb and made contact with Hamilton's car, sending his own car airborne, and it landed on top of Hamilton's.

If not for the recent addition of a titanium "halo" that protects the head of the driver, Hamilton might have had his head separated from his body on this sunny afternoon outside of Bologna. The relationship between the drivers was not helped by Verstappen's behavior during the incident. Max accelerated, causing the wheel to spin dangerously just centimeters from Lewis's head. After the Dutchman exited his car, he didn't bother to look at Hamilton to see if he was alive. Instead, Max was heard on the radio to his team saying, "That's what you get when you don't leave the space, ****!"[1] What Verstappen called Hamilton during this broadcast has been censored into oblivion. Max had found himself on the wrong side of both racist and ableist language in the past, a practice that had been largely ignored by the Fédération Internationale de l'Automobile (FIA), the governing body of the sport. During the 2020 season, after the Mongolian government had penned a scathing letter denouncing Verstappen's use of the word "Mongol" as an insult, Jake Boxhall-Legge of Autosport .com wrote an article called "Why Do Verstappen's Offensive Comments Get a Free Pass?"[2]. Boxhall-Legge goes directly at the problem, writing, "Verstappen has been able to publicly use ableist, borderline racist language without any fear of sanctions from those in charge. There's been no apology from Verstappen, and the matter has been rather brushed under the carpet without any further inquiry from those involved."[3] The FIA and broadcasters have provocatively gone to great lengths not to reveal what Verstappen said here, which leaves open the possibility that he may have used language that is beyond commonly used curse words.

To say that the two drivers weren't friends would be to understate the atmosphere of animosity between them. Adding to the negative dynamic between the two was Max's reputation for aggressive driving, what some would characterize as reckless disregard for safety and the rules. This culminated in the implementation of what became known as the "Verstappen Rule," which prohibited drivers from "moving under

---

1. "Verstappen Furious at Hamilton: 'This Is What You Get Without Giving Space,'" GPblog.com, September 12, 2021, https://www.gpblog.com/en/news/93904/ver stappen-furious-at-hamilton-this-is-what-you-get-without-giving-space.html.
2. Jake Boxhall-Legge, "Why Do Verstappen's Offensive Comments Get a Free Pass?" Autosport.com, October 27, 2020, https://www.autosport.com/f1/news/why-do -verstappens-offensive-comments-get-a-free-pass-4977790/4977790/.
3. Boxhall-Legge, "Why Do Verstappen's Offensive Comments Get a Free Pass?"

braking." This means that when a driver is defending against another driver's attempt to pass them, the leading driver cannot make a second move once the attempt has been established, especially in curves where the braking point determines whether the cars make it around without leaving the track or worse. For instance, if a car approaches another and intends to pass on the right side as they enter the curve, the other driver cannot show space on the right side and then suddenly "close the door" at the last possible moment to cause the other driver to have to make an evasive move.[4] The pressure for Max to win his first championship while at the same time denying Hamilton his eighth created a toxic atmosphere.

Some chalk up the crash at Monza to Verstappen seeking revenge for a high-speed crash at Silverstone four races before. In that incident, Lewis and Max came together, and the Red Bull driver ended up in the wall with a force of 51g's. For perspective, that would make a 200-pound person's body feel as if it weighed 10,200 pounds. Max ended up in the hospital, while Lewis was able to continue and eventually win the race. Lewis celebrated after his win, which infuriated Max, his team, and his fans. The situation was not helped when race officials determined Lewis was "mostly responsible"[5] for the crash.

Hamilton later called the hospital to check on Verstappen, though Max was not placated. After the wreck that ended both drivers' participation in the Italian Grand Prix a few weeks after Silverstone, Verstappen was found to be predominantly at fault[6] and was penalized with a three-place reduction in his qualifying position in the next race. There is no evidence that Max ever found it in his heart to check on Lewis after the crash at

---

4. Henry Valantine, "The Three Rules Introduced by the FIA Because of Max Verstappen," PlanetF1.com, July 3, 2024, https://www.planetf1.com/news /max-verstappen-fia-rule-introductions.

5. Jonathan Noble, "FIA Explains Hamilton Blame for Verstappen F1 Collision," Motorsport.com, July 19, 2021, https://us.motorsport.com/f1/news/fia-explains -hamilton-blame-for-verstappen-collision/6633217/.

6. Laurence Edmondson, "Why the Stewards Blamed Max Verstappen over Lewis Hamilton," ESPN.com, September 13, 2021, https://www.espn.com/f1/story/_/id/32203367 /why-stewards-blamed-max-verstappen-lewis-hamilton.

Monza, though he could have tuned in to the red carpet coverage of the Met Gala to see that Hamilton was discharged in time to make it to the event with his head where it belonged and seemingly no worse for wear.

Elle magazine reported that Hamilton was there to find ways to "put these Black designers at the top of people's minds." The article, entitled "Lewis Hamilton Paid Over £60,000 for Young Black Designers to Attend the Met Gala," identifies the three designers as Theophilio, Kenneth Nicholson, and Jason Rembert. The article makes no mention of what the driver was up to days before the Gala, but focuses only on the positive and inclusive message Hamilton was promoting with his appearance and sponsorship.[7]

In addition to the designers whose work he was dedicated to center, Lewis was accompanied by others whom *Elle* described as "Black innovators" including Zendaya's stylist Law Roach, Alton Mason (model), Kehlani (singer/songwriter), and athletes Miles Chamley-Watson (fencer) and Sha'Carri Richardson (sprinter). Several paragraphs of the article are devoted to describing the diversity problem in motorsports and how the driver's Mission 44 initiative was designed to understand the problems and solve them. Hamilton has the same concerns for the world of fashion, and he apparently had no difficulty separating the two worlds when necessary and combining them when it proved productive.

———————

LEWIS HAMILTON ARRIVED IN FORMULA ONE WHEN THE WORLD HAD fully embraced the digital revolution in communications that made stars of everyone, even if it was only in their own minds and to those who tagged along in the virtual world. For those who were actually public figures, celebrity was supercharged, and the notion of the boundary stars had enjoyed between the public and private were hard to discern or maintain if they exist at all anymore. Formula One, up until the present moment,

———————

7. Katie O'Malley, "Lewis Hamilton Paid Over £60,000 for Young Black Designers to Attend the Met Gala," *Elle*, September 15, 2021, https://www.elle.com/uk/fashion/a37603807/lewis-hamilton-paid-black-designers-attend-met-gala/.

had enjoyed a wealthy as well as niche following. The residents of the Principality of Monaco were inconvenienced for several days in May so Formula One could conduct its event, and then it was gone. Hard-core fans could follow their heroes, but the distance granted celebrities made it difficult to know what these people were up to away from the races, if they were up to anything at all. This is obviously no longer the case.

Every moment of every day is subject to being documented and broadcast around the world at the speed of light. Every utterance, no matter how well or poorly considered, can be scrutinized by the world. Bad news travels fast and tends to overwhelm any holistic consideration of the person, situation, context, or revision. Lewis Hamilton embraces all of this. His appearance at the Met Gala demonstrates how he will use the platform of Formula One as a point of departure rather than an end so he can get involved in other causes he cares about. Fashion is a common thread through all his affinities, as are questions about diversity and opportunity.

Hip-hop became a global phenomenon in the 1990s. One of its major themes is the desire for luxury and conspicuous consumption. Fast cars, glittering jewelry, exotic locations, and beautiful people. In short, everything that goes on in the small and exclusive world of Formula One. The concurrent global phenomenon of Modern Black Celebrity served as the fuel in the engine of the global expansion and explosion in the popularity of Formula One. If F1 didn't have Lewis Hamilton, it would have needed to invent him.

———

Lewis's presence at the Met Gala signals his complete awareness of what he means to F1 racing. Lewis is hip-hop in a way that could not have been anticipated. He is creating what some might call a modern form of Black cosmopolitanism. He isn't a basketball or football player, but the biggest stars of both sports make their way to F1 circuits all over the world to cheer him on. The same goes for actors, models, celebrity chefs, musicians, authors, and more. Everyone who is anyone wants to be around Hamilton, turning Formula One racing into a 200-mile-per-hour ride driven by fear of missing out. As the orbit around Lewis becomes full, F1 is affected in a new way: the tastemakers gravitate to other drivers in the sport, and the sport necessarily expands. Not everyone can fit in Lewis's side of the garage on a race weekend.

Formula One is unlike anything else. Every few weeks from February to November, they hold a sporting event that is a cross between the World Cup and the Oscars with a healthy dose of the Prêt-à-Porter, also known as Paris Fashion Week, to go along. All of it revolves around the twenty or so drivers who pilot these cars, and it is not possible to have a conversation about the greatest in the history of the sport without Hamilton's name near the top of the list. The mixed-race kid from Stevenage, about twenty-seven miles north of London, has become an inspiration for people across the world who have dreams that don't seem to fit things as they are. What Sir Lewis Hamilton has done—he was knighted in 2021—is show the world that *the possible* is only limited by *the possibility of access*. He and his family burst open the gilded doors of Formula One and the sport has been the better for it.

This book traces the ascendency of Sir Lewis to the top of the sport and tells the story of how and why he has become a worldwide tastemaker. The ups and downs, the triumphs and struggles, and the history-making campaign at the end of his career to win his eighth title. Along the way, we will also examine and critique every institution Hamilton is involved with from a perspective of race, ethnicity, religion, gender, sexuality, and class. Hamilton cares about all of it, and in so doing, creates the space for a new generation of athletes and fans to see themselves in the sport—or any other endeavor—and express what matters to them.

SIR
LEWIS

CHAPTER I

THE ILLUSTRATED SON

Formula One DHL Turkish Grand Prix
Istanbul Park
Tuzla, Turkey
November 15, 2020

The year 2020 is known as a year of crisis. For those who lived through it, the world will be perceived in parts: the way things were before the pandemic, during it, and after. Even as the world shut down, the annual global traveling circus that is Formula One carried on. The season was not immune to the cancellations and changes of the pandemic but round fifteen in Turkey arrived with Lewis Hamilton eighty-five points ahead of his Mercedes-AMG PETRONAS team- mate, Valtteri Bottas, the only other competitor who could possibly challenge him for the title. Everyone else was mathematically elimi- nated. A win by Hamilton would secure the crown for the 2020 sea- son. Winning a single-season championship is hard enough. Winning one while a global pandemic rages in a sport that requires hundreds of people to travel to five continents adds a layer of difficulty. This championship would also be Hamilton's seventh, which would tie him with former driver Michael Schumacher atop the all-time list, a feat even the ultimate dreamer Hamilton did not have on his vision board. At the same time, the driver was preoccupied with using his platform to show solidarity with the victims of police brutality in the United States.

It had been a long road to this point. Something of what we might call the beginning of this phase of his career is captured in a video clip of the young Lewis in 2006, a year before joining Formula One and on the threshold of his championship in Grand Prix-2, better known as GP-2, a series that is one of the "minor leagues" for big-time Formula One. During the wide-ranging interview, the subject of Schumacher and his seven world titles came up, and Lewis said, "I don't know whether it would be possible for me to win seven world championships, but I would be happy with one."[1] At that point in his career, he was aware that he was on a magic carpet ride of his own making with the assistance of his family, but not even Lewis could imagine that on this day in Turkey he would find himself sharing the top spot in the history of Formula One with Schumacher, a driver who had defined an age of motor racing.

Just after the GP-2 season, Hamilton found a seat in a Formula One car teamed up with former world champion Fernando Alonso with McLaren Racing, the team that had supported his career for years. Lewis's aspiration from that interview for one world championship almost came true in his rookie season when he came within one point of the title in a season full of controversy, much of it because the rookie driver did not come to play around and immediately found himself in competition and conflict with the veteran Spaniard Alonso. This pairing, in the mind of Alonso, was supposed to cast Lewis in a supporting role. After Hamilton ended up celebrating on the podium in his first Grand Prix in third place behind his second-place teammate, it was clear to everyone that the rookie was

---

1. Lewis Hamilton 2006 Interview: "Young Driver on His F1 Hopes and Dreams," November 17, 2020, by Formula 1, YouTube, https://www.youtube.com/watch?v =T3TAySZNq_g.

not there to be a tackling dummy for Alonso or for show. Something special was happening.

Hamilton won the world title in 2008 in his second season by a single point, then after a six-year drought, won again in 2014, 2015, 2017, 2018, 2019, and in 2020, he was poised to tie Michael Schumacher in Turkey. During the race, Lewis built a lead, and Peter Bonnington, predictably nicknamed "Bono," his race engineer—the team member responsible for keeping the driver updated on strategic and technical concerns— broadcast to the driver congratulations as he crossed the finish line thirty seconds ahead of the car in second place. "Get in there, Lewis!" Bono radioed. "What a way to do it, mate! What a way to win your seventh world title!"

Lewis answered. Kind of. First with a visceral, drawn-out victory cry somewhere between agony, relief, hysteria, and unbridled joy. He was overwhelmed, and his hysterical laughter finally landed tearfully on words: "Thank you so much, guys! Woo! Woo! That's for all the kids out there who dream the impossible! You can do it too, man! I believe in you guys. Thank you so much everyone for your support." The kid from Stevenage, a town about twenty-seven miles north of London, the Black British son of a man of Grenadian descent and a white English mother, who had himself dreamed the impossible had outdistanced even his wildest fantasies.

Lewis Hamilton, in the aftermath of his seventh world title, would soon be knighted by then Prince Charles. He now stood next to Michael Schumacher, the same driver whom he marveled at during the 2006 interview as arguably, at least in terms of world championships, one of the greatest drivers in the history of the sport. After Turkey, as we will see, he was back to his initial concern from the GP-2 interview. After number seven, he would "just be happy with one" more: his eighth to separate himself from Schumacher. It had been a tortuous path to get to this success—not just this race, this season, or this championship but a life that did not seem to have Formula One world champion listed as potential options. Lewis and his family made it to Formula One despite having neither the financial resources nor experience in the sport. All of this happened while they also managed the pressure that comes with being the only Black family in what had been an exclusively non-Black world.

———

THIS STORY IS LEWIS HAMILTON'S STORY. THAT MEANS IT IS ABOUT dreams. Impossible dreams. Not because they are impossible to dream; as we know, anyone can dream up anything. But what Hamilton means when he says "dream the impossible" is to push beyond whatever horizon or limit you think exists for yourself and do it. He literally says it at the moment of dreams coming true that he did not even dare to dream. "You can do it too. I believe in you guys." And then, in typical Lewis Hamilton fashion, he moves immediately to gratitude for all of the people who have become irreplaceable companions to the success. As much as this is Lewis's story, it is part of the magic that is Hamilton that it is ours as well. Lewis is a person who cares about people, especially those who seem to be forgotten and are having a difficult time believing in themselves. While all of this is going on, the marketing departments at corporate interests all over the world can't get enough of him. His persona sells cars, clothes, food, drinks, luggage, watches; you name it, he can sell it, but more than that he makes it possible to put your faith in the impossible. Even with this kind of uplifting and positive message there are those who want him to disappear, but not before he fails spectacularly.

Lewis Hamilton, the driver and cultural icon, is the product of a collective. People like his parents and Ron Dennis, the McClaren executive who took the institutional risk on the teenager, are impossible to ignore in getting to some understanding of the international phenomenon that arrived on the world-scene from a background that is part of the "impossible" part of this dream.

The other part of the Hamilton brand of dreaming is the sharing of it. He is willing to put his money and his mouth and anything else necessary behind demonstrating that he really does believe in the dreamers. All of Hamilton's efforts at diversity, equity, and inclusion seem to me to be the product of his knowledge that he could very easily be going to a wage-earning job every day—not that there isn't dignity in that, watching races on the weekend that he should have been winning. He is committed to diversity and opportunity in every aspect of motor racing, from the cockpit of a Formula One car to the broadcast booth, to the garage, to management, and the wind tunnel. Everywhere. Hamilton demonstrates that there should be no child dreaming of participation who is blocked by a lack of opportunity rather than drive and talent.

Lewis Hamilton has forever altered the face of Formula One, literally and figuratively. Before the Lewis of GP-2 could wonder if he would ever win a single Formula One world title, he had to wonder if he would be the first Black driver in the sport, a sport that is arguably the whitest and most elite in the world, not a place where a mixed-race kid from a town north of London would be able to find role models who look like him.

There are those who will want or maybe need the symbolism of Hamilton's success to be only about class because race is too hot an object to hold on to for very long. That would be nice in some sense, but it isn't the world we live in. Just as fans will cheer for their nation in the Olympics or the World Cup, it is undeniable that identity drives us: sometimes in positive ways but far too often in ways that are harmful. Lewis is aware of the attention his race gets, positively and negatively, and he seems always to be committed to being proud of who he is. This book will honor that by being real about it.

———

LEWIS OFTEN STATES HOW HE NEVER FELT LIKE HE FIT IN. HE RECENTLY told *Vanity Fair* magazine that he "didn't feel like I was welcome" and "I didn't feel like I was accepted."[2] His story can't be told without taking care to understand what that means to him and to our society.

Sports in general, and especially the Olympic Games, are designed

———

2. Chris Heath, "Lewis Hamilton: The F1 Superstar on Racism, His Future, and the Shocker That Cost Him a Championship," *Vanity Fair*, August 8, 2022, https://www.vanityfair.com/style/2022/08/cover-story-lewis-hamilton-never-quits.

so loyalty is built on the good feeling fans get from the sensation of belonging or feeling that they are part of the game. The medal count that serves as the intro and outro of a day's coverage of the Olympics is meant to feed the hunger of citizens of a particular city, region, or country to measure themselves against their rival, or the world, depending upon how well they are doing. At the most basic level, a sporting event like the Palio di Siena in Italy pits ten bareback riders representing ten of the seventeen wards of Siena against one another in a no-holds-barred race around the square for local honor. The same goes for a person who has grown up in Detroit, Michigan. Even though the Lions have been, until recently, perennial losers in the NFL, fans continue to root for them because of their identification with the city and its team. These associations are an essential part of the way western culture—not just sports culture—is formed, from the nation state down to the neighborhood. When you tune in to ESPN for the endless loop of scores from the night before, fans are always interested in the big rivalries, and many of them are regional. The Lakers fans can't stand the Boston Celtics supporters. Philadelphia is particularly hostile to Dallas. In the city of Chicago, the South Siders don't journey north to Wrigley Field to support the Cubs because that would be a betrayal of the White Sox.

Naturally, the sports hero assumes a profound sense of importance in addition to these other associations. Heroes of the gridiron, court, or ball diamond come to be the representative and aspirational figures for the neighborhood, city, state, college, team or even nation. The athlete exemplifies the relationship of belonging, and in an ideal circumstance, becomes the "prototypical" citizen of that neighborhood, city, state, and ultimately nation.

Babe Ruth is a classic example. He was a native of Baltimore who was traded early in his career to the New York Yankees by the Boston Red Sox. Ruth eventually came to exemplify New York City and everything that the Big Apple meant for American culture in the early twentieth century and beyond. Ruth's outsize persona and league-leading statistics situated him in American culture as the exemplar of the ideal participant in baseball, what was then the American pastime. Turning athletes into heroes is all well and good until someone who doesn't fit becomes the standard-bearer. The outsider who becomes the hero can throw into crisis how people feel about a sport, a team, a nation, or even types of people. Another baseball legend, Jackie Robinson, is the prime example of such an outsider.

———

IN ITS CURRENT FORMATION, FORMULA ONE, AN *INTERNATIONAL* sport, appears on every continent except one: Africa. The Formula One season reads like a luxury traveler's bucket list. A typical season makes stops in Bahrain, Saudi Arabia, Australia, Japan, China, Italy, Canada, the United States, Monaco, Spain, Austria, Great Britain, Hungary, Belgium, the Netherlands, Azerbaijan, Singapore, Mexico, Brazil, Qatar, and the United Arab Emirates. As noted, Africa is absent, a problem Hamilton vowed to fix.[3] But to be clear, Formula One has never been a sport where you would expect to see working class or, in the case of Hamilton, Black people as even spectators, let alone drivers.

Africa as a site for F1 disappeared in the wake of the death throes of apartheid in 1993. What that means is that the presence of Formula One in South Africa from 1967 to 1993 was much about the lack of diversity of that way of running a country. The event disappeared as apartheid was discredited and abandoned. Diversity is an ongoing concern for Lewis both in the sport and outside of it. This goes for class as well as other ways of being in the world.

Formula One did not have formal rules and traditions that excluded Black people from participation the way other sports have. (For instance, Major League Baseball in the United States was explicitly segregated until Jackie Robinson joined the Brooklyn Dodgers in the spring of 1947.) But it didn't need them. The structure of Formula One, mostly the steep economic cost of the entry level go-kart league, stopped Black

———

3. "Lewis Hamilton Says Africa Needs a Formula 1 Race," November 21, 2023, by Pan African Lifestyle, YouTube, https://youtu.be/M9WmEH8oRug?si=6FAZJZggoqQE7_zZ.

participation before it started. Hamilton did not share the familial wealth that virtually all other F1 drivers enjoy, having grown up in working class Stevenage, Hertfordshire, England.

Imagine for a moment that it cost $11,000 per season for an American child to play high school football. If that were the case, there would be virtually no Black college football players and likely few to none in the NFL. Anthony Hamilton, Lewis's Grenadian father, was having none of it, and in the tradition of Black parents of world-changing athletes in unlikely places set about dealing with the part of the impossible that he could make possible. His father's actions make perfect sense in the aftermath of seven world championships and all that Lewis Hamilton has come to represent, but at the time, there must have been those who wondered if Anthony Hamilton had lost his mind.

The story of Lewis's father's support of his son's ambition must be considered next to other similarly improbable stories in sports and entertainment. Joe Jackson must have believed the band of children he was disciplining to the point of abuse in a garage in Gary, Indiana, would become, arguably, the most influential group of the era. Not to mention that his son Michael would one day need no further identifier than his first name from the shores of Lake Michigan to the Yangtze River and back.

The same goes for the visionary in Compton, California, Richard Williams, who knew nothing about tennis except that you could make a lot of money at the game. His daughters, Venus and Serena, having won a total of sixty Grand Slam titles (singles and doubles), proved his relatively uninformed point, and the sport cannot be understood without thinking about the two of them.

Another visionary father is the Green Beret, Earl Woods. He named his son Eldrick and gave him the nickname "Tiger" after his colleague, the South Vietnamese colonel Vuong Dang Phong, who fought with Woods deep in the jungles of Southeast Asia. In keeping with that DNA, Earl applied mental and physical stress to his son that made Tiger's chip-in on the sixteenth hole at the Masters in 2005 like just another night with his dad hitting balls in a cemetery.

Gymnastics is another expensive sport that has had its struggles with diversity. When she was six years old, the grand- and adoptive parents of the older Biles sister took seriously a note from the coach at a day-care field trip that said the child was notably skilled at gymnastics.[4] They enrolled Simone in classes immediately. The fact that she has won a total of forty-one (and counting) world and Olympic championships probably makes that note the most important one in the history of that sport.

Let's leave Michael (Jackson, not Jordan) to the side, not because he's not important but because music exists as a field, particularly in the modern world, that is comfortable with, if not necessarily equitable, when it comes to the contributions of Black people. That is not the case when it comes to endeavors like tennis, golf, gymnastics, or Formula One, sports for which the terms "exclusive" and "expensive" are understood and almost redundant. So, for parents Williams, Woods, Biles, and Hamilton, the leap of faith was immeasurably farther from Gary to Motown as compared to the one from Compton to Wimbledon.

Anthony Hamilton, as a practical matter, had no hero for his son or himself to serve as a symbol for success in F1 racing. For example, Dianne Durham, also from Gary, won the national championship in gymnastics in 1983, missing the Los Angeles Olympics because of injury. Dominique Dawes won an Olympic gold medal a year before Simone Biles was born to add to her bronze in Barcelona in 1992 with another for good measure in Sydney in 2000. Simone had shoulders that looked a lot like hers to vault from. Anthony and Lewis had no such shoulders.

Golfer Charlie Sifford was born in 1922, and he competed in the 1959 US Open and became a member of the PGA Tour at the age of thirty-nine after winning the National Negro Open six times. President Barack Obama awarded Sifford the Presidential Medal of Freedom a year

4. "This Is Simone: Read the Story of Simone Biles," *TIME for Kids* and *American Girl*, August 16, 2020, https://www.timeforkids.com/g56/this-is-simone-biles/.

before his death, the capstone of a career that enjoyed financial support from singer Billy Eckstine and heavyweight champ Joe Louis, making him something like the Jackie Robinson of golf.

In 1979, when Tiger Woods was about four years old, Calvin Peete won the first of his twelve PGA Tour victories in the Greater Milwaukee Open. So, when Earl's golf prodigy won his first title at Augusta National in 1997, the Fuzzy Zoellers of the world were predictably surprised and perplexed at the same time when they should have expected it would happen sooner or later. There were Black golfers around but none who "mattered" to people who support the de facto apartheid of Augusta National. Zoeller, after not making the cut at Augusta and watching Woods from the spectators' gallery, said what a lot of people must have been thinking in one way or another.

> He's doing quite well, pretty impressive. That little boy is driving well and he's putting well. He's done everything it takes to win. So you know what you guys do when he gets here? You pat him on the back and say congratulations and enjoy it and tell him not to serve fried chicken next year. Got it. Or collard greens or whatever the hell they serve.[5]

There is good reason to forget Fuzzy but also good reason to remember him. Sports are a continuum. You can't understand the way an athlete fits into a sport without understanding the context that surrounds them, including rules, other competitors, and various forms of difficulty. The cultural context that Lewis entered when he joined Formula One was an echo of the space and time of Tiger.

The "fried chicken" comment wasn't isolated to self-styled "jokester" Fuzzy, who was born three years before *Brown v. Board of Education*. Spanish golf pro Sergio García, born in 1980, when asked if he might have dinner with his rival Woods, assured the press that if he did "we will

---

5. "Golfer Says Comments About Woods 'Misconstrued,'" CNN.com, April 21, 1997, http://www.cnn.com/US/9704/21/fuzzy/.

serve fried chicken." These "jokes" reveal the uncomfortable disruption athletes like Tiger, Simone, Venus, Serena, and others have caused in enclaves that evidently declared themselves safe from the ravages of soul food. The preoccupation with the common exoticism of fried chicken has nothing to do with "driving for show and putting for dough." It reveals that in many sports, Black athletes must fight messages that they don't belong and that they are bringing their "Black crap" along with them and messing everything up.

The fact that Black golfers were facing such obvious prejudice, even though Black golfers had been around for the better part of the twentieth century, reveals how put out people must have been when the Hamiltons showed up. Formula One didn't have the benefit of a century or so to still be scared of fried chicken and collard greens or whatever the hell else Black people eat. When Lewis showed up, it was in many ways like Charlie Sifford winning the US Open six times instead of the National Negro Open.

Of his arrival in Formula One, Lewis said, "I didn't feel like I was welcome. I didn't feel accepted...This is not how you do it. Tattoos?"[6] Despite it seeming out of character for an F1 driver to have tattoos, Lewis clearly was not enrolled in "Intro to Worrying About What People Think About You." He doesn't care what people think about how he decorates himself. To understand Lewis's thinking more deeply, let's focus on one tattoo on his left shoulder, an image of a silhouetted dad throwing a child in the air against a clock that reads 11:10.

In an interview with *GQ* in 2018, Lewis gives a frankly intrusive journey around his body art (but I get the motivation) and says that getting tattoos takes thought and should be a way "to display your story, your journey to where you are." Obviously, none of us would be anywhere without parents one way or another, but the relationship between Lewis and his father, Anthony, is complicated for reasons we'll unpack in later chapters. The clock tattoo, Lewis says, is "dedicated to my dad. I wouldn't

---

6. Heath, "Lewis Hamilton: The F1 Superstar on Racism."

be doing what I'm doing without my dad...from the age of four he would pick me up and throw me in the air, like you do with kids. And it was the single most special moment that I would really have with my dad. He's a very serious man. He's very tough but in this particular moment he was the happiest. There was no business. There was no discipline needed. There was just pure love."[7]

Lewis doesn't leave much room to guess about how complicated the situation was between a kid and his dad who wanted to do something that neither of them really understood and that quickly became a business relationship. The effort and sacrifice all make sense when it works out, but it is worth spending some time discussing what got Anthony Hamilton to Great Britain in the first place. Anthony's story has a lot to say about the drive to get his son to Formula One.

ANTHONY HAMILTON'S FAMILY MIGRATED TO ENGLAND FROM THE Caribbean in the 1950s. They were part of what became known as the Windrush Generation. In the aftermath of the devastation of World War II, Caribbean people were invited to Great Britain to rebuild the country. The Hamiltons were from the small windward island of Grenada in the Lesser Antilles. The current population of the island is about 126,000. In the 1950s, when the Hamiltons departed the island, it was about 50 percent smaller. Its population has remained about 80 percent Black since the genocide of the indigenous people and the Atlantic slave trade. Grenada's main exports, since being spotted by Columbus on his third foray into the unknown (by Europeans), were nutmeg and mace. The possibilities for trade were severely limited for the citizens of Grenada. So Anthony's family, like many people of African descent around the Caribbean, imagined that things might look better in Europe or even the United States.

Leaving Grenada sounded great on the brochure, but as a practical

---

7. "Lewis Hamilton Breaks Down His Tattoos," May 17, 2018, by GQ, YouTube, https://youtu.be/—5-4WPEs6Y?si=bGIQ1Su3tGYp2YW4.

matter, anti-immigrant tension reached a crescendo in 1968 with member of Parliament Enoch Powell's "River of Blood" speech that sounded the alarm about Great Britain becoming a non-white nation.

> Here is a decent, ordinary fellow Englishman, who in broad daylight in my own town says to me, his Member of Parliament, that the country will not be worth living in for his children. I simply do not have the right to shrug my shoulders and think about something else. What he is saying, thousands and hundreds of thousands are saying and thinking—not throughout Great Britain, perhaps, but in the areas that are already undergoing the total transformation to which there is no parallel in a thousand years of English history. We must be mad, literally mad, as a nation to be permitting the annual inflow of some 50,000 dependents, who are for the most part the material of the future growth of the immigrant descended population. It is like watching a nation busily engaged in heaping up its own funeral pyre. So insane are we that we actually permit unmarried persons to immigrate for the purpose of founding a family with spouses and fiancées whom they have never seen.[8]

The migration to Great Britain was about economic and educational opportunity, despite the preoccupation of Enoch Powell and others with interracial relationships. The economic prospects for the residents of Grenada who chose to migrate were significant compared to those available on the island. The most recent gross domestic product on record was around $1.1 billion. By way of comparison, the business that is Formula One had total revenue in excess of $2.5 billion in 2022. The per capita income in Grenada is currently around $10,000. So one can see why the prospect of movement around the world for Black people in the 1950s would be attractive. Anthony Hamilton was born in 1956 in England

---

8. "Enoch Powell's 'Rivers of Blood' Speech," *The Telegraph*, November 6, 2007, https://www.telegraph.co.uk/comment/3643823/Enoch-Powells-Rivers-of-Blood-speech.html.

and apparently never allowed himself to forget his roots in the Caribbean. Yet England was where he would establish himself personally and professionally.

Anthony met Lewis's biological mother, Carmen Larbalestier, and the two married. Living outside of London as a mixed-race couple was their choice and undoubtedly had implications for their relationship and the way Lewis was raised. The two welcomed the birth of Lewis Carl Davidson Hamilton on the seventh of January in 1985. Lewis was born a few months after runner Carl Lewis matched Jesse Owens's four-gold-medal performance at the Los Angeles Olympics which, we can imagine, made an impression on Lewis's parents. Speed of one kind or another was clearly in the mind of Anthony. Anthony and Carmen divorced in 1987 when Lewis was two years old. Though he remarried and had another child with his second wife, Linda, Anthony was never absent from his son's life. Lewis's brother, Nicholas, remains close to him and became an inspiration to his big brother in the way he has worked to overcome many of the obstacles presented by having cerebral palsy.

Mr. Hamilton, as the story goes, bought Lewis a remote-controlled car after he showed interest in cars when he was five years old. There is hardly a more auspicious toy that ever appeared as a gift for a kid than this one. Not unlike the Simone Biles story, Lewis showed such interest and aptitude in driving the remote-controlled car that his dad signed him up with the British Racing Car Association (BRCA), which conducted a competition series that pitted children against adults. Some say the adults involved in BRCA take it too seriously. Lewis won the championship at six, and there are still those who are more than a little bit pissed off about it. Lewis posted a picture on his Facebook page on November 6, 2020, to memorialize the event with the following caption:

> I was 6 years old when I earned my first two trophies remote control car racing. The small trophy was 2nd place in the electric car championship, against grown men. The bigger was for

best newcomer in the bigger petrol cars against men. I was the youngest by at least 15 years. We were also the only people of color there in a much smaller field. I was so proud, these were some [*sic*] best days of my life spending time with my dad out the back of the old car we had with our pot noodles soup and bacon sandwiches which was very much an English thing. #1991.[9]

This seems nice enough. It's full of statements of fact, without judgments made about anyone or anything. There are lots of positive "I" statements, for those who keep track of such things, never casting aspersions on anyone or anything else. However, the comments from the public about the post draw out what we commonly refer to as "Haters."

Haters are important for understanding Lewis Hamilton in the same way that Fuzzy Zoeller is important. Hamilton's comments about the pressures he felt as he was made into an outsider cannot be properly understood without understanding his experience with social media. It is obviously a powerful tool, but social media is also potentially devastating to even the most secure person. In posts like this one, Hamilton speaks in vague terms. He avoids punching down, but also, pointedly, he does not remove these posts as he could. They are a major part of his story. Stories like these speak to his concern for even the most common type of bullying and show that it happens even to him and that you can get past it.

Dan Tomlinson, whose Facebook/Meta profile describes him as "2x motorcycle club racing Champion, Dad & Husband, life is good" writes in response to the seven-time world champion's post: What's colour got to do with it? You're all racers. Same people with the same passion. But are they? One might be tempted to write back to Dan, racer, champion, dad, etc., something like, "Who cares about your wife and kids? All families and championships matter!" but that wouldn't be nice, right? One thing

9. Lewis Hamilton, Facebook, November 6, 2020, https://www.facebook.com/Lewis Hamilton/photos/i-was-6-years-old-here-when-i-earned-my-first-two-trophies -remote-control-car-ra/3871477899600176/.

to note about Dan's self-awareness is that he is careful to leave skill off the table when speaking to the "sameness" of "all racers." Dan, however, is not alone in his dislike of Lewis's post.

Another Facebook user, Andrew Bottomley, had something to say about this as well and serves as an example of countless others who reacted negatively to Lewis's post. In a post on his page from February 8, 2024, Andrew expresses his regard for Formula One drivers, in this instance James Hunt and Barry Sheene. Andrew describes the two as being part of an era of drivers who competed …in the days before men could get pregnant. Whatever. He said of Lewis's throwback trophy post:

> I was the white guy with the white family parked next to you in the
> early 2000s lifting your zip go cart off your Vauxhall cavalier roof
> rack at PF kart track funny that as your dad had no issue using
> our white kettle water while he rode your box stay on track don't
> loose track of your roots son shine.[10]

There's a lot going on here. First, there is no reason to believe that Andrew has ever been near the Hamiltons or that he gave them "white kettle water." That being said, it is the subtext of Andrew's screed that is worth thinking through. There is a narrative that Lewis and his family were given things by white people that they didn't deserve, and that they remain ungrateful and unrepentant. This narrative will emerge again and again as Lewis's story unfolds. Whether that be the kettle water that the white folks are good enough to give out to under-provisioned Black people or major sponsorships from multinational corporations, it is all undeserved.

As Lewis points out, as far as he could tell, he and Anthony were the only Black folks around these remote-control car events. It must have been particularly difficult for the adults who worked really hard at being

---

10. Lewis Hamilton, Facebook, November 6, 2020, https://www.facebook.com/Lewis Hamilton/photos/i-was-6-years-old-here-when-i-earned-my-first-two-trophies -remote-control-car-ra/3871477899600176/.

experts at piloting these toys to have their asses handed to them by a six-year-old Black kid. If this aggression were limited to angry posts twenty-plus years later, or better yet, if people just seethed in their own private hellscape, it would be one thing. But unfortunately, both Lewis and his dad describe instances of physical aggression that escalated along with Lewis's success.

The BRCA's website now includes a tab called "Race with Respect." It's not hard to imagine that this is an attempt to get out in front of the type of issues that occur in places where adults place too much emphasis on trying to "win" something that really speaks to their own mediocrity.

This is all part of why Lewis said he didn't feel like he "fit in" in the *Vanity Fair* piece. Racism and exclusion haunt and motivate Lewis to this day, as both affect him and others. There are many ways to deal with the feeling of not fitting in, whether it is real or imagined. Over the history of Formula One, the sport had developed a culture, and the center of it, as with every sport, was the top-performing athletes. Formula One drivers were understood to be daredevils who relaxed off the track with hard drinking and partying. Lewis is not proposing that if only he spent more time partying, he would have fit in. What he means is that to have a Black person in the sport would bother some people. Lewis pushes it further by not making any attempt to tone down who he is, whether it be his tattoos, braids, fashion choices, or activism. The mechanics of the way cultures are created, maintained, and defended is always reactionary. Lewis causes a reaction, some of it positive and some negative. Culture is moved forward by those who refuse to conform to standards, many of which are designed to refuse progress. As Lewis begins his career, he cannot avoid taking a stance on what it means to be a Formula One driver who is Black and what he decides to do about people who don't want him around.

Anthony's answer to this problem is a classic in response to racism: professionalism. There is not a Black person on Earth who at one time or another has not been told something like, "You have to be twice as good as everyone else." This statement is similar to what former first lady

Michelle Obama set as the edict, "When they go low, we go high."[11] Such responses are important, ethical, and marginally efficient notions to get through these problems, but they don't do much of anything about them. It is delusional to think that folks like Dan and Andrew will come around to having some sense and grace because Lewis is doing well. It is unfortunately exactly the opposite. We will see that as things get better for someone like Lewis, the racist backlash from folks like Dan and Andrew only grows exponentially. (One wonders what other Black people who have the misfortune of encountering people like Dan and Andrew must have to put up with.) But Lewis, at some point, decided he was going to go high just like his dad and First Lady Obama propose, while at the same time he was going to *do* something about the whole mess.

---

11. Kate Ng, "Michelle Obama Explains Her Catchphrase 'When They Go Low, We Go High,'" *The Independent*, 15 November 2022, https://www.independent.co.uk/life -style/michelle-obama-stephen-colbert-catchphrase-b2225386.html.

CHAPTER 2

SLOW DOWN, LEWIS, YOU'RE KILLIN' 'EM

SEVEN-YEAR-OLD LEWIS APPEARS FOR THE FIRST TIME IN POPULAR media on an episode of *Blue Peter*, the world's longest running children's show, to talk about remote control car racing.[1] The journey to this short segment of Lewis during his radio control car days is best reached by way of Bed-Stuy and the teenage, pre-discovery Christopher Wallace, aka the late, great Notorious B.I.G., rhyming on a street corner in front of a bodega. Wallace is battle rapping. One-on-one lyrical combat against all comers. The video lasts about sixty seconds. Christopher rides the beat like the pro he already was and would become, driving his opponent away from the contest because the gathered crowd can't help but laugh at the way Biggie is clowning him.[2]

The Biggie of the 1997 hit "Hypnotize," about eight years after this battle, lets the listeners know that "Poppa been smooth since the days

---

1. "Lewis Hamilton R/C Car Champion," posted December 21, 2014, by eville84, YouTube, https://www.youtube.com/watch?v=knuYY8oiDZU.
2. "Notorious B.I.G.—Brooklyn Freestyle at the Age of 17 (1989)," posted January 27, 2013, by Fernando Quintero Gonzalez, YouTube, https://www.youtube.com/watch?v=zSx03q1-1KA.

of Underoos," as if we didn't know that already based upon the event in Bedford-Stuyvesant. In 1989, Wallace is as refined as he is in 1997. The presence, the swagger, the confidence of a megastar in waiting, fresh off sending a want-to-be rapper running for cover. A rapper with so much flavor, it is told, that the late hip-hop mogul Andre Harrell pointed at a glass of water on a restaurant table and said that if Biggie dipped his pinkie finger in it, it would turn to Kool-Aid.

The Netflix documentary *Biggie: I Got A Story To Tell* from 2021 assists in understanding the point here. There are several instances in the documentary of Christopher Wallace's school classmates who made it their business to take a picture with him back in the 1990s, when pictures weren't as easy to take, much less keep, as they are now. What these kids were tasting is the flavor that Harrell was describing. People wanted to be around the young Biggie. Even in grade school he was a transcendent personality. The only question at the time was whether and how he would be discovered.

The young Lewis Hamilton also had *flavor*. The *Blue Peter* segment with seven-year-old Lewis is short on words but long on charisma. The segment begins to explain some of the negative reaction we have been looking at along the way.

Anthony Hamilton has arranged for Lewis, the RC car phenom, to race his toy among hay bales that the staff of the show set up as a racecourse. It is worth watching it without the sound for a lot of reasons, not the least of which is because Lewis's answers to the interviewer's questions consist of: "About a year" to the question of how long he has been racing. "No" to the whether it's easy to do. "Yes" to whether the host can "have a go." That's it. Somewhere around fourteen words. The rest of the story is told by the imagery.

Even in this first television appearance, Lewis is about fashion and makes a statement with his clothing. The jacket Lewis has on at seven is the same color scheme that he would one day sport in Formula One: royal purple. Most prominent is the intensity of his focus. He has no intention of losing to the host or anyone else in this moment and pretty much any other. When you think about what Anthony has set up for his son and what Lewis understands about the interview is that there is a complex relationship between three things: time, opportunity, and skill. Lewis understands that no matter how much skill you have, it is meaningless without the opportunity and time to take advantage of it. The sixty-five-second *Blue Peter* segment doesn't allow the time for long answers to silly questions, but what it does allow for is the opportunity to display his skill, which is driving. Lewis wins the staged race easily, and the host, trying to be funny, which is his job, makes reference to Nigel Mansell, the 1992 F1 world champion, "warning" the driver that "the radio control model racers are hot on your heels." Truer words have never been spoken.

Lewis and his dad do not linger long in radio control racing. There is a world where, without the opportunity and tenacity to take advantage of it, Lewis sticks around radio control cars and at thirty-nine wins his thirtieth or so championship and puts the trophy on the shelf next to the ones that he'd been winning since the 1990s. Fortunately, things played out differently. The mission to make it to Formula One, if you should choose to accept it, is impossible. It is complicated, full of barriers, dependent upon luck, and profoundly expensive. The last thing, the expense, is something at the outset of this journey that the Hamilton family was ill-equipped to afford.

The drivers who find themselves sitting in one of the twenty seats available in Formula One have made it to the top of the sport. They have navigated a series of car types and race series that lead to the big time, and there is nothing but off-ramps. Some leave the sport. Some get left by the sport. Most don't get anywhere near an F1 drive, and in the effort, they leave behind a pile of cash, broken dreams, and woulda, shoulda, couldas.

After Anthony Hamilton remarried, in affirmation of his son's domination of RC racing and, in an attempt to have something that they share together, the two decided to get into karting. It is not long before the financial commitment to the hobby that was a major sacrifice for the Hamiltons meant that Anthony began to believe his son was capable of finding a place in professional motorsports.[3]

The next step in the journey to F1 is kart racing. Go-karts are basically souped-up versions of the ones you might see at a carnival. They are low to the ground, gas-powered carts that strip racing down to its most fundamental component parts. The move from "driving" a remote-controlled car to driving a go-kart is obviously significant in an athlete's development. Racing a toy car never allows the driver to actually *feel* all the forces that are acting on the vehicle as it races around the hay bales. The "driver" of the toy car can't feel *any* of the forces of going fast or not. Once racing aspirants lower themselves to the ground to sit in the unprotected driver's seat of a go-kart, they can't help but feel *all* of them.

At this point, we can look back at this moment and Lewis's talent to begin to understand an important element of his brilliance as a driver that we will hear more about as he evolves in Formula One. NFL great Tom Brady is a fan and friend of Hamilton's and gives his take on this in *USA Today* of August 9, 2022:

> I think he's an artist. I think when he sees the racetrack, he sees it different than everyone else does. Like any great athlete, you have your unique way of doing things—everyone else looks at something one way and you look at it a different way. And you create strategies and you execute under pressure in ways that other people can't. I just think he probably sees lines on the track no one else can see.[4]

3. "Anthony Hamilton The Man Behind Lewis Hamilton's Success," RN365, June 23, 2021, https://racingnews365.com/anthony-hamilton-the-man-behind-lewis-hamiltons-success.
4. Victoria Hernandez, "Tom Brady: Lewis Hamilton's 'Unique Way of Doing Things' Wins Championships," *USAToday*, August 9, 2022, https://www.usatoday.com/story/nfl/tampa-bay-buccaneers/2022/08/09/tom-brady-lewis-hamilton-long-term-competitiveness/10271776002/.

Six-year-old Lewis, who had never driven a car, was able to imagine the forces that act on the toy car as he "drove" it around the track, choosing the correct line, acceleration, and braking points in ways that were superior to adults who had the advantage of having driven cars in the real world. What Brady is saying is that this skill apparently evolved once he was in the car, allowing him to see things that aren't apparent from the driver's seat, almost as if he is beside the car watching it like a toy. (The driver's seat in a Formula One car is designed to fit the driver alone. It's not like just anyone can just hop in an F1 car at a dealership and take a spin. We'll see that, as Lewis develops as a driver, he will eventually learn to translate what he is feeling in the car for the engineers and technicians who have never been behind the wheel of a Formula One car.)

All of this talent and skill needs to be nurtured, and at this point in the move from toys to karting, money and time are in short supply for the Hamilton family.[5] The typical racing kart costs about $8,000, and a family would need to spend a minimum of about $10,000 in addition competing in a European Karting season. There is hardly any profile about Lewis that doesn't at some point get around to talking about the problem the financial burden of Formula One, at least the path to it, posed for Anthony. That is of course true. It is also true that really only the wealthiest people in the world can frankly afford the cost and the risk associated with this ambition on the part of a kid. Saying that this hobby/career is prohibitively expensive for most everyone is meant to do two things at once. First, to demonstrate the amount of sacrifice it took for the Hamiltons to participate and second, to undertand that Mr. Hamilton must have believed that this effort was more than a hobby because of that same sacrifice and risk.

In narratives about the early moments of Lewis's career, it is common to see class referenced because of the expense of the sport. Race is also periodically gestured at if not taken up carefully. There is obviously financial risk that comes with this large investment in a sport for children that

5. "Hamilton Says F1 Is Now a 'Billionaire Boys' Club,'" ESPN.com, May 21, 2021, https://www.espn.com/f1/story/_/id/31481456/hamilton-says-f1-now-billionaire-boys-club.

is even more acute for people who are not wealthy. For Anthony and his son, there was also the risk that showed up as both physical and spiritual violence based upon their race. It's likely that even if Anthony could have funded a Formula One team out of his play money, there would still be the same resistance to the presence of Lewis and what he was doing to disrupt the environment that had been closed off to Black people for a variety of reasons.

Karting, as noted, is an expensive and time-consuming sport. The "car" is expensive on its own but, as is usually the case with this kind of hobby, it's all the stuff that goes along with the hobby that damages bank balances. Tires. Fuel. Racing gear. Helmets. Transportation. Entry fees. Lodging. Food. Repairs if you crash the car. Fortunately, the British enjoy universal healthcare, so medical bills won't bankrupt a family when a kid almost inevitably gets injured racing. For a working-class person, even the time away from doing the work of a working-class person makes this all very difficult, and it quickly goes from hobby to sacrifice. Anthony scraped together the money to get his son his first kart and made a deal that so long as Lewis did his job in school, he would support his racing.

To deal with this, Anthony took on multiple jobs to keep Lewis driving until someone, somewhere would take the ride with them. A 2021 Business Insider article by Sam Cooper has the provocative and frankly ridiculous title: "When He Was a Kid, Lewis Hamilton's Dad Asked People if They Wanted to 'Support the First Black F1 Driver' to Try and Attract Sponsors." The effort, like the title of the article, didn't work. Cooper writes, "[s]peaking to the *Wall Street Journal Magazine* Hamilton said, 'it went nowhere.'"[6] The failure of this effort is worth keeping in mind for a couple of reasons. First, Anthony was mindful of the possibility here and understood Lewis's race as being a component of it. Second,

6. Sam Cooper, "When He Was a Kid, Lewis Hamilton's Dad Asked People if They Wanted to 'Support the First Black F1 Driver' to Try and Attract Sponsors," Business Insider, October 28, 2021, https://www.businessinsider.com/lewis-hamiltons-dad-offered-chance-sponsor-the-first-f1-driver-2021-10#:~:text=Lewis%20Hamilton's%20dad%20tried%20to,still%20managed%20to%20enter%20F1.

as we watch Lewis's efforts to diversify motorsports from top to bottom, the failure of his dad to find people willing to invest in the ambitions of underrepresented people is exactly the point, especially when it comes to accessing what Lewis would one day call the "Billionaire Boys' Club"[7] of F1.

According to Frank Worrall's well-written *Lewis Hamilton: The Biography* from 2021, the first sponsor to join what we can call this early version of the "Hamilton Project" was a kart chassis sponsor. The chassis provides the structure of the kart, with the engine, wheels, brakes, and safety equipment accounting for the majority of the additional expense. This sponsor provided access to the Zip go-kart that Andrew Bottomley was so eager to remind us he lifted off the back of the Hamiltons' car. Again, the risk all makes sense in the aftermath of his success, but the shot in the dark that Anthony makes with his son speaks to the vision of Anthony and gets to the second of the reasons that it is important to spend time on Anthony's finances in a more complicated way than just a strict debit-over-credits problem with a foray into a common narrative around Black folks and their money, or lack thereof.

The public is always preoccupied in a strange way with how much money Black people have. Black celebrity, as with Black people's legacy in sports, is a continuum. Celebrity is relative, and so much of the way we understand an individual's fame has to do with how it is related to famous people who have come before them. A 1989 *60 Minutes* segment with the late Miles Davis demonstrates the point.[8]

Harry Reasoner, perhaps the corniest person on planet Earth, shows up to interview Miles, arguably the least corny person on planet Earth. You have to wonder where Ed Bradley was that week, but it is what it is. The predictably stupid questions Reasoner asks include but are nowhere near limited to whether Black people play on beat because of slavery, whether Miles is "anti-white," and to the point here, whether "You got

---

7. "Hamilton Says F1 Is Now a 'Billionaire Boys' Club.'"
8. "Miles Davis on Sixty Minutes," posted May 3, 2024, by Jazz Video Guy, YouTube, https://youtu.be/miOU6SZG1Ac?si=DYH5z10Fzxigy5Py.

enough money?" Miles gets right to the point of the question by asking quickly, "For what?" Reasoner tries to stick the landing by saying "to live comfortably," which doesn't help at all. Recall I said that Harry "shows up" to interview Miles. More to the point, he films the segment at Davis's beach house in Malibu where he spent time with the cameras caressing the artist's knee-high Ferrari Testarossa and references the fact that he, Miles, sells his paintings for $15,000–$25,000 a pop, which wasn't a small amount of money in the 1980s. The entire point of the interview was to deal with the fact that Miles was a superstar for most of the twentieth century, but Harry was so distracted by Miles's Blackness and maybe the din from the surf on the musician's private beach to see and hear that he was living "well" or, not to oversell it, lavishly. Maybe Harry was wondering who was paying for it all.

What that means to me is that after a career that spanned almost fifty years and changed the course of music at least three times, the press can still ask a Black person if they have "enough money" as if that is the most important thing to get to or, more to the point, as if he wouldn't. If even a celebrity as recognizable as Miles Davis was subject to bizarre questions regarding his finances, there is no reason to believe a similar level of scrutiny of the Hamiltons' finances wouldn't be present, too. As Lewis continued to develop as a driver, Anthony Hamilton's finances, and eventually Lewis's, would be of bizarre and illogical interest to people.

It's not a leap to imagine that at these early moments of what becomes this improbable and impossible ride, Anthony's requests for what we understand as "sponsorship" for his talented son, the unavoidable "Black thing" makes it look to some like a handout rather than an investment.

After Lewis secured a sponsorship from Zip Carts when he was ten years old, we can see how the shift goes from the fact that he had too little money to the fact that he has too much—the former and latter being because he didn't deserve to have it. A since deleted Instagram post from "Alan," who went by the handle @Asmclean on that platform, was captured by another social media racing fan and is quoted here:

I was there when Lewis Hamilton was in go karts. He was handed everything because he stood out because of his colour. There was an expensive motorhome and support from a top-team called Zip Kart before he was ever part of McLaren's junior project. He was never poor and had more than most of his competitiors. There were drivers who beat him and outclassed him but they didn't get to F-1. Once McLaren put investment into his equipment, he won everything. He is the ultimate recipient of "Black Privilege" given by many white British men but now claims he has been discriminated against throughout his career. Nothing could be further from the truth. He is nothing more than an entitled hypocrite.[9]

This post has to be examined against reality. Let's be honest, if we put ourselves back in the time when Anthony Hamilton was trying to raise money for the "first Black F-1 driver,"[10] there is a risk that the arrival of Lewis in the sport with this framing might be seen as him being a token and just there for representation, not competition. Alan seems to be arguing that if not for Lewis being Black, other, more deserving white drivers would have collected these championships. This is as absurd a way to think about this as it is common.

According to this line of reasoning, all of Lewis's accomplishments have nothing to do with his talent. He was handed everything he needed by well-meaning white people who felt guilty about white privilege, and so they tried to fix things with the racist yin and yang phantasm of "Black Privilege." The problem is, according to the Alans of the world, that world champions like Lewis are actually losers who refuse to acknowledge that it's all a con. So Alan needs the world to know that Lewis is not a talented driver and never was. Rather he's a Black Privileged driver.

9. "The Nitty Gritty of the BLM Movement," not606 Comment Debate Create, July 6, 2020, https://not606.com/threads/the-nitty-gritty-of-the-blm-movement.384383/page-17.
10. Cooper, "When He Was a Kid, Lewis Hamilton's Dad Asked People."

The supposed hypocrisy stems from the fact that Lewis knows he was never poor. This reasoning is morbidly funny. What he means is that poor Black people don't realize the untapped commercial potential that rests in exploiting white guilt. But supposedly Lewis and Anthony did. They were rich the entire time—if not monetarily then rich in Blackness, and once they found out how to use that to assuage the guilt of rich white men, their efforts all start to bear fruit.

Cutting to the chase, of course Anthony couldn't afford to fund Lewis's path to Formula One, and he shouldn't have had to. Lewis's obvious talent deserved serious sponsorship, and it shows up in the form of McLaren and their "junior program." The pitch for the sponsorship actually came from Lewis himself, again manifesting his hyper-developed understanding of skill, time, and opportunity when he is ten years old. At the 1995 Autosport Awards young Lewis is there collecting his awards for the Cadet Championships when he runs into the director of McLaren's Formula One team, Ron Dennis. Lewis relates the incident in his 2007 biography, an account that neither Dennis nor anyone else refutes:

> "Hi. I'm Lewis Hamilton. I won the British Championship and one day I want to be racing your cars."[11]

Ron Dennis told him to call him in nine years; but then in the classic positive outcome of the "don't call me, I'll call you" thing, three years later it is McLaren that comes calling and gives Lewis the type of support necessary to make a serious run at his dream: full support from the McLaren Young Driver Programme. This kind of sponsorship is what every young driver craves, not just for the money but for the validation, training, and mentorship that comes with joining a professional racing team, even at the most basic level.

One of the enduring critiques of Lewis Hamilton as a driver is the continuation of the narrative found in Alan's unhinged post: that Lewis

---

11. Lewis Hamilton, *Lewis Hamilton: My Story* (Harper Sport: 2007), 79–80.

is not a talented driver at all, he has just been given (again, Black Privilege) not only money but the best equipment. This is a not-so-subtle racist trope that is the text and the subtext of one form of argument against affirmative action and diversity initiatives: basically that because of the enduring and dynamic incompetence of Black people, anytime you find them "accomplishing" something, it's because they were "given" it in some form or fashion.

But it is demonstrably false that there were other, better drivers than Lewis who just didn't get their shot in karting and beyond because he takes up all the space because he's Black. But all of this crap is what drives Lewis's social activism, particularly as it relates to diversifying motorsports. There very well could have been a lot of people who had zero representation in the sport until he showed up who could have been as good or better than anyone who happened to have made it to the big time. That is the point of diversity: not to privilege the undeserving but to make sure that everyone who deserves it gets the opportunity to compete and participate.

Think about a similar scenario in a statistics-based sport like baseball. For all of the apparent dominance of Babe Ruth, his numbers really can't be taken seriously because the sport was rigged to ensure that some people (Black) didn't get to challenge the Babe. The name Josh Gibson immediately comes to mind, a power-hitting catcher in the Negro Leagues who might've hit more home runs than Babe Ruth, but who was never allowed the opportunity to compete in Major League Baseball.[12] In response to this discrepancy, Major League Baseball announced that the statistics from the Negro Leagues would be incorporated into their records, and as of May 2024, Josh Gibson's .466 batting average for the 1946 Homestead Grays is the highest in league history.[13]

---

12. Brian Murphy, "Reality of Josh Gibson's Incredible Talent Transcends Even His Legend," MLB.com, June 24, 2024, https://www.mlb.com/news/josh-gibson-s-stats-talent-transcend-even-his-own-legend.

13. "Statistics of the Negro Leagues Officially Enter the Major League Record," MLB.com, May 29, 2024, https://www.mlb.com/press-release/press-release-statistics

The notion that Hamilton is playing with the house's money will show up again and again. Black people everywhere, from college admissions to the space program, often find the prevailing sentiment that everything is given rather than earned when the reality is generally the opposite. No one is actually given anything. They earned it. The best stuff goes to the most talented people when the world works the way it is supposed to, whoever they are. Period. There is a really good reason for this. They get the most out of whatever the thing is. The Stradivari Society put this simply on their website: "Great instruments in the hands of rising stars thanks to generous patrons." It doesn't say, "Great instruments in the hands of mediocre musicians, because, well, whatever!" Secretariat was the greatest thoroughbred of all time, but he doesn't win anything with an incompetent jockey on his back.

Ron Dennis sees that young Lewis is burning up the road, literally, in karting with limited resources and makes the momentous decision to take Anthony up on his offer to "support the first Black Formula One Driver."

And just like Biggie, Lewis won't slow down. And it's killing them.

-of-the-negro-leagues-officially-enter-the-major-league-record#:~:text=Josh%20Gibson's%20.,Famer%20Hugh%20Duffy%20in%201894.

CHAPTER 3

F— AROUND AND FIND OUT

ONCE A DRIVER BECOMES AN ACTUAL "DRIVER," MEANING THEY ARE NO longer guiding the car remotely but inside or, in the case of karting, more like on top of the car, the sport becomes dangerous. RC racing, however competitive, is a hobby and is not part of the official pathway to Formula One. Karting is, and even though it is a minor league compared to driving open-wheeled race cars, it is expensive, time consuming, and dangerous.

Speed is all that is at stake when racing remote control cars...that and having to fix a broken toy. But, unless the plastic vehicle somehow hurtles off the track and becomes a deadly projectile, there is no danger to speak of in remote control racing.

Karting is different than toy racing, obviously, because the driver is actually part of the car. Being part of the car in the way a first-rate professional driver is means that the mechanical operations of the car—steering, acceleration, braking—are mastered and applied to a comprehensive understanding of the forces outside of the car: the track, the weather, all of the other cars. Add fuel, tire quality, mechanical problems and advantages, and driver fatigue to the mix, and you see what "part" means here.

It's reasonable to imagine that all drivers who make it to F1 have an uncanny mastery of these mechanical aspects of the cars and how they get applied to driving fast. Meaning even the "worst" driver on the grid is doing things with a car that would never occur to the average driver. And, honestly, it's best if these ideas don't crop up in the minds of the average driver, because they would probably kill themselves or someone else.

The difference in a driver who can compete for a world championship is the intangible "something" that shows up in tangible results. It is something like fearlessness in the face of heart-stopping risk that is a significant part of what we are talking about. It's not enough to say that the best drivers are not afraid to drive fast, because there is a thin line between being brave and a fool. A dead fool, to be exact. The other side of this is being too cautious to the point of being noncompetitive and actually not doing anything that comes close to racing, let alone winning. The greatest drivers occupy the razor-thin place where skill and mechanical knowledge of the stuff of racing allow for that extra something-something that separates the good from the great.

There are highly skilled drivers who have flirted with the razor's edge over the abyss. They did not live to tell the tale. The names of those who have sacrificed themselves is lengthy. Not so long a list is the names of world champions who have died racing. This is an interesting fact, which means that the best drivers have figured out the limits of the sport. They have mastered the proper balance between fast and foolish, because only two of them, Jochen Rindt in 1970 and Ayrton Senna in 1994 are the unfortunate souls etched on that memorial wall. Paying attention to the example of a world champion who crossed the line and lived to tell the tale is useful.

————

THE AUSTRIAN DRIVER, NIKI LAUDA, WORLD CHAMPION IN 1975, 1977, and 1984, is the test case. During the 1976 season, following his first world championship with Ferrari, the driver found himself with a decision to make at the German Grand Prix held at the notoriously dangerous Nürburgring. Before the race, Lauda's instincts told him that the combination of factors—the car, the competition, the weather, and the course—had tipped the scales to the point that he did not feel safe. Lauda describes this as an understanding that he had a 20 percent chance of being killed in any given race; an 80 percent chance of surviving, for the glass-half-full crowd. When the circumstances indicated that this balance was out of whack, when the survival rate dipped below 80 percent, it was time to do something different. In this circumstance, prior to the race, Lauda implored the other drivers to boycott the race. The vote failed, and the race was held, with catastrophic consequences for Lauda.

On the second lap of the race, Lauda's Ferrari hit an embankment and crashed into another driver and burst into flames. Burt Lunger, whose car Lauda ran into, escaped but the Austrian was trapped inside of his burning car. His suffering was compounded by the fact that he did not have on a helmet that fit, leaving his head and face relatively unprotected from the flames. An Italian driver, Arturo Mezario, among others, risked their lives trying to free Lauda from the rapidly burning car. In a *BBC Radio 4, Live* interview in May 2019, Niki said the following about the rescue.

> There were basically two or three drivers trying to get me out of the car, but one was Arturo Mezario, the Italian guy, who had to stop there at the scene, because I blocked the road; and he really came into the car himself, and uh, triggered my, my seatbelt loose, and then pulled me out.[1]

If not for this heroism, Niki Lauda would have been killed in this crash. The damage the fire did to his skin and lungs sent him into a coma. Niki Lauda, despite all of this, only missed two races and returned from this trip beyond the limit with a new understanding of risk. Lauda was

---

1. Radio 4, "Niki Lauda, The Fearless Racing Driver Who Survived a Terrible Crash to Make a Dramatic Comeback on the Track," *Last Word*, May 24, 2019, https://www.bbc.co.uk/programmes/p07b8ddz.

three points behind his friend and competitor James Hunt in the scoring for the world championship when the series found itself in Japan.

As is often the case at the Japanese Grand Prix at Suzuka, the course was flooded because of torrential rain. After two laps, the same number that caught Lauda out in Germany, Niki parked his car because the risk was too great. This resulted in him losing the world championship by a single point, some say damaging his relationship with Ferrari, but making it possible for him to live long enough to win another world title and become an important mentor to Lewis. To put it simply: Niki had F—ed around and found out, and wasn't going to do it again.

This "analysis" was wildly popular via a viral X (formerly Twitter) video posted in 2022 by Roger Skaer, who bills himself as the F— Around and Find Out Guy.[2] Roger proposes that there is an equal amount of finding out that comes from how much you F— around. Formula One and other dangerous activities don't work that predictably. In the real world, there is not a constant and predictable one-to-one relationship between F—ing around and finding out. Second, things can go wrong very quickly and often unpredictably.

Lauda sensed this before the German Grand Prix but did not act upon the information, which was to do something about his concern and back out of the race if it wasn't canceled altogether. In Germany, in spite of that lapse, he made it to the other side. After missing two races because of his injuries, Lauda made it back to the grid in Japan. There, unlike in Germany, the driver walked away before he crossed the line and risked ending up with another catastrophe. All Formula One drivers, good, great, bad, or indifferent, are always thinking about this at some level.

The fact that F1 is much "safer" in the aftermath of what happened to Lauda, or after the deaths of Rindt and Senna, doesn't mean it is anywhere near "safe." As Lewis transitions from the absolute safety of driving a toy car to driving/racing a kart where he is physically exposed, safety isn't just something he needs to think about but something the

---

2. "Roger Skaers the F around and Find Out Guy," October 6, 2022, https://www.tik tok.com/@eunicemathis/video/7151328158631873835?lang=en.

Hamilton family has to think about for him and themselves. Parents are always having to navigate the question of safety for their children until they become old enough to make decisions for themselves. This must be particularly poignant as Lewis moves up in racing and danger... F—ing around, while his parents are on the sidelines, powerless, and hoping that he has learned enough to avoid finding out too much. That is one thing. There is another safety concern that is unique to Lewis and his family.

Even in the remote-control world where there was supposed to be no danger, the Hamiltons were threatened with physical and other kinds of risk. At no point in his "career," even when he was playing with what might be considered toys, was Lewis or his family ever safe, physically or emotionally. This is true of all Black people who cross boundaries, whenever or wherever those boundaries happen to be.

Visiting the *On Purpose* podcast, Lewis tells Jay Shetty, podcaster née monk, that at some point a father of one of his "competitors" cornered him and told him it was best for him to just quit the sport because, wait for it, *things were going too well and nothing good could come of it all.*[3] Linger with the "nothing good can come of it" warning. The intimidator can't mean that Lewis won't win, which is "good," because he already is. The threat is that the winning will cause a backlash. Obviously, this man's attempt to get rid of Lewis didn't succeed, but it's worth considering the negative energy that it takes to *threaten children* and at the same time their families. Attempts to get Lewis to quit occurred not only at races but also during his education.

Lewis tells another story of a situation in school that occurred when he was sixteen years old. It too could have led to all of his promise on the track being ruined. For some reason, a fellow student was beaten to the point of fractures and soft tissue injuries in a bathroom at the school. Without evidence, the headmaster (another villain who has been granted much undeserved anonymity) kicked Lewis out of school, saying

---

3. "Lewis Hamilton: Everything You've Been Taught About Success Is a Lie," posted January 23, 2023, by Jay Shetty Podcast, YouTube, https://youtu.be/AyiWK XTd9aY?si=1nTq95sk4KZ619PN.

something to the effect that he "finally had enough to get rid of" him. Lewis was expelled for two months. Only because of his father's advocacy was it proven that Lewis had absolutely nothing to do with the beating, and he was allowed back in school.[4]

As parents make decisions for their children that are meant to keep them safe, it is also a sort of training for the child to make good decisions on their own. Just as a parent can't be at school with a child as they navigate the good and the bad, this is even more true for children and sports. The white lines that serve as the boundary of the field of play, or in this case racing, are everything that is good and bad about sports. What is bad is that once the athlete is inside of those boundaries, no one can help them. The good thing is that once an athlete is inside of those boundaries, no one can help them. All of the racing decisions are hard enough on their own. All of the things most kids have to put up with in school are hard, too. Most parents just hope that it goes okay for them. The Hamiltons and those like them have a whole other set of risks that may not be apparent but must be taken seriously.

Lewis certainly does. Remember his comments about how tattoos tell an individual's journey. Consider the clock as the backdrop for the child whose only risk is the moment of weightlessness between the toss and the catch. Lewis says that he is memorializing a time when there was no "business" between him and his dad. I want to propose that it was a time, however brief but more meaningful because of the brevity of it, that the two weren't F—ing around and didn't have to worry about finding anything out. Not in karts or trying to fight their way from the parking lot to the starting line or to escape with their trophies without punishment for their excellence. Also not being blamed for fights that they weren't involved with or reading social media posts years later that say that it is all a con. The story that Lewis is telling with his body art is that he had found a place of rest and peace where he and his dad could really live the

4. "F1 Ace Hamilton Wrongly Expelled from School for Breaking Pupil's Fingers," *The Standard*, April 12, 2012 https://www.standard.co.uk/hp/front/f1-ace-hamilton-wrongly-expelled-from-school-for-breaking-pupils-fingers-6591001.html.

opposite of F—ing around and finding out. It's 200 miles per hour in an open-wheeled race car inches off the ground while having to deal with a bunch of crap that had nothing to do with making that happen.

Anthony was always trying to balance the dad part with the manager part, and a racing tragedy demonstrates the problem.

———————

BRAZILIAN DRIVER AYRTON SENNA IS ONE OF THE TWO WORLD CHAMPIONS who was killed racing. In Lewis's 2007 autobiography, *Lewis Hamilton: My Story*, he grants us a window into his awareness of the physical danger posed by racing. The year before he met Ron Dennis while celebrating his British Cadet Championship, tragedy struck the sport. He describes it this way in his book.

> The year before, I'd experienced the real dangers of motor racing for the first time. I remember it was early May and I was at Rye House. I had just finished a race and my dad quietly came over to me and said, "Lewis, Ayrton Senna's just died...He'd had a terrible crash at Imola..." I remember how I did not want to show emotions in front of my dad because I thought he would have a go at me and so I walked round the back, where no one was looking, and I just cried. I really struggled the rest of that day. I could not stop imagining what had gone on. I was only nine years old. The man who inspired me was dead. He was a superhero; you know and that was him...just gone.[5]

Take note of the brevity with which Lewis deals with this tragedy in his book. This is the entire treatment of the death of his hero, except for a mention later in the book that he never got to meet him and a paparazzi-foiled attempt to pay homage at Senna's grave in Brazil. Senna's

———————

5. *Lewis Hamilton: My Story*, 61–62.

legacy continues to be part of Lewis's journey in Formula One and has particular importance for his activism. The clipped way that he deals with this loss is directly related to the way drivers deal with death.

Obviously, this account of his reaction to Senna's death is told from the perspective of a driver whose Formula One dream had come true recalling what he felt when he was nine years old. But it reveals something interesting about the complexity of the relationship between Anthony and his child. What Anthony Hamilton knows is that the world, with or without racing, can be a cruel place and more so for Black people. That is thing one. The hard exterior and tough love that Lewis recalls here is a common way of relating to children for Black parents, who can be harsh to their children to "prepare" them for the world. Part of that is to learn not to let the world see that you are hurt, even in the face of unspeakable tragedy. You don't have to be a psychologist or somatic healer to know that this isn't the best way to develop emotional health, but it is an all too common experience. Black people are often brought up to understand that the world doesn't care about their feelings. The world may not care about the feelings of Black people, but another way to see this episode is as proof that Anthony cared deeply about his son's emotional and physical safety. Lewis's account can be understood to be the story of a father who loved his son and who needed him to be clearheaded and take care while taking the same sort of risk that killed his hero. Anthony might well be saying in his own way that maybe on this racing weekend the fates could be cruel, and rather than placing laurels on the heads of once and future champions they were swinging scythes at their necks. Lewis has his private cry that his dad pretends not to see, and I'll bet Mr. Hamilton had one of his own; and by his own admission, Lewis backed off for the rest of the weekend.

The questions in the form of statements that finish off Lewis's account—"I could not stop imagining what had gone on...The man who inspired me was dead...He was a superhero..."—are the voice of the professional cheater of death. Lewis is someone who has seen another virtuoso of the form come to ruin and has to do his own cruel calculus of what his hero must have done wrong. It can't be that it just happened, that when you play dangerous games, part of the bargain is that things just happen, and people end up dead. It can't "just happen," because that would mean that the real answer to Niki Lauda's death calculus was to park the car forever, and neither Lewis nor his dad had any intention of doing that.

What "happened" to Senna, to Lewis's point after the fact, is of real importance for Formula One and something that approximates safety. The San Marino Grand Prix at the Imola Circuit in the Emilia-Romagna region of Italy was cruel that weekend. The day before Senna's death, during qualifying, the Austrian driver Roland Ratzenberger was killed in a wreck. Ratzenberger's death should have been a wakeup call, because it was the first in the sport in more than a decade. The violence of the crash that killed Ayrton Senna is not worth rehashing here. Let it suffice to say that he ran into a concrete barrier going 130 miles per hour. Grisly photos of the devastation have never been seen by the public because the photographer who was on the scene was a friend of Ayrton's, and his family has agreed to keep them hidden. The crash ushered in a new era of safety concerns for Formula One. The sport had raced on borrowed time for twelve years in the aftermath of the death of one of its greatest stars; that, along with a handful of other serious crashes at the same circuit, made it clear that something had to be done. The governing body, at the time that Lewis is headed for the top series, begins to take seriously the safety of the drivers, mechanics, and spectators as the twenty-first century looms, and the cars keep getting faster, and danger mounts.

CHAPTER 4

THE TECHNOLOGY ARMS RACE

As soon as there were cars, there were people who wanted to race them. But a race necessarily requires rules. Safety is an obvious concern, but there are many other things to consider to make sure the competition makes sense. It's not enough, for instance, to decide on the distance of a marathon without coming to some agreement about how it is supposed to be run. It wouldn't make sense for some people to be on foot and others out there on Rollerblades. The same goes for motor sports.

It probably wasn't long after the second horseless carriage showed up that the two owners began to wonder who had the faster car. Drivers A & B might try to come up with ways to modify their cars to get more and more performance out of them, but as human innovation goes, it would only be a matter of time before one car may be completely unrecognizable from where they started. One way to think about motorsports might be to imagine it as a kind of technological arms race where pretty much anything with an engine and wheels that mostly stays in contact with the ground would be acceptable.

This is one way that car racing exists in the popular imagination, perhaps especially for people who grew up rushing home from school to watch the

Speed Racer cartoon in the 1970s. Speed, the likewise predictably named son of his father, "Pops" Racer, was always adding stuff to his car, the Mach 5, to make it competitive with whatever weirdness showed up to line up against him: cars with wings that could basically fly, some with rocket boosters, even a "Mammoth Car" that was about the size of a locomotive.

This imagined race world reveals the challenge is just to get from one place to the other as fast as possible; pretty much anything was acceptable. Kids didn't want to see much in the way of alteration to the body of the Mach 5, so Pops outfitted it with at least five James Bond–like gizmos that were activated by buttons on the steering wheel. The website Jalopnik.com has an article by Jason Torchinsky that lays out what each button in the car did.[1] For instance, Button A activated these mega jacks that Speed could use to leap over obstacles. My personal favorite has always been Button C, which released huge spinning blades that could mow down trees or slash the tires of his competitors. As ridiculous as Speed Racer's buttons may have been, there was an era of Formula One when regulations were less stringent, when there could be a lack of uniformity to the point of just plain weird cars on the grid. The 1976 six-wheeled Tyrrell P34 is one that sticks out for its engineering, which figured that adding two more tires would improve traction and for the fact that it actually won a Grand Prix.

Today, the parameters are much more stringent, and the governing body of all motorsports, the FIA, works hard to make sure engineers can innovate while at the same time avoiding a grid that looks like it was drawn by super creative sixth graders who are into cars, or by cartoonists in the 1970s.

———————

The Fédération Internationale de l'Automobile (FIA) was created on June 20, 1904, and maintains all the standards that make modern

---

1. Jason Torchinsky, "Finally, Here's a Guide to Those Buttons on Speed Racer's Mach 5 Steering Wheel," Jalopnik, August 19, 2020, https://jalopnik.com/finally -heres-a-guide-to-those-buttons-on-speed-racers-1844768068.

racing as different from *Speed Racer* as it can be while at the same time setting it up as a laboratory for automotive engineering that shows up in the cars we drive.

The FIA structure and the global series of races, Grand Prix, are designed to crown two champions at the end of each season: a world champion driver and what is known as the constructors' champion. The latter is awarded to the team that has accumulated the most points. Generally, the math means that the team with the best driver accumulates the most points, but that is not always the case. Though the world is focused on the individual driver at the end of season who reigns supreme, the teams relish the Constructors' Championship as much if not more because it comes with money...lots of it. In 2021 constructors' champion Mercedes-AMG PETRONAS received $61 million as compared to the relatively paltry sum of $13 million to the last-place team. This all sounds great, but as we know, there is a long and winding path to worrying about world titles that includes figuring out how to grab hold of one of the twenty available seats in Formula One.

The existence of this governing body not only speaks to technological issues but also establishes a predictable, though fraught, path to the big time. Recall that between 1993 and 2001, Lewis and his dad are competing in karting, which is likewise governed by the FIA and represents the first tentative steps on the path to glory.

This path necessarily and fortunately has guardrails and regulatory hurdles that ensure that someone doesn't somehow show up on the grid at Monaco and not know what they are doing. This is mostly obvious in the case of someone who has too much money and not enough skill. A person like this could, theoretically, have enough loot to get themselves a team and a car and enter Formula One as a deadly vanity project. What the FIA understands is that this would turn whatever race this individual appeared in from a grand prix to a one-and-done episode of *The Death-Styles of the Rich, Famous, and Foolhardy.*

To avoid this scenario, there are standards for drivers that ultimately require them to earn an FIA Racing Super License. There is a requirement to pass a FIA theory exam on the sporting regulations, which may sound strange. It's hard to imagine drivers working through the theory of rules, but that is what it is called. Obviously, racing is a thinking endeavor, but most obviously a physical one, so there are some rigorous experience and performance standards that must be adhered to.

There is also the basic requirement that you must be eighteen years old for a Super License. Then the difficult part: an aspirant must manage to complete 80 percent of the races over two seasons in a qualifying single-seat championship series. They must also accumulate at least forty Super License points over the course of three seasons. These regulations are laid out in gross detail of Appendix L of the FIA's International Sporting Code.[2] The theory behind these time frames is related to the point allocation across the various sub-series to F1.

For instance, the championship in Formula Two awards forty points to first, second, and third place. Formula Three gives out thirty points to the champion, twenty-five to the runner-up, and twenty to the third-place driver. Either of these series, according to the thinking of the FIA, would give a driver sufficient experience over the course of three seasons at the upper ranks to be eligible for a Super License. That license is most likely to stay in that person's pocket and never see the light of day in Formula One, but that is what it takes to meet the minimum requirements.

There are also Super License points to be had way down in the karting ranks. The three-season rule requires that a driver make progress up the ranks, learning the things that will keep them from killing themselves or someone else when the races get much faster. These regulations also prevent a person from hanging out in the Senior Karting World Championship for a decade and collecting a championship every year at four points a pop and arguing they have met the requirements for the coveted Super License.

---

2. "FIA Statutes and Internal Regulations" (link to PDF), FIA, n.d., https://www.fia .com/fia-statutes-and-internal-regulations.

Lewis joined the McLaren Young Driver Programme in 1998 when he was thirteen years old, which meant he had at least four-plus years to deal with karting before the window would open and make it both possible and sensible for him to move up to race cars. Lewis and his dad started on the path in earnest in 1999 in the Intercontinental A series. In 2000, they moved up to Formula A first and then directly to Formula Super A in 2001, where Lewis won the European Championship. He was sixteen years old and within the window to make a run at forty points in a race car to begin to push for a seat in F1. Lewis's karting days would soon be over.

In 2001, he moved closer to F1 via the British Formula Renault Winter Series, which folded its tent in 2011. McLaren set him up for a seat with Manor Motorsport, meaning that he was finally going to have an opportunity to drive a "real" race car, in this case a single-seat, open-wheeled car. Lewis said of this test:

> McLaren arranged for me to have a test with Manor Motorsport in their Formula Renault car. It was going to be tricky, never having been in a racing car before, and I crashed after about three laps, taking out the right corner of the car. It did not put them off too much though and after they fixed the car I got straight back in and did okay.[3]

If there was a notion that karting success would translate into readiness for a race car, the Hamiltons were quickly disabused of that notion on day one, lap 3. Imagine if Anthony were footing the bill when Lewis cracked up the Formula Renault. A vintage 2000 Renault racer costs around 90,000 euros today. Without the financial backing from these institutions, these few laps would have been the grand opening and grand closing of this venture for the Hamiltons. Fortunately, the good people at Manor fixed the car, and they moved on.

Despite the financial support, this was a difficult time for Lewis and

3. *Lewis Hamilton: My Story*, 65.

his family, personally and professionally, both as separate ventures and as the lines between the two things became increasingly difficult to discern. They had weathered the storm caused by Lewis's expulsion from school because of the accusations surrounding the fight, but at this stage, Lewis admitted that he considered giving it all up as he struggled to adjust to race cars.[4] He pulled it together by the end of that season and finished third in the competition in 2002.

The following year, 2003, was a much better year for Lewis. He won ten of the fifteen races that season, and the next step for the Hamiltons was the British Formula Three series and then on to the Formula Three Euroseries in 2004, still with Manor Motorsport. In his autobiography, *My Story*, Lewis described 2003 as "the absolutely worst year of my racing career both because of the car and the relationship with the team."[5] Lewis attributes this to the fact that this was Manor's first year in Formula Renault, so driver, team, and Lewis's management (Anthony) were dealing with a steep learning curve. All of that is fine, but in Lewis's estimation he was given the vast majority of the blame for the poor showing. At this critical moment in the path to F1, Lewis and his father could not come to an agreement with McLaren about the way forward. This was a serious problem. Lewis did not want to spend another year with Manor, and McLaren stood firm on requiring another year in Formula Three with that team.

The last two races of the 2004 season saw Lewis without the financial support of McLaren. While he was attending college (at the same time all of this racing is going on), he had begun a relationship with Jodia Ma, whose father owned a corporation in her native Hong Kong. Jodia offered to have her dad back his race in Macau. Lewis initially said he wouldn't accept that help before finally relenting and went to the race.

The Formula Three Euroseries typically has two races per day, and Lewis won the first but crashed out of the second from pole position.

---

4. *Lewis Hamilton: My Story*, 66.
5. *Lewis Hamilton: My Story*, 67.

Not an auspicious return on the investment of Mr. Ma and an even worse setup for the season's last race in Bahrain.

Somehow, Manor agreed to foot the bill for the Formula Three Super-prix final in Bahrain; it seemed to both Lewis and his dad that this was the critical moment for this situation and the end of the road for the Formula One dream. The complicated dad/manager relationship exacerbated the already difficult task Lewis had in front of him after screwing up qualifying and starting the race in twenty-second place. Things weren't looking good, and Lewis lays out the difficult details in his book.

> We were both devastated but my dad in particular because as usual he felt responsible for everything, the loss of McLaren, the situation we were in, and he was worried about where he would find the money to keep my career going and to fund the following year's racing. He was so depressed and worried that he booked an early flight home so that he could make better use of his time making calls and focusing on getting help. I know he was really feeling the pressure because I had no sponsor and at that stage not enough good performances to attract new ones. Before he left, he made sure I knew all about it, leaving me to kick myself for the rest of that day and all night.[6]

Despite this negative energy and financial instability, Lewis was able to pull it together. He ended up eleventh from his twenty-second place starting position in the first race, and ended up going from eleventh to first place in the second. And then the phone rang. Again.

> The next thing I knew, Martin Whitmarsh from McLaren came on the phone to congratulate me and said, "We'll decide where we can go from here." That was typical of Martin and Ron, they were always there somewhere in the background

---

6. *Lewis Hamilton: My Story*, 69.

keeping an eye on me. They really cared and wanted to help but also wanted us to learn the hard way.[7]

With Lewis back in the McLaren fold, some decisions had to be made. A figure who will become another central player in Lewis's career, Frédéric Vasseur, shows up at this critical moment in his role as the owner and operator of the Formula Three Euroseries Championship team ASM. In his first year with ASM, Lewis won fifteen of twenty races and the series, and in 2006 made his way to the GP2 Series with ART Grand Prix, which was also under the management of Vasseur. This was his last campaign outside of Formula One. He won the GP2 and pressured McLaren to give him the seat he had worked toward since *Blue Peter*.

A seat as the teammate of world champion Spaniard Fernando Alonso with McLaren was his. He had fulfilled his dream of getting to Formula One. Now the question was, what he would do with the opportunity?

7. *Lewis Hamilton: My Story*, 70.

CHAPTER 5

"HELLO, WORLD"

THE WAY SPORTS ARE PRESENTED TO THE PUBLIC THROUGH THE MEDIA doesn't accurately depict the journey from the amateur ranks to pro. Even the Little League World Series, a broadcast of children playing an amateur sport, takes place on a field that bears no resemblance to what a baseball diamond looks like at your local park district. The public only sees sports at its most refined state: venues like center court at Wimbledon, with six officials, an equal number of ball fetchers, and as many perfect balls as a player can caress until finding the one they like the best and smacking the rest back for someone to retrieve while they get on with their match. The thousands of hours spent with substandard equipment, incompetent officials, overworked coaches, and poorly maintained venues is not something the viewing public has to endure. When we turn on a baseball game, even Little League on ESPN, all the balls are white. In the major leagues, the used balls are sent down to the minor leagues, where they don't have the luxury of the single use of a baseball. At every level of the sport balls get reused. In the major leagues, the balls, like the fields, the clubhouses, the hotels, the flights, the buses, the food, the drinks, everything is as perfect as a ball straight out of the box, and once it gets a speck of dirt, it is shipped away to be used by lesser beings. If the balls are white in the major leagues, then they must be platinum in Formula One.

––––––––––

The March 2024 issue of ROAD & TRACK magazine had an article by Kate Wagner that carries the title "Behind F1's Velvet Curtain." The article has since been removed from the Road & Track website. One might speculate that the class arguments Wagner made in the piece were deemed controversial. The well-done piece tries to make sense of the all too calculable wealth that sloshes around the sport from the perspective of a person who styles themself as what I would call "poor-ish" or "poor-like." Not poor at all, but perfectly willing to act as if they are, particularly the way everyone is "poor" compared to a person who watches Formula One qualifying while jogging on a treadmill from their superyacht docked trackside in Monaco. (Don't ask. You can't afford it.) Wagner poetically equates the precision of Formula One to fencing, writing, "One thing that strikes me about Formula One is its unexpected resemblance to fencing—it is an absolutely poised and disciplined affair. Recently for my 30th birthday, I took up medieval sword fighting." Let's be clear, the poor don't fence now and didn't back then, but we will play along with the piece because it gets the sport right. The gist of the article lingers on the author's time pressed up against the glass of a Formula One weekend from the perspective of a person who generally covers cycling, where professional riders make about $50,000 a year. (Still, the winner of the Tour de France makes about 6 million euros a year, while the average salary of a person doing essential and generally unglamorous work is about $59,000 a year.) Behind the velvet curtain of Formula One, Wagner finds the seedlings of the vanguard of communist world revolution.

> I think if you wanted to turn someone into a socialist you
> could do it in about an hour by taking them for a spin around
> the paddock of a Formula 1 race. No need for corny art sing-
> ing tribute to the worker or even for the *Manifesto*. Never

before had I seen so many wealthy people gathered all in one place. If a tornado came through and wiped the whole thing out, the stock market would plummet and the net worth of a country the size of Slovenia would vanish from the ledgers in a day. I used to live in Baltimore and remembered the kind of people who would go to the Preakness in their stupid hats and Sunday best while the whole swath of the city it was situated in starved and languished for lack of funds. This was like that, but without the hats. I saw $30,000 Birkin bags and $10,000 Off-White Nikes. I saw people with the kind of Rolexes that make strangers cry on *Antiques Roadshow*. I saw Ozempic-riddled influencers and fleshy, T-shirt-clad tech bros and people who still talked with *Great Gatsby* accents as they sweated profusely in Yves Saint Laurent under the unforgiving Texas sun. The kind of money I saw will haunt me forever. People clinked glasses of free champagne in outfits worth more than the market price of all the organs in my body. I stood there among them in a thrift-store blouse and shorts from Target.[1]

As mentioned, it seems that the explicit left-wing critique of capitalism ended up causing the story to be pulled by *Road & Track* magazine.[2] For all of its perceived radical potential, if you wanted to encourage someone to embrace socialism, it would be better to have them visit an under-resourced school in a decimated census tract in Detroit, not a Grand Prix. But Wagner's type of analysis can find itself landing on the form of player hating that shows up again and again in the criticism of Lewis. He just doesn't belong here because a) none of us or maybe no one belongs, b) he's a

---

1. Jacqui Shine, "Behind F1's Velvet Curtain: Kate Wagner on Formula 1 Racing," Well, Actually, Substack, March 4, 2024, https://wellactually.substack.com/p /behind-f1s-velvet-curtain-kate-wagner.
2. Kate Wagner, "Behind F1's Velvet Curtain," Longreads, March 7, 2024, https:// longreads.com/2024/03/07/behind-f1s-velvet-curtain/.

hypocrite because he comments on being Black and working class when he was granted privileges because of that, and/or c) people who are serious about social justice, the environment, etc., wouldn't participate in a sport like this. All Black athletes have had to face similar criticisms. In order to fully understand what Lewis was going through, let's look again at how another boy and his father navigated similar circumstances.

———————

"HELLO, WORLD." WHEN TIGER WOODS SAID THIS AT THE PRESS CON-ference about his announcement that he was turning pro, it was a greeting to a closed space that he, like Lewis, would alter forever. The territory that Lewis would enter had in some sense already been mapped by Tiger years before in the path to the moral crisis of Black folks eating fried chicken in the American South. In 1996, at the Greater Milwaukee Open, ironically, or perhaps purposefully the same event that had hosted Calvin Peete's first PGA Tour victory two decades before, Tiger spoke to the press.

Like Lewis, the telltale signs of the force of nature that is Woods had been spotted on the horizon of the PGA for many years. Think about the "forecast" of Tiger's arrival as similar to the way a weather alert about a coming blizzard is received by kids who want to have school canceled and parents who have things to do and need these kids to be out of the house. Some people were excited about the arrival of Tiger, and others hoped it was just overhyped and would end up in no measurable accumulation. Of course, there is a lot of space between these two extremes, but there are also those who hate snow just because it's snow or maybe because it's August or South Beach where it "doesn't belong."

Tiger, like Lewis, had been a media figure for a long time before turning pro. At two years old, Tiger and his dad, Earl, showed up on *The Mike Douglas Show* for a segment with the host and Bob Hope and Jimmy Stewart. This was 1978. There is a short, heavily redacted clip of the segment online. It is a complicated event.[3] The video shows how uncom-

———————

3. "Tiger Woods' First TV Appearance with Mike Douglas, Bob Hope, Jimmy

fortable the child is. In Jeff Benedict and Armen Keteyian's book *Tiger Woods*, the two write:

> It's easy to see this as a funny moment, but Tiger's appearance on *The Mike Douglas Show* revealed that he shared textbook attributes of what child psychologists refer to as the gifted child: quiet, sensitive, isolated. There was the incessant, nervous pulling at his ear; his obvious desire to please his father; and his need to succeed, indicated by his determination to ensure he didn't miss his final putt.[4]

These authors lean into this event and ones that follow, proposing that Earl Woods, in pushing his son in this way, caused people to think along the same lines as what actor Jimmy Stewart intimated to Mike Douglas backstage: "I've seen too many precious kids like this sweet little boy, and too many starry-eyed parents."[5] The concern here was, according to Benedict and Keteyian, that "Stewart had been around show business for almost sixty years and had seen his fair share of little children who had been put onto the big stage by parents who failed to recognize or appreciate the long-term consequences of early stardom."[6] This might well be true, but I want to propose another understanding of what Earl Woods was up to based upon what we know about his training and time in the Special Forces in Vietnam.

I think Earl fully recognized and appreciated the long-term effects of putting a two-year-old under this type of public pressure. I think he was perfectly comfortable with Tiger missing putts and worrying about pleasing him at two because at thirty when he has the chip-in of all chip-ins before him at the Masters, he will make the shot. Tiger had lived under

Stewart," posted June 13, 2016, by Eclecto Tuber, YouTube, https://youtu.be/6XupL9h0DOc?si=rb8Kpb067wJJk2pX.

4. Jeff Benedict and Armen Keteyian, *Tiger Woods* (Simon and Schuster, 2018), 24.

5. Benedict and Keteyian, *Tiger Woods*, 24.

6. Benedict and Keteyian, *Tiger Woods*, 24.

extreme pressure his entire life, both personally and professionally, and the complexity of parsing what it all means for him, those around him, and us as spectators to the triumph and tragedy, remains.

The editing of the YouTube segment removes a complicated part of the interaction. The YouTube segment is only thirty-six seconds long. There are commentators who claim to have seen the original broadcast and elements of it that are important to think with.

YouTube handle @imbees2 posted two notes of their remembrance of the show. The first reads: Mike Douglas said on camera, 'look at that little monkey go!' And patted tigers[sic] head. The second: In that video, Mike Douglas said on air, 'look at that monkey play.' I saw it myself on tv. They cut that part out. Notably, no one refutes this claim. Someone called @laverite9082 added this note: Adults would say that in an endearing fashion to youngsters at play; it was not considered to be an insult, as some today might construe.

Armed with this speculation, there is another way to consider this show, and it's not so much about what Earl Woods intended or what the long-term effects on Tiger may have been. The show was known for its gimmicks, the kind of campy stuff that passed for entertainment on daytime TV in the 1970s. They saw this as just that kind of thing. A kid playing golf is one thing. A Black kid playing golf is another and would cause the audience and the hosts to focus on the novelty of a Black person of whatever age playing golf and have no idea that it had anything to do with mastery of the entire sport in the mind of the father. By the time of the "Hello, World" press conference, the golf world had been anticipating the arrival of Tiger, and this was the start.

The press conference is vintage Tiger: the big smile, carefully scripted, thoughtful, and his dad weirdly sitting in an easy chair next to the lectern. Two things stick out that are important for situating Lewis in relation to Tiger. The first is the golfer's response to a question about representation. Chris Collins from CBS in Milwaukee frames the question by asking Tiger about his appeal to groups who have "hardly been associated with golf" who are coming out to see him. Books could be written on Tiger's (mis)understanding of things regarding race, but here he makes a fairly coherent statement about the exclusionary nature of golf and notes that his dad and others were working to increase minority participation.

The other point of commonality between the experiences of the Woods and Hamilton families is obviously this question of access. The Woods family couldn't afford membership, even if all these places let Black folks into the clubs where the best courses are found. Like the journey to Formula One, a golfer needs to learn what it's like to play the game on world-class courses. Earl Woods's marketing plan, the first most public step being the *Mike Douglas* segment, was about using the novelty of Tiger to get him free access to the best course and instruction possible, and it worked.

In the same press conference, when Tiger is asked what he had found different about the move to the PGA, he echoes the luxury of Major League Baseball. All the balls in both places are white. You can only imagine what it must have been like for Lewis to step behind the velvet curtain of Formula One, not as a spectator or a potential driver but as a member of one of the premier teams in the sport.

Did anyone say, "Look at the monkey go!" to Lewis? When people mobbed a track in Barcelona dressed as gorillas with shirts that proposed they were part of the "Hamilton Family" and threw bananas, we find that the racist primate trope would become part of Lewis's reality as well.

By design, Lewis's arrival to the public at his F1 debut was a quieter affair. The team principal of McLaren, Ron Dennis, had restricted the media's access to the rookie driver so he would not be distracted from the task at hand.

The months since the end of his GP2 campaign and the opening of the Formula One season had been filled with work. Lewis describes the half-year of preparation in his 2007 biography:

...for six months leading up to my first Grand Prix in Australia, I was in the factory every day, from eight in the morning until six or later in the evening. Ron and Martin had basically given a number of people at McLaren the task of transforming me from a GP2 driver into a Formula One driver.[7]

Despite all of this documented hard work, critics of Hamilton came up with yet another demeaning explanation for his success. It is reminiscent of ridiculous theories like "Aliens must have built the pyramids" because people can't figure out how *those people* did it. One of the people tasked by McLaren to get Lewis ready for the demands (physical and mental) of Formula One was mathematician and astrophysicist turned neuroscientist and sports performance guru Dr. Kerry Spackman. *The Guardian*'s Richard Williams checked in with the performance coach and wrote about the encounter in an article entitled "The Brain Rewiring and Supercharging that Makes Hamilton a Master" in May 2007. While chatting over a model described as "Lewis Hamilton's brain," which is actually a model of everyone's brain, Dr. Spackman throws back this layer of the veil over the secrets of this newcomer's success:

> "We didn't evolve to drive racing cars," he is saying. "Our brains have developed over millions of years and in some ways they're incredibly sophisticated, but in others they're very ill suited to some of the tasks we want them to do. In most sports now, the modern athlete is pushing his brain to the limit. Today's formula one car does things almost instantaneously, and the brain can't keep up. The idea is to rewire its circuits, to supercharge its processes, so that it's more suited to the task. To turn it from a computer into a supercomputer, if you like."[8]

---

7. *Lewis Hamilton: My Story*, 90.
8. Richard Williams, "The Brain Rewiring and Supercharging That Makes Hamilton a Master," *The Guardian*, May 25, 2007, https://www.theguardian.com/sport/2007/may/26/motorsports.sport.

Many people would read this and think that it makes sense to be attentive to this element of the sport (and that there must be a lot of PhDs out there who would trade their classrooms and faculty meetings for the klieg lights of Formula One). Humans have evolved over the course of roughly 6 million years, and we have been driving cars for about 150 years. Outside of the speed of a horse, human hand–eye coordination was a matter of reacting to objects that arrived at pedestrian speeds: literally. In the case of driving a Formula One car, or piloting a high-performance aircraft, the mind and body are asked to do things that exceed the performance that was necessary for more than 5 million years. Teams are seeking to extract every bit of performance out of both driver and car, understanding that the vehicle's capabilities are likely beyond those of the operator. Part of closing that gap is training the brain to process information differently, not just faster. The brain must be trained to resist reactions that would tend to say "stop" when the key to winning is "go."

The effort to assist Lewis in developing this part of his skill set is added to the list of reasons that Lewis is nothing more than a product of being rewarded and awarded things other drivers deserved and weren't given. Adding insult to injury, some will say Lewis is also ungrateful and falls back on the "race card" to explain it all at the same time. Worrell covers this in his book.

> There was suggestion by some pundits that Dennis played Frankenstein to Lewis, that he was making his Formula One creation. This theory was backed up, they claimed, by the fact that Big Ron had hired Dr. Kerry Spackman, a New Zealand-born neuroscientist, apparently to turn the boy into a race-winning machine.[9]

It is important to note that the twenty-one-year-old is repeatedly called "boy" in various accounts. More on this later.

---

9. Frank Worrall, *Lewis Hamilton: The Biography* (John Blake, 2021), 72.

Ron Dennis, upon hearing this nonsense, attempted to correct the record by noting that Lewis is one of several drivers who have access to this kind of sophisticated training. Despite this fact, some continue to see Lewis as a product or figment of Dennis's imagination and expertise. Ron Dennis was positively protective of his investment in Lewis, and the decision to keep Lewis away from a frenzied media scrum was the right approach.

There is an interview that Dennis allowed with Hamilton during the days preceding his debut at the Australian Grand Prix that sheds light on what the driver felt was possible. The rookie sits down with an interviewer who lobs a few softball questions that he handles easily. They are mostly questions about the jump from GP2. Lewis presents himself as confident, not arrogant. He is eager to take ownership of his work ethic and skill but goes out of his way to recognize that he is only the most visible element of a team. In short, he is gracious. He talks about the extreme level of preparation he's embarked upon and the sharp learning curve that is the entire point of Formula One.

The interviewer presses beyond the boilerplate questions and asks him whether the first half of the season would and should be devoted to learning and the second part to competition. Lewis pauses almost imperceptibly and then agrees, all of this in the context of him joining a team that included a double world champion, Fernando Alonso. Lewis buys into the notion that he wasn't expected to compete during the first half of the season, but he must have had his fingers crossed, because as the world would see as the weekend in Melbourne unfolded, he was not there to be tutored by any other driver, especially not his teammate.[10]

Most important, and this is also a window into the strategic thinking of Ron Dennis, Lewis was uninterested in being symbolic, or more precisely, "only" a symbol of diversity and progress. Branch Rickey, the Dodgers' executive who successfully broke the color line in the baseball major leagues with Jackie Robinson, comes to mind. According to Ken

---

10. "Fernando Alonso Interview Melbourne 2007," posted March 14, 2020, by F1 World, YouTube, https://youtu.be/Dn2VOocGHTo?si=9JEUXNTCCoM0ueJz.

Burns's documentary *Baseball*, part of Rickey's legacy of innovation came from a business perspective, and a genuine concern with the immorality of segregation motivated his efforts.

Ron Dennis was dedicated to putting McLaren in a position to win world championships, and that meant putting the best drivers he could find in the best cars he could engineer. Lewis, race notwithstanding, certainly showed the aptitude to be a first-rate driver. There is no direct evidence that Dennis was working, like Branch Rickey, to right a wrong. Unlike the open and documented segregation of Major League Baseball, Formula One didn't have to care for all of the reasons that we have traced. Dennis was obviously aware that there were no other Black drivers, so his effort to support Lewis through good times and bad could not have been only about Lewis's skill. What it does illustrate is what advocates of diversity, equity, and inclusion set as the goal for these efforts. Ron Dennis found a talent in a place and situation and body that Formula One was predisposed to ignore. He did the opposite, and it paid off.

To the extent that McLaren had pulled its support from the Hamiltons, there was literally zero chance that another team would have stepped in to embarrass Ron for not hanging in there. Lewis would have disappeared from the sport, and it would have moved on. Ron Dennis made the decision that it was time for the sport to open its lens and its wallet. And he meant for it to lead to the winner's circle, not as a short-term project in social engineering by way of automotive engineering.

This did not sit well with Fernando Alonso.

CHAPTER 6

FORMULA ONE 101

A GRAND PRIX WEEKEND BEGINS ON THURSDAY AND ENDS ON SUNDAY. In most cases, the weekend is divided into three distinct phases. Phase one is called "free practice," and each session is designated sequentially FP1, FP2, etc. This first phase is meant to allow all the drivers to familiarize themselves with the racecourse and how the car performs with various setups. These include tire compound (more about this later), fuel load, aerodynamics, etc. This is analogous to the early stages of a driver's career when they are essentially starting from scratch and dealing with basic questions of driving fast. Well-run teams and experienced drivers know what they do and don't know about the car and how it will perform at different venues. Some of this is as basic as the profound differences between running a car on a street course like Monaco or a track like Silverstone, so their performance week to week, for better or for worse, is often predictable.

These drivers have all come up through the ranks where GP2 and Formula 2 races are often held on the same courses as Formula One. But the first ride in an F1 car on any course can present even the most talented driver with a steep learning curve. Teams will hope to get their drivers as many laps as they can on the various setups to develop a plan for the next two phases of the event, qualifying and the race. All the while, as they push the limits of the car's performance, the driver, more than anything, needs to keep from crashing and losing valuable practice time to repairs or, worse, injury. By the time the teams have had several rounds of practice, they should be ready to get the most they can out of car and driver during qualifying.

All this effort and thinking is only worthwhile if it puts the driver in a position to do the best over the fifty or more laps of the actual races, unlike qualifying, where the question is speed over one lap. What drivers call "race pace" can be very different from "qualifying pace." Hundred-meter sprinters and 400-meter sprinters are both "fast," but they have to apportion that speed over different distances. The same goes for a Formula One car. During qualifying, the car's setup and the mindset of the driver are about maximum speed over one lap. Race day requires a different approach. The purpose of qualifying is to establish where each of the twenty drivers will start the race on the grid. The fastest driver from qualifying will have "pole position" or P1, and the slowest P20, which doesn't have a name except "last." Some racecourses do not lend themselves to passing or overtaking, so lining up in the front of the grid can determine the result on Sunday.

Qualifying has three phases: Q1, Q2, and Q3. Q1 is eighteen minutes long, and the top fifteen drivers, meaning the best fifteen times over one lap, move forward to Q2, with the last five slotted into spots sixteen to twenty on the starting grid.

Q2 is fifteen minutes long and, just like Q1, the bottom five are shown the door and will start in positions eleven to fifteen on Sunday. Finally, Q3 lasts for twelve harrowing minutes and determines positions one to ten.

It all sounds simple. It isn't. The time limits of each session are one of the variables that makes qualifying complicated. Basically, this comes down to a driver finding position on the track at the most opportune time to get the best result. As you might imagine, during Q1 with twenty cars participating in the session, a driver can have a lap ruined by being impeded. This is one place to really be cognizant of how you just can't have drivers who don't know what they are doing on the track. A car doesn't come blasting out of the pits while an official hits a stopwatch to see how they did. Generally, a driver will typically take one or two "out laps" to get the tires warmed up and try to find track space before embarking on a hot lap. If Driver A is on a hot lap and Driver B is on an out lap, it is of life-threatening importance that Driver B's car is not scouting out a position at 90 miles per hour on the wrong side of the track—what is known as the "racing line"—when Driver A's car comes around a blind corner going 180.

Also, with respect to when a driver goes onto the track, most raceways get faster as more cars do laps. This is because they leave rubber on the racing line, and grip improves as the session goes on, which means times are faster at the end. This sounds great, but it would be foolish for a driver to leave themselves with one shot at getting out of a session, because a lot can go wrong, including a driver being caught in a line of cars vying for position and the time running out. There could also be a crash that causes the race officials to slow everyone down (yellow flag) or even stop the session (red flag). That means that the last, best moment may not be there to take advantage of, so a driver must time the number of runs they can squeeze into a session to maximize attempts at the best time to be on the track.

Then there is the weather. Imagine Driver A goes out early in the session, and midway through their hot lap a rain squall kicks up on half the track. The first part of the lap is fast, the second part much slower, but the drivers after don't have the benefit of the dry first part, so Driver A posts a top time. With four minutes left, while our early driver watches the other drivers struggle around the soaked track, the sun comes out and rapidly dries the surface. The challenge now is to get back out there with enough time to take advantage of the dry conditions.

The other major variable is tire wear. All the teams receive the same allotment of tires for the entire Grand Prix. There are several tire compounds—relative texture of the tire—that make up the tire allotment. The soft compound is typically the fastest but doesn't last as long as the others. The medium compound is between soft and hard for speed and durability. The hard compound lasts the longest but is the slowest. In addition to these three, teams also have access to intermediate/rain tires for the worst weather conditions.

With this information, the newly minted Formula One armchair strategist might think, okay, the soft tires are fastest, you only need a few laps for qualifying, so stick to those, right? Maybe. Except recall that a driver only has so many of each type of tire for the entire weekend, which means you don't want to be starting the race on a worn-out set of soft tires because you used them up in qualifying. Teams that can make it through the early rounds of qualifying on harder compound tires will do so to save the best for Q3 and the race on Sunday.

———

RACE DAY. NOW TEAMS HAVE SELECTED THEIR STRATEGY FOR THE race. Some are concerned about winning, others finishing. Will they start on medium tires, run for as long as possible, and then change late in the race to softs to have the fastest tires at the end of the race? Or do the opposite? Some might think that it must take time to change tires, so why not just put on the hards and gut it out without stopping. It can't be done. Every car has to use two different tire compounds unless the race is run in the rain.

This means F1 teams need to think about the pit stop in their strategic planning. A well-drilled F1 pit crew changes all four tires in about three seconds. Consider this next time the local mechanic quotes six or more hours to change the tires on your car. Likewise, a local body shop may spend three weeks fixing your rear quarter panel. F1 pit crews do it in about five seconds. Since the FIA stopped the profoundly dangerous process of refueling during the race, the majority of stops are for tires, and even the worst crews can usually pull this off in about four seconds. Despite taking the danger of fires and explosions out of the pit stop without rocket fuel splashing all over the place, the pit lane is still a place of danger roughly equivalent to the deck of an active aircraft carrier.

People must know what to do, what *not* do, and when to do or *not* do it. Cars can be released unsafely, and people can be in the way, or they can crash into other drivers entering or leaving the pits. The pit stop is a well-orchestrated ballet between all of the teams that requires uncompromising professionalism. Drivers are not allowed to enter the pit lane at top speed, and they can't blast out of there like they have been shot out of a cannon, either. Some of the most severe penalties in the sport are often given out for pit lane safety violations, and for good reason.

It's finally time to race. At the appointed time on Sunday all the cars take off on the formation lap, which usually features the drivers swerving back and forth to warm up their tires. Drivers have crashed during the formation lap. The cars at the front of the grid finish the lap and must wait for the back markers to get in position, which cools off their tires and messes up their grip, so they will often back up the field to spend as little time as possible waiting. Once every car is in position, a person will run behind the nineteenth and twentieth positions waving a green flag to signal the starter to start the countdown, which isn't the "on your marks...set...gun" of track meets nor the 10-9-8-7-6-5-4-3-2-1 of space missions. Instead, two rows of five red lights come on in sequence, and when they go off...the race is on.

CHAPTER 7

TO THE FATHER GO THE SPOILS

THE FIRST RACE OF A NEW FORMULA ONE SEASON IS A LOT LIKE THE first day of a new school year. Everyone has plans to do all of their homework, ace all of their tests, make friends with interesting people, and be the hands-down front-runner for the homecoming court by Thanksgiving. Then reality sets in. Trigonometry sends your GPA into a tailspin. Your locker is next to the school bully, and he colonizes your space to hide makeshift weapons and contraband. And alas, the phone never rings for a homecoming date. But then there is always next year.

Lewis spent his entire life, along with his father, preparing for this "first day of school," his F1 debut, and it was immediately apparent that he had already graduated. Despite telling the interviewer that the first part of the season was a time for getting his feet under him, it was clear that Lewis had successfully made the transition from GP2 to Formula One.

What does this mean? It is not just that the cars are faster; that is a given. The "faster" part comes with a lot of demands. *Wired* magazine posted a video titled "Why the Average Human Couldn't Drive an F1 Car" that lays this out with commentary by Clayton Green, the former performance coach for Lewis during the 2010 season.[1] First there is the reaction time required to get a good start. According to *Wired*, the average reaction time of an F1 driver is about 200 milliseconds. For a point of reference the video uses Usain Bolt's 160-millisecond reaction time in the 100-meter dash, while the typical human being's time is around 500 to 600 milliseconds. This is not just important at the start but throughout the race; at these extreme speeds, staying alive depends upon being able to react before it is too late.

Next, a driver moving up to Formula One needs to be prepared to deal with the extreme forces that are generated in high-speed corners that the *Wired* piece compared to an eighty-plus-pound force pushing your head away from the direction of the turn. This means that the neck strength of a Formula One driver, unlike that of the normal person, is such that they will be able to hold their head in position to see where they are going instead of having their eyes looking at their lap.

Braking requires that the driver generate 220 pounds of force to move the brake pedal. That is like going to the gym and pushing 200 pounds on the leg press with one leg hundreds of times over the course of a few hours. If the average person got the car moving, they would be unlikely to be able to stop it.

These are just the physical elements. Mental capacity and the ability to manage the stress of driving, competing, and obligations that are team-related but off the track can grind a driver down. Much of this is generated by the expectations placed on the driver and the team.

McLaren was not a team that was unused to success. The Spaniard, Fernando Alonso, had already notched two World Drivers' Championships with Williams Racing and joined McLaren fully expecting more. The fact that Hamilton, an unproven rookie, was joining him indicated to Alonso and his fans that the youngster was there to support his championship run and maybe learn something along the way, not to try to win it himself.

---

1. "Why the Average Human Couldn't Drive an F1 Car," posted July 6, 2023, by Wired, YouTube, https://www.youtube.com/watch?v=FVlEaCrC3IM.

In the annals of sporting history, Formula One and beyond, you would be hard pressed to find a rookie who was as impactful to the sport as Lewis, though Magic Johnson comes immediately to mind. When the leader of the team, Kareem Abdul-Jabbar, went down with an injury in the NBA finals, Magic stepped up. In the deciding game against the Philadelphia 76ers, the rookie played every position on the floor on the road. Magic scored 42 points, grabbed 15 rebounds, and had 7 assists, winning the championship and the series MVP. Lewis would have that type of season.

The media was not afforded the type of frenzied access they would have liked prior to Lewis's first race. This allowed Lewis to spend a great deal of time in close communication with his team. This was most evident in photographs of Lewis closeted with Ron Dennis talking about who knows what. Commentators noted that Fernando Alonso must have wondered why he was pressed up against the glass instead of in the champagne room whispering with the talent. The rub here is that it is clear that no one at McLaren ever promised Fernando he would be the number one driver, and here is the problem: no one told him that he wasn't, either. As far as the two-time world champion was concerned, he probably felt that it would be bizarre for someone to say something like, "Our two-time world champion is the number one driver over the unproven rookie."

Likewise, no one assured Lewis of anything except a competitive car. He certainly wasn't given any direction at this point that he ought to be thinking first about supporting his accomplished teammate—a practice known as "team orders" that can very quickly violate the principle that the race is a competition. In some ways, a Formula One team can function the same way a cycling team in a grand tour would, with other members dedicated to getting the principal rider to the front and keeping them there.

With their two stars in the dark about the team's expectations, what were Hamilton and Alonso supposed to do other than compete? Unlike in Johnson's "magic" rookie year, the "Kareem" of this team wasn't injured. Alonso was still racing. What did McLaren expect?

———————

THE 2007 SEASON IS BEST UNDERSTOOD AS A TRANSITION POINT FOR
Formula One. The seven-time world champion, Michael Schumacher,
had hung up his helmet at the end of the 2006 season. His departure left
two open questions for the sport: first, whether his replacement at Ferrari, the laconic Kimi Räikkönen, could begin to fill the giant hole left
by the German driver's departure, and second, who would be the face of
the sport.

Alonso's move from Williams to McLaren was designed to answer
both questions, first by keeping the ambitious Ferrari drivers behind
him, and second, by adding a third world championship to his tally and
establishing him as the driver of a new era. The view on all of this from
the perspective of Alonso was that the team, including Ron Dennis and
Martin Whitmarsh, were there to make this happen. Lewis was necessary because you need two drivers on a team, and while he was there, he
might as well take some notes, stay out of the way, help when he could,
and maybe find a place somewhere else that needed a primary driver.

There are lots of ways a driver can help a teammate when they aren't
worried about winning for themselves. These "team orders" usually take
the form of doing all they can to hold up rivals to create the type of
gaps that allow pit stops without losing a place. Or, during the qualifying rounds, a secondary driver will punch a hole in the air so the lead
driver gets an aerodynamic tow to have a speed advantage over qualifiers
who are in it for themselves. The most complicated practice is when two
drivers are both able to be competitive, and they are ordered to refrain
from "racing" each other and hold position; there have even been times
when a driver has been told to swap positions with a teammate. Fernando
Alonso apparently fully expected to be able to choose from this menu of
self-beneficial options. If there was an internal McLaren memo to this
effect, Lewis didn't get it, or he decided it didn't apply to him, because
Alonso was going to have to worry about the rookie before dealing with
the challenge of drivers on other teams.

As the weekend evolved, Hamilton was quiet yet competent on the track during practice sessions. The top times of these sessions were all put up by veteran drivers, and Lewis was feeling his way around Albert Park in the McLaren. Qualifying featured a landmark performance from Kimi, who was the first Ferrari driver since 1956 to qualify on pole in their first race for the team, when the legendary Juan Michael Fangio did it. Fernando was stalking him in a self-assured P2.

Just like Räikkönen with Ferrari, Alonso was in his debut race for McLaren. In the post-qualifying press conference, he was asked about his experience with the team so far. He expressed confidence in himself and the car. The interviewer asked him about his thinking on strategy for the race the next day, and Fernando had his attention firmly focused on the Ferrari, making no mention of Lewis, who had qualified in fourth behind the BMW of Nick Heidfeld.[2]

In a pre-race interview on the same platform that Lewis had visited, Fernando talks about his excitement to join McLaren, even after the team had struggled for performance in the 2006 season. He downplays the importance of making a big splash at the beginning of the season, offering assurances that as he and the team become more comfortable with each other, things would pick up. He is next asked about Lewis.

INTERVIEWER: We're all interested, of course, in how your teammate is going to perform as well. What do you make of Lewis Hamilton? What do you know of him and how are you getting on with him so far?

ALONSO: It's very good. It has been a very good relationship. He can be a very strong driver in 2007. I see him like a very good teammate. He is pushing the team a little bit with some fresh ideas and fresh mentality that is only help for the team and for me as well.[3]

---

2. "Fernando Alonso Interview Melbourne 2007."
3. "Fernando Alonso Interview Melbourne 2007."

All innocuous stuff and what you would expect to hear from a more experienced teammate talking about a teammate who had never driven in a F1 race before. This would be as good as it got between Lewis and Fernando.

On race day, Lewis's P4 position from qualifying placed him right behind Fernando in P2. The chaos of the start of the race saw Lewis taking advantage of the type of daring move only an experienced driver would make and getting in front of Alonso after the first corner. He described the moment in his 2007 memoir.

> It was a heart-pounding moment for me. I was really in it. I was in the middle of everything. I had just overtaken Fernando, the World Champion, with an outside manoeuvre and it was one of those feelings where you are really on the limit. You either pull it off or you don't. And, realistically, there was far more chance of me not pulling that off, but it all went well. And it was not luck. I just timed it to perfection, and I got in there and it was like, "Phew!" That's a much better place to start.[4]

Lewis had arrived. On the first corner of the first race, he had announced with that move that he was not there to play. Despite what some might have thought or even wished, he was not in the sport only to be the first Black F1 driver. The race ended with Lewis gaining a place on his start, finishing P3 with Fernando getting back to second as the result of a pit stop strategy that didn't serve Lewis well. Kimi had won his first race as a Ferrari driver, and if not for the eruption of Lewis on the podium, the race had a fairly conventional storyline.

Even with the success of that great start, Lewis doesn't allow himself the space to let that be what people would remember of him. He is restless to the point of self-doubt and is self-aware enough to question

4. *Lewis Hamilton: My Story*, 110.

whether it was just beginner's luck; a combination of being reckless and having it actually fixed by a more experienced teammate who saved him from himself because everyone was caught by surprise.

> Then, other thoughts started entering my mind, like "Is this a one-off thing? How do I maintain it?" I was standing on the podium thinking that, but at the same time feeling great and thinking "I've done my parents proud."... "My dad's smiling down there," I thought, "so I know he's happy and that's all that matters to me. There's one thing I can do that made my dad smile and this is it."[5]

This aspect of the relationship between Lewis and his dad must be taken seriously. The driver expresses in his own words what he thinks guides their relationship. This statement is thoroughly considered. It is not the product of an unthoughtful answer in the middle of a press scrum but in a published memoir. Lewis, at this stage of his life, does not think that there is any other way he can please his dad besides being a highly successful Formula One driver. In Lewis's mind and perhaps that of his dad, Driver = Son and Son = Driver. The stakes, emotionally, for Lewis and his family could not be higher. There is no reason to believe that Lewis's wouldn't love him if he weren't a driver. The term "love" is notably absent from what Hamilton says. What he seems to believe, and this is not the first nor the last time similar thoughts appear in his thinking, is that in order for his dad to be happy with him, to "like" him, is within the four corners of Formula One success, as a goal or reality.

This is not an uncommon state of affairs between fathers and sons. August Wilson centers the problem in his play *Fences* when the father is asked by his son, "How come you ain't never liked me?" The father, predictably, replies, "Like you? Who the hell say I got to like you?" This goes on, but the unspoken question is about love.

---

5. *Lewis Hamilton: My Story*, 111.

Maybe Anthony Hamilton is really only responding to what he understands as the thing that really matters to his son. If he thought Lewis was
similarly passionate about being the world's greatest third-grade teacher,
Anthony would be smiling just as brightly at the plays and recorder
recitals put on by his son and his class. Or it could also be that Anthony
knows that in the game, motor racing, if you are in for a penny, you are in
for a pound, or at least you'd better be. Lewis can't half-ass Formula One.
It is likely clear to Anthony from his life experience that if Lewis made
it all the way to being the first Black Formula One driver as he proposed
way back when and didn't accomplish anything but being there, it could
be worse than never having made it in the first place. But here the two
were, improbably, with Lewis on the podium bathed in champagne at his
first grand prix, and the question for Anthony, just like his son, was: what
was next?

The way the schedule was set up, the world and the drivers had two
long weeks to think about it before the next race. The time allowed Lewis
to reset. The media frenzy that Ron Dennis was eager to avoid was now
unstoppable. When the wandering circus that is Formula One made it to
Sepang for the Malaysian Grand Prix in the middle of March, everyone
was on watch to see if Lewis could show that his first race success was not
a fluke.

—————

QUALIFYING AT THE CIRCUIT AT SEPANG REQUIRED EXPERIENCE,
because the weather didn't cooperate as it had in Australia. Recall the
chaos that rain brings to a qualifying session; that is exactly what happened in Malaysia, and the more experienced drivers fared better. Felipe
Massa, the other Ferrari driver, took pole position. Fernando Alonso
matched his position from Australia in P2, and Kimi Räikkönen put his
Ferrari in the third slot. Lewis was fourth again as a result of his inexperience at qualifying in the wet in an F1 car, ending up a distant half
second (a lifetime in this sport) behind the top three qualifiers.

But, just like in Australia, Lewis didn't allow himself to get comfortable in fourth place. In similar fashion to his move in the first round, he passed Kimi to move into third at the first corner. But Fernando pulled away in the closing laps to win by seventeen seconds over his teammate. With both McLaren drivers on the podium again, the team padded its lead in the Constructors' Championship over Ferrari.

The post-race show gave all the credit for Fernando's win to Lewis. This could not have sat well with the vastly more accomplished Spaniard. The ITV post-race commentator spent 70 percent of the two-and-a-half-minute setup for the driver's press conference on the brilliance of Lewis with Fernando's win serving as an afterthought.

The presser allows Fernando to describe his race and his glee at the early return on his investment in the move to McLaren. Then the focus shifts to Lewis, who describes the difficulty he had in keeping the lighter and faster Ferraris, piloted by more experienced drivers, behind him, and then, as is his pattern, carefully thanking the team for their support. The ITV broadcast then cuts away from the podium interviews, depriving viewers of Kimi Räikkönen's characteristic indifference, to check in with Anthony Hamilton.

The show sets up the segment with: "That was the brilliant Lewis Hamilton and to the father go the spoils." Anthony is bursting with pride and cradles the second-place trophy like...a child. Anthony is hardly able to talk through his smile. He says that he and Lewis had expected sixth or seventh place in Australia and were both over the moon with the results so far. The questions predictably turn to whether progress from third to second would find Lewis at the top of the podium for round three in Bahrain.[6]

But that was not the case.

———

AFTER A HARD-FOUGHT RACE IN THE DESERT, LEWIS ENDED UP IN SECond place behind the Ferrari of Felipe Massa. Fernando's fourth-place

6. "2007 F1 Malaysian GP ITV Post-Race Show," posted November 18, 2023, by Race Day Replay, YouTube, https://youtu.be/dUERRKpx3Ns?si=3uYiZDaLeX7AjnB3.

finish meant that after the first three races, he, Kimi, and the rookie were tied with twenty-two points for the Drivers' Championship. The transcript from the post-qualifying press conference reveals how quickly the coverage of Lewis was evolving.

Q: How do you feel about the race and the spotlight that you, too, have been under?

LEWIS HAMILTON: I feel quite relaxed about it. It feels natural. I'm extremely happy to be where I am. I've worked for thirteen years to be where I am and finally to be here, and to be performing quite well, I'm really happy with myself and I think the team has made some good steps forward. Going into tomorrow's race, it will be tough. The first corner here is always tricky, because it's so tight, but we'll see what happens.

Then the question of race comes up explicitly in an off-topic reference to Tiger Woods.

Q: This question is to Lewis; a lot of people are comparing you with great sports personalities, with Tiger Woods for instance. What do you think of these comparisons? They're saying you're the Tiger on wheels...

LEWIS HAMILTON: I don't really take much notice of that sort of thing. I'm not Tiger Woods, I'm Lewis Hamilton, I'm completely different. I do think he's a sensational athlete and it's an honor to be compared to someone of such great caliber. But I'm here in Formula One, I'm here to do a job. I hope I can have a similar impact on Formula One as he has had in golf.[7]

---

7. "2007 F1 Malaysian GP ITV Post-Race Show."

Lewis takes this up in his memoir, writing:

> Tiger Woods is one of the greatest golfers ever and he com-
> pletely changed the way that sport is perceived by millions of
> people...I know where the Tiger Woods comparison questions
> were heading; so I just answered them in the way I always did.
> I have said that for me, race is not an issue at all...I do not
> want to be the Tiger Woods of motor racing—just being the
> Lewis Hamilton of motor racing will be cool enough for me.[8]

This is clearly a continuation on Lewis's father-approved way to deal with questions of race. Which is fine. But it is demonstrably not useful as a response to racism. It is not difficult to see how at the furthest extremes of class distinctions, a person can be so completely isolated from the question of race to the point that race isn't apparently a thing. A person could be so desperately poor or fabulously wealthy that the hard barrier around those facts renders race something that doesn't much matter. It is in the space between those two extremes where there are many ways that a person contacts the world that race can matter, positively or negatively.

Racism, however, is like gravity. It doesn't make any difference if you feel it's an issue for you or not, because it's always an issue for everyone. It takes a while for Lewis to conclude that deciding that race was not a thing was neither productive nor ethical. Lewis takes a much different path than Tiger's explicit rejection of anything having to do with the complexities of race or racism.

The focus on racing excellence is certainly what Lewis should be doing, but as his star rises the dislike of Lewis becomes more complicated and amplified. Fernando Alonso clearly becomes fed up with Lewis, and their relationship becomes a negative part of the story of the 2007 season.

After a poor showing in Bahrain, Fernando was excited to be heading to his home grand prix in Barcelona, where he fully expected and needed

---

8. *Lewis Hamilton: My Story*, 146–147.

to redeem himself. The track at the Circuit de Catalunya had been altered prior to the race. Fernando, the resident and self-proclaimed expert on the course, commented that he thought the changes would allow for more overtaking on the course, which had a history of making it difficult on drivers seeking to move up the ranks.[9]

Alonso did not have the race weekend he had been expecting. The Spaniard had thrown down the gauntlet by qualifying first and looked to be in perfect form to begin to take control of the title race and put his teammate in his place. On the first lap, Fernando tangled with Felipe Massa and ended up in the gravel, falling to a distant fourth from his pole position. Ultimately, Fernando clawed his way back to third place, but Massa collected the win, and Lewis scored another second-place finish. That result put Hamilton alone in the lead for the Drivers' Championship, two points clear of his veteran teammate and headed to one of the most iconic races, Monaco.

Lewis had raced on the course before in other race series and had never been defeated, but Formula One was a different animal. His rivals at the closely fought title race were vastly more experienced on the streets of Monaco, but Lewis had proven himself to be a quick study. The race, as usual, was exciting enough, but a bizarre incident involving Ferrari was the first indication that the season was headed for controversy beyond the internal conflict at McLaren. A disgruntled Ferrari employee, angry that he wasn't promoted to technical director for the team, was caught trying to sabotage the team's cars before the proceedings began.

While all the Ferrari drama played itself out, Fernando and Lewis aced qualifying and ended up P1 and P2 for the race on Sunday. If passing was considered difficult in Barcelona, it has always been nigh on impossible on the narrow streets of Monaco. The course is 3.337 kilometers long, just a touch over two miles. The race is scheduled for seventy-eight laps around a course that features nineteen turns and boasts the slowest corner in the sport, the Fairmont Hairpin, which drivers navigate at an agonizingly

9. "Alonso Backs Spanish GP Changes," BBC Sport, March 4, 2007, http://news.bbc .co.uk/sport1/hi/motorsport/formula_one/6624093.stm.

slow 30 miles per hour, considering that the same racecourse has other kinks that are taken at well over 150 miles per hour. All that being said, drivers who complete the race have made more than 1,482 direction changes at an average speed of 100 miles per hour, a feat described by former world champion Nelson Piquet Sr. as being like "riding a bicycle around your living room" except you're going about 100 miles per hour.[10]

This meant that Lewis had his work cut out for him if he wanted to finally pick up his first race win at perhaps the sport's most iconic event. Fernando Alonso was known to have sharp elbows when it came to defending against rivals, and the narrow roads in Monaco made the risk of a full-on fight between the two McLaren drivers a big risk for both. As the race progressed, the two McLaren drivers distanced themselves from the field, and the question that was percolating and left unanswered this entire season was in front of everyone. Was Lewis in a support role? Since the rookie was leading the championship, should Alonso be about making sure Lewis had some breathing room? Were they allowed to race each other? It is clear that none of this was ever openly discussed, and when Fernando came in for a pit stop from first place, Lewis took the lead and was doing everything he could to make sure he held on to the position.

The Brit was as surprised as everyone else when the team called him in early for a pit stop and prevented him from building a lead, restoring Fernando to first place. Lewis didn't give up, and as the race came to a close, he was within striking distance of his teammate. This forced McLaren's hand. The decision was not to the rookie's liking. He was told to hold his position, *giving* the victory to Fernando. There are several ways to look at this, and in the years that have passed no one has given an answer as to what was really going on with McLaren ordering Lewis to hold back.

The most controversial read of the decision is that the upper management of McLaren had spent a lot of money bringing the two-time world champion to the team. It didn't take a whole lot of imagination to think that betting on the experience of Alonso to bring McLaren a

---

10. Brad Spurgeon, "Monaco Grand Prix Is Glamorous and Grueling," *New York Times*, May 25, 2008, https://www.nytimes.com/2008/05/25/sports/othersports/25prix.html.

championship as the season wore on was far less risky than putting all their chips on the newcomer, no matter how talented he had proven to be.

Another possible explanation is based upon accepting Ron Dennis's take on the situation as the gospel truth in the wake of the controversy that exploded after the race. Monaco is obviously a difficult course for passing. Ron Dennis said that the priority of the team was picking up the top two spots, so whoever was in front was going to stay there. In that way there were no risks that overzealous tactics would end the race for both. That makes sense if you allow yourself to forget that Lewis was ordered to return to the pits just as he was in a position to build an insurmountable lead for himself. That move ensured Fernando was going to stay in front.

Whatever the reasoning, Lewis didn't like it and made it clear in the post-race press conference.[11] His father felt or at least expressed a positive view of the situation and made clear during his post-race interview that holding position was the right decision based upon his son qualifying behind his teammate and rival.[12] The commentators on ITV took this as an opportunity to propose that the race represented a master class on the part of Alonso and that the master–pupil relationship between the two McLaren drivers was established.[13]

During the drivers' press conference, Fernando gave innocuous answers, sticking to tires and being grateful for the finish by both drivers that was putting some distance between the McLarens and the Ferrari. Lewis was more interested in reasserting that he was there to race, not to study or serve as a support mechanism for his teammate's ambition for a third championship. The team's ineffective communication to the drivers and the public about this one way or the other contributed to the confusion, and the FIA got involved by launching an investigation into the team's practices.

11. "Monaco 2007 F1 GP Press Conference," posted August 3, 2023, by jayjayletho8, YouTube, https://youtu.be/NrnACXuePbU?si=sy7_gN9-jGDY3CDu.
12. "2007 F1 Malaysian GP ITV Post-Race Show."
13. "2007 F1 Malaysian GP ITV Post-Race Show."

The FIA has rules against team orders that predetermine the results of what is supposed to be an actual race. McLaren had tiptoed up to the line in Monaco. The investigation forced the team to have to declare that the team did not have a hierarchy, real or imagined, and that the drivers were free to race. Dennis, in an interview with Reuters, tried to put this to rest, saying, "Everybody feels, I'm sure, that there is some favouritism or some penalisation that is given to either Lewis or Fernando. But we are scrupulously fair at all times in how we run this grand prix team. We will never favour one driver, no matter who it is. We never have, we never will."[14] With that declaration and with a two-week break before the next race, the public was eager to see what would happen between the two McLaren drivers, especially since the rookie had not been off the podium, but most important had not won a grand prix.

---

14. "McLaren: We Will Never Favour One Driver," Crash, May 28, 2007, https://www .crash.net/f1/news/58712/1/mclaren-we-will-never-favour-one-driver.

CHAPTER 8

NEVER AS GOOD AS THE FIRST TIME

Formula 1 Grand Prix de Canada
Circuit Gilles Villeneuve
Montreal, Quebec, Canada
June 8–10, 2007

As the season moved to the other side of the Atlantic, the racing world still wondered if Lewis had what it took to win a grand prix. Hamilton had found a seemingly permanent place on the podium in the first five races of the season, but he had not made the final leap to the top spot, and the buzz was that he was not ready to snatch a victory from more experienced drivers and was becoming content with second and third place. In a very short time, the conversation had gone from whether Lewis would spend the first part of the season as an apprentice to whether he might win a world championship without ever winning a race: something that was mathematically possible. Lewis was frustrated because he felt he had the pace in Monaco, and one can imagine that as he was closing on his teammate during the last few laps, he might have allowed himself to think about standing on the top step on the podium in the principality. But the team robbed him of the opportunity to compete for the victory. He would have no more of it. Lewis went to Canada, a course he had never seen before, with the bit in his teeth.

The raceway in Montreal is named after the legendary driver Gilles Villeneuve, who tragically died in 1982 during qualification at the Belgian Grand Prix. His son, Jacques, followed in his father's footsteps to motor racing and won a world championship in 1997 with Williams Racing. The former world champion was a frequent commentator on the sport, and as the teams left the confusion of Monaco and headed to the course named after his father, Jacques had a strong critique of the rookie and McLaren. In an interview with *Autosport* magazine, reported by the BBC, Villeneuve voiced his concern about what he understood as the overly aggressive driving that Lewis had exhibited and so far been allowed to employ to improve his position early in the race. Villeneuve asked rhetorically in the pages of the magazine "when will these chopping moves stop? So far, he (Lewis) has been lucky, so we'll see if he carries on...Lewis is very fast but he still has to step up and beat Alonso. And we still haven't seen how he reacts under pressure."[1]

This sharp criticism was in contrast to what had been going on in the thinking of other former F1 drivers, who had generally been supportive of what they had been seeing from Hamilton. The pundits, in contrast to Villeneuve's take on the matter, had leveled nothing but praise for Lewis's driving, so some felt that Jacques's comments were coming from a place of jealousy. The Canadian had wowed the world of motorsport himself in his rookie year in F1, actually taking pole position in his first grand prix and finishing second in the race. Calling Villeneuve a rookie is in some ways a stretch, because he had come to Formula One having been an IndyCar Series champion, where he had won the iconic Indy 500. Also, his father had been a successful Formula One driver, so Jacques had

1. "Hamilton Criticised by Villeneuve," BBC Sport, June 6, 2007, http://news.bbc.co .uk/sport2/hi/motorsport/formula_one/6726711.stm.

come into the sport with a parent with real experience in every facet of F1, which the Hamiltons did not enjoy. Whatever the case, Jacques felt that Lewis was all hype and unlikely to continue his streak of luck since the other drivers would settle into the season and the race stewards would start penalizing the rookie for his tactics.

Coming off his victory in Monaco, Fernando believed he had captured the momentum and had set himself up to get down to the business of winning the world championship. Fernando, despite the explanation from Ron Dennis on why the team had ordered Lewis to slow down, as a practice distinct from team orders that violate the rules, believed the team had come to understand that the rookie was there to support his championship run.

Lewis felt differently. After only a handful of races it was becoming obvious that Lewis had that rare quality of most pathologically driven people. He was never satisfied. At each step along the way there were a series of fairly obvious and fairly defensible off-ramps or excuses that would have allowed him to back down and use his neophyte status as a safe haven.

He could have gone with the narrative from his pre-race interview in Australia, simply being content to get a feel for the premier series in motorsports. He didn't.

Lewis might have looked himself in the mirror after finding himself tied with drivers with vastly more experience for the title and felt he had demonstrated he belonged and left it at that. He didn't.

After Monaco, even a competitive person could find a way out of the intensity that was ratcheting up by leaning into the narrative that, for the good of the team, it was time to support the two-time world champion. Lewis did not.

Perhaps even larger than all of these possibilities, he had come from "nowhere" and as the first Black Formula One driver, he had every reason to lean into that as an achievement in and of itself. Lewis was apparently never really concerned about any of these options.

As the season progressed, it became a microcosm of the career that would unfold, this unwillingness to be content with success that drives Hamilton. This, along with an almost bizarre level of modesty, confounds Lewis's detractors and commends him to his fans. No one would have taken it seriously if, at the interview prior to Australia, instead of agreeing that he had ten races or so to get his footing in Formula One, he announced he considered himself to be in the running for a world championship. In the interview, he agreed with the lowered expectations but apparently had something completely different in mind.[2]

Professional athletes, for the most part, all think they could win the title given the right circumstances, which is different from being in a real fight for the championship. Joining a team like McLaren took the question of the necessary equipment and corporate experience necessary to compete for a championship off the table, which then put the onus on the athlete. Lewis never allows the expectations of the public and the media to limit his expectation for himself. That also goes for the expectation of his partner in this dream, his father. Anthony had been committed to a slow and steady start to this first season and found himself, like everyone, surprised by his son.

Lewis owns the moment. Not as an isolated event but as a link in a chain to owning all the moments. This goes back to his appearance on the kids' show *Blue Peter*. He is prepared to take care of the moment when it presents itself. In the case of the Canadian Grand Prix, Lewis was competing on a course he had never driven before and one that is notoriously deceptive in its complexity. Hamilton wrote about this in his 2007 memoir:

> Luckily, though the challenges of racing on new tracks never really bothered me. Even though it looks a simple circuit, Montreal is actually quite demanding physically, and also quite technical, so it took a while to learn in practice on Friday.[3]

2. "Lewis Hamilton—Interview Melbourne 2007," posted March 14, 2020, by F1 World, YouTube, https://youtu.be/VoeyKYEtXBs?feature=shared 14 March 2020.
3. *Lewis Hamilton: My Story*, 139.

The complex simplicity of Lewis's statement here is worth noting as an expression of his professional method. First is the notion that he wasn't "bothered," which doesn't mean that it wasn't something to be concerned about but rather that he was committed to doing what had to be done to unravel the mystery. Practice for Lewis is just that, and his goal on the Circuit de Villeneuve on Friday was to stay away from the wall and crashing the car, wasting time and opportunity. By the final practice session on Saturday morning, Lewis felt armed and ready for quietly delivering what he called a "very consistent lap" in qualifying: "I did not make any mistakes at all and I got the time. I remember thinking to myself: 'Wow!' I qualified pole and I did not put it in the wall!"[4]

Fernando had been fast, but Lewis had been faster. When the lights went out on Saturday, once again Lewis used turn one to assert his dominance. Fernando ended up running off the track, losing his second position and sliding to fourth place. After several more mishaps, the Spaniard continued to move backward, picking up damage on his car while Lewis drove into the distance. The race was far from straightforward. His lead was placed in jeopardy four times when the safety car was deployed but, in the end, after seventy grueling laps around the Circuit de Villeneuve, Lewis had proven not only that he could beat his teammate, but he could win a grand prix. Despite what seemed like an inevitable outcome at some point, there was no shortage of pundits who were stunned at the lightning strike success of Hamilton. Niki Lauda was shocked and the British racing icon Damon Hill, like many, found it hard to grapple with the rapid rise of Lewis to the top of the sport. With this victory and Alonso's abysmal seventh place result, Lewis found himself eight points ahead of his teammate. The question about the possibility of the rookie grabbing the Drivers' Championship without winning a race had been resolved.

––––––––––

4. *Lewis Hamilton: My Story*, 139.

THE PRESS WANTED TO KNOW, HAVING DREAMED THIS IMPOSSIBLE
dream since he was six years old and seen it come true, what was next? In
keeping with his endless need to overcome himself, Lewis said out loud
what people were daring to think. Worrall's book quotes the driver's bold
and at the same time self-deprecating pronouncement:

> The next dream is obviously to win a Formula One World
> Championship but at the moment we have to be realistic
> again. It's always good to bear in mind that I'm still a rookie
> and this is my first season.[5]

"Realistic" was a new term in Lewis Hamilton's vocabulary as it related
to Formula One. None of this has ever been "realistic," but now, from the
top of the podium, he demonstrated his profound maturity. The frame-
work had shifted. Prior to making it to Formula One, a seat with a team
was a dream that became more and more real as he moved closer to that
goal. Now as a Formula One driver with a top team, grand prix winner,
and points leader, he purposefully placed the notion of the championship
just beyond his reach.

Lewis's endless need to chase goals seems to require that he never
allow even the obvious to be quite realistic. It becomes realistic when it is
real. He didn't quite think that he was in a position to defeat Alonso in
Montreal, and now that "Grand Prix Winner" was something that could
never be taken away from him or speculated about, it was his understanding of the "impossible dream" that allowed him to activate a competitive
mode that made the impossible possible. He had arrived, and somehow it
is important that he did it in the New World. North America was ready
for an international motor racing star.

---

5. Worrall, *Lewis Hamilton: The Biography*, 190–191.

CHAPTER 9

ALL THE CRITICS LOVE YOU IN NEW YORK...

On April 12, 2024, Lewis was in New York City to be honored as one of *GQ* magazine's global innovators and, as these things go, he was interviewed on the red carpet at the event. The interviewers asked him a popular TikTok/pop culture question that had been going around for a few years now: whether he would rather have $500,000 or have lunch with Jay-Z. As any rational person would, Lewis said he would take the loot and do something positive with it since, to be honest, it wasn't a lot of money to him. He went on to say that he had had the chance to meet the rapper many times, mostly in New York, where he kept a place that he really hadn't had much of a chance to sleep in, but he was planning to spend more time there. This, Lewis said, went back to his love affair with the city that began when his mother brought him on a three-day visit when he was a kid. From that moment on, Lewis knew he wanted to make a home in New York City.[1]

Following his first grand prix victory in Canada, the series was remaining in the hemisphere for the US Grand Prix in Indianapolis. In

1. @GQ on TikTok, April 11, 2024, https://www.tiktok.com/@gq/video/73568 40102326291755.

2007, Lewis hadn't quite caught on with American popular culture, but it wouldn't take long.

The Brickyard in Indianapolis, the home of the legendary Indy 500, is the center of gravity for motorsports in the United States, and at the time Formula One enjoyed a fringe following with race fans who spent their time watching NASCAR or the IndyCar Series. Some of this was because there really hadn't been a driver from the United States who mattered in the series for many years. Some race fans remembered that Mario Andretti, the Italian American immigrant, had raced Formula One, but no one who cared about the Indy 500 thought that his 1978 Formula One World Championship meant as much as his success at the Brickyard. Phil Hill was successful in the 1960s, and Eddie Cheever was a marginal performer in the 1980s, neither of whom could likely be picked out of a lineup by American sports fans. It is also worth mentioning that in 1986 Willy T. Ribbs, an African American sports car racer, tested a Brabham Formula One car for Bernie Ecclestone's team, but things never went beyond those three laps.

Frankly, the popularity of the major domestic sports in the United States, along with interest in international sports like golf, tennis, and boxing as well as the Olympics every four years, left little space in the American psyche for Formula One. And Indianapolis, while a great city, is not New York City. Formula One isn't set in the Midwest because it's home to tastemakers. But American culture is personality-based, and Lewis Hamilton was set to open a new market in many ways for the sport of Formula One. Nothing attracts the interest of American audiences like luxury.

———

LEWIS, LIKE EVERYONE ELSE, HAD BEEN PROFOUNDLY INFLUENCED BY Black American hip-hop culture. It doesn't matter if you are in Brooklyn or Katmandu, at some point at the club you are going to hear rap music, and Lewis, as a kid who came of age during the 1990s, was into it. At the same time, as hip-hop evolved past its beginnings in New York

City, it picked up personalities and interests that were more and more international. Pharrell Williams of the hip-hop production duo the Neptunes and the band N.E.R.D. was already a Lewis fan and reached out to him before he had come to the Americas. Unlike many in New York and West Coast rap culture, Pharrell was not from a major city or from an under-resourced background. Pharrell is from Virginia Beach, Virginia, and had met his partner, Chad Hugo, at a camp for gifted children in 1992. By the time Lewis got his start in Formula One, Pharrell was an international superstar, and he was eager to meet Lewis.

You can't think about the international footprint of hip-hop and luxury as the object and goal without thinking of Sean "Puffy" Combs. Despite his recent legal and moral difficulties, Puffy/Diddy/P-Diddy/Love, whatever, had been defining a form of Black luxury since the late 1990s. The rap mogul had been spotted over and over again at venues like the Prêt-à-Porter in Paris, New York's Fashion Week, etc., and all of these roads ultimately found their way to Monaco, a place synonymous with Formula One. Lewis was a part of an as yet unknown form of global Black culture that was inseparable from what Combs and others were up to, which was based on conspicuous consumption: cars (fast and European ones), diamonds (big ones), watches (rare ones), houses (in exotic places), champagne (flowing), all of which sounds like every Formula One weekend.

Lewis had grown up being fascinated at a distance with Black American culture, and in 2007 suddenly he found himself on the must-meet list of tastemakers like Pharrell. The worldwide project of Black cultural dominance was gaining a valuable partner in Lewis Hamilton, who, even at the earliest stage of his career, was creating a new form of luxurious Black internationalism.

Pharrell Williams, producer extraordinaire and fashion-forward cultural icon, served as Lewis's point of entry and guide into this world. The quirky kid who was dominating hip-hop got Lewis, and Lewis got him in a way that would not have been possible for other brands of rap music. Other brands come from a completely different space and have much different sensibilities. It would be hard to imagine Lewis taking up with Cash Money Records out of New Orleans at the time.

There was a short turnaround between the euphoria of his first win and having to figure out another new raceway at the Brickyard. Lewis had proven he was able to win in Canada, so the "aw shucks, I'm a rookie" demeanor was over. The attention on the driver had reached a fever pitch in Europe, and the Atlantic Ocean couldn't blunt the enthusiasm. Lewis had very little time to himself. He had to attend sponsor appearances before he even got to Indy to prepare for the race.

Lewis was at the early stage of celebrity, when it all still seems so surreal that he couldn't find the energy to be sick of it. With all of that atmospheric pressure, little of which had anything to do with driving a race car fast, the rookie demonstrated that he understood that what he did on the track was what made this new world go around. It would have been all too easy for the wunderkind to get distracted by his newfound fame and friendships with famous people. That mistake could easily have derailed his career and caused him to lose a grip on the thing that had made him famous in the first place.

Once the business of the weekend got underway, Lewis found himself feeling his way around the unfamiliar raceway. Fernando placed himself at the top of the time sheets after the first round of practice, and Lewis was upbeat about the progress that he was making. Qualifying on Saturday was off to a similar start, with Lewis finding himself third after Q1 with his teammate continuing to lead the way and Nick Heidfeld in second position. At the close of Q2, Lewis was still behind Alonso, who seemed intent on digging himself out of the hole he had found himself in after Canada.

Q3 saw the ground shifting unpredictably as the session progressed. Lewis went onto the course first and put himself at the top of the timing for the first time that weekend with his first hot lap. Fernando was a few tenths behind Lewis, and it was clear that if he smoothed out the lap he would easily move ahead of his teammate. Over the next several minutes, upstarts from the middle of the pack reshuffled the deck, forcing Lewis and Fernando down to third and fourth position. Two Ferrari drivers showed themselves to be back among the top teams seconds later with Felipe Massa a few ticks ahead of his teammate Kimi Räikkönen. Lewis saved his best for his last run, clawing his way around the Brickyard and ending up a few tenths of a second ahead of Fernando, who had made his way back to the pole competition with time for another run. Lewis had returned to the pits and was not able to get himself back out for a final run. That meant he had to hold his breath while Alonso teed up a last-ditch effort for the pole. Fernando failed and ended up a razor-thin two-tenths of a second behind his ecstatic teammate. Felipe Massa's Ferrari rounded out the top three. In the post-qualifying press conference, Lewis hurled a backhanded compliment at his faltering teammate.

Q: Lewis, a brilliant performance from you on a circuit on which you've never been before.

LEWIS HAMILTON: Yeah. Quite a surprise, to be honest. Going into qualifying, we hadn't really found the best, the optimal setup, and I knew that Fernando is obviously extremely quick here. But it's great to see that the team is so quick and ahead of the Ferraris obviously, but going into that qualifying session I just had to pull it all out and my two last laps in Q3 were spot on and I think I just beat my best lap at the end. So, I couldn't be happier. I didn't really expect to be on pole. I thought Fernando would have been quicker, but obviously not.

Q: Yes, your second lap just quicker but not purple on any sector, but a slight drama last night when they had to change the race engine before you came out this morning and we hear also you've got a little bit of hay fever.

LH: No, I wouldn't say I've got hay fever. Yesterday...I haven't been getting much sleep lately, probably just enjoying it too much! But yesterday I didn't feel great. But yeah, they had to change the engine. I think it was an assembly problem or something, but the engine performed very well, so obviously I'm ecstatic. I really didn't expect to get pole again but I am very, very pleased and happy for the team.

Q: Fernando, in many ways commiserations to you: fastest in every session so far except the all-important Q3, just beaten for the pole.

FERNANDO ALONSO: Yeah, it has been a good weekend for me, no doubt, and I was fastest in P1, P2, P3, Q1, Q2, but not the important one, Q3. But being fastest all weekend gives me a lot of confidence for tomorrow. Yes, Q3, we know, is a different matter and you place many, many factors in Q3 so...I think we can have a strong race tomorrow and I have confidence.

Q: What were those last five minutes of Q3 like for you in terms of the two laps you were able to do on those tyres?

FA: They were okay. I think both sets of tyres were really, really close to a timed lap and I didn't improve too much in the second. I think it was a little bit worse and I had quite good grip in the car and I was quite happy with the laps as well, so I think tomorrow we can do really well.

Q: Felipe, it looks as if Ferrari are definitely closer to McLaren Mercedes than they were in Canada. I guess it's a surprise that we have to say that. What's the car like from your point of view?

FELIPE MASSA: Well, for sure a bit closer but not enough, so we need to be in front, not be closer. But for sure, the situation is a little bit better than in Canada. Canada was a pretty difficult weekend for us. Here, starting third, second row, is not a disaster.

We know that McLaren is going to be strong in the race as they were in every session, so we need to work hard. We need to fight until the end and that's what I'm going to do tomorrow.[2]

Sunday's race found a tense Anthony Hamilton joined in the pits by Lewis's new famous friend, Pharrell. At the start, Alonso put on fierce pressure, but Lewis was razor-sharp and placed his car in a defensive position that shut the door on the Spaniard. These positions held, but toward the middle of the race, Fernando put serious pressure on Lewis, but he was again denied. Lewis repelled the attacks and saw the checkered flag for his second win in as many races. The post-race press conference featured Lewis, as usual, bringing attention to the invisible workers who made his victory possible.

LEWIS HAMILTON: What a dream. To come into two circuits that I didn't know my first time, you know, to really come out with such pace to see the team moving forward always and being competitive, and just to see how much work the team back home in Brixworth and Woking and Stuttgart, how hard they all worked to produce a car and to develop it. They have done a fantastic job, and I am really so thankful to them because it wouldn't be possible without them. The guys here are a great bunch of guys and did a fantastic job on strategy, setting up the car. It's a perfect team, and I'm really happy I could put the icing on the cake.

MODERATOR: Very, very close race with your teammate Fernando throughout the race distance. He took the lead at the, start but on Lap 38, Fernando was right there, and there was pressure all the way.

2. Principessa, "FIA Post-Qualifying Press Conference—US GP," F1 Technical, June 17, 2007, https://www.f1technical.net/news/6085.

LEWIS HAMILTON: There was, and especially the middle stint. The first stint, the first couple laps were really close, and I managed to pull a slight gap and maintain that. And going to the middle stint, the first two laps were very good and then my tires started to grain, so maybe I pushed too hard on them immediately and so Fernando was right up my tail. It was extremely difficult. He was in my slipstream the whole time, so he would always catch me down the straights. So, whatever I gained midfield, I would lose on the straight. So, it was very, very tough but he fought very well, very professional. At the end I managed to pull a gap, and we both sort of, are—I was able to maintain that gap and control the rest of the race.

MODERATOR: As you say, second successive win but a win here in Indianapolis. Talk us through the closing laps. Did it seem like a long, hot day for you?

LEWIS HAMILTON: It did. Obviously, it was great to see that there's a big crowd here, and they're all very, very supportive. A lot of British flags out there, which is fantastic for me. I get a lot of energy from that. But the last few laps, it just seemed to be very long. They came across the radio and said 15 laps, and I was like, "Yeah." And the 15 laps just seemed a lifetime, especially when you're out in the lead, trying to maintain it, not to push too hard and not to damage the car. But I was able to do it and, as I said, just very, very emotional.

MODERATOR: Congratulations to you, Lewis.[3]

The conversation moved to Fernando, who was clearly displeased with his result.

---

3. June 16, 2007, https://www.grandprix.com/races/united-states-gp-2007-sunday -press-conference.html.

MODERATOR: Fernando, ran one lap longer into the first stint, looked as if you might have a fuel advantage, very, very close on lap 38, as Lewis said.

FERNANDO ALONSO: Yeah, very close. Also, at the start was very close. But I did (sic) manage to overtake Lewis and then from then on when you follow someone you lose a little bit of downforce, and it is difficult to get the tires in conditions to push all through the stint because you damage the tires maybe a little bit more when you run behind someone. So, I think I try in the middle stint, and I was side by side once here on the main straight. But, again, it was not enough to overtake him. The last stint was just maybe a conservative one, very difficult to overtake, very difficult to follow anyone. So just start thinking in the French Grand Prix.

MODERATOR: If I could ask you, how would you describe your start?

FERNANDO ALONSO: Well, I think it was good, but, you know, I think we both brake more or less in the same point. The start is always risky. I remember Canada going off in the grass and losing one position. So obviously was with my teammate, you know, you try to overtake but you don't want to finish the race in the first corner. So, eight points are better than nothing. So, you know, we increase the gap to Ferrari, which is one of the main things in this first part of the championship.[4]

Fernando, for his part, seemed resigned to taking this beating and turned his attention to getting back to Europe. He saw the next race as an opportunity to get back to competing for a championship. Heading back to the Continent, the McLarens put more distance between themselves

4. June 16, 2007, https://www.grandprix.com/races/united-states-gp-2007-sunday-press-conference.html.

and Ferrari, and Lewis had managed to find himself with fifty-eight points to his teammate's forty-eight in the Drivers' Championship race.

The post-race frenzy wouldn't have been complete without a moment with Anthony, especially since the United States was celebrating Fathers' Day. Lewis's dad said his son remained calm the entire week and was pleasantly surprised by his pole position from qualifying. Lewis had systematically and almost sublimely dealt with the problem from Monaco. Passing is always difficult, and if a driver cares for personal or team reasons about the racer they are trying to overtake, it becomes even more complicated. The rookie had mastered making up places at the start where chaos is common and had learned that being in front of the entire field from qualifying meant he was in the position to have his drive respected and supported.

Also, it is important to take stock of the unique interest in Lewis's father. All drivers have friends and family attending races, but the media didn't seem to care as much. The media's preoccupation with the Hamilton family would prove to be interesting and quaint to some and laborious if not downright triggering for others. As the season wore on, both of these ways of seeing this situation would become more acute.

As the post-race show headed to a close, the same commentators who were doubtful that Lewis was ready to win a race following the debacle in Monaco had to admit that it was time to think of Lewis as the favorite to win the Drivers' Championship, however improbable that had seemed just a few weeks or perhaps even days before. The best laid plans of the two-time Spanish world champion for his first season at McLaren had crashed on the rocks of a rookie driver who didn't seem to feel pressure or make mistakes. The two weeks between Indy and the French Grand Prix at Magny-Cours only ratcheted up the media attention on the British upstart.

THE RELATIONSHIP BETWEEN FERNANDO AND LEWIS, WHICH HAD begun to get overripe after Monaco, was positively rotten, though not quite at the point of being toxic. Yet. *Motor Sport* magazine's July 4, 2023, edition revisits this brewing controversy in an article entitled "How Alonso and Hamilton's 2007 Feud Erupted: 'It's Going to Be a Fight.'" An interview with a McLaren engineer, Steve Hallam, reveals that after Hamilton's "brilliant" maiden win in Canada, "Alonso made comments about his British team favouring its British driver—and again at Indianapolis, during which the Spaniard gestured to McLaren that it should let him have the win due to apparently being faster, which it didn't."[5]

To be clear, it is hard to imagine that Fernando was "apparently faster" when Lewis had out-qualified him and kept him behind him through every phase of the race during wheel-to-wheel racing without intervention by the team. The gesturing part should also not go unremarked. Formula One drivers are connected to their teams via a radio link. The problem is everyone can hear it, and Fernando had no intention of having the commentators and the public, or probably more important the FIA officials, hear him begging the team to rig the race so he could win. Lewis mentions Alonso's wild complaints in his book, clearly as confused as everyone else as to what on earth he could be talking about.

> . . . in the first press conference in Indianapolis it was the first time that Fernando made comments about the team helping me more than him. I found that strange when he said that especially after what happened to me in Monaco.[6]

Lewis did not win his third straight grand prix in France, but he continued his unbroken streak of podium finishes, taking third behind the two Ferraris at Magny-Cours. His ever more taciturn teammate continued to deliver substandard results; falling to seventh place. From the cheap seats of barely point earning finishing position, Fernando made

---

5. "How Alonso and Hamilton's 2007 Feud Erupted: 'It's Going to Be a Fight,'" Motorsport, July 4, 2023, https://www.motorsportmagazine.com/articles/single-seaters/f1/how-alonso-and-hamiltons-2007-feud-erupted-its-going-to-be-a-fight/.
6. *Lewis Hamilton: My Story*, 147.

it known that he was glad to see that the Ferraris had beaten his team-mate. Even if you think something like this, it is probably better not to tell the public. This is a pretty wild statement, demonstrating that he was ever more unhinged. He just couldn't seem to make peace with the fact that he couldn't bend the team and Lewis to his will. The team order in Monaco was a short-term victory for Fernando, and what followed in the races immediately after was nowhere near the floor of the behavior barrel that the Spaniard would prove determined to scrape. From this point forward, the 2007 season would explode in multiple controversies, all of them seeming to be linked to McLaren.

CHAPTER 10

MO' MONEY, MO' (POTENTIAL) PROBLEMS

THE SILVERSTONE CIRCUIT IS ONE OF THE MOST LEGENDARY IN RACING. The 5.9-kilometer (3.6 mile) circuit is built on the footprint of a World War II–era Royal Air Force (RAF) base and lived in the imagination of the young Hamilton. Now he was a Formula One driver and headed to his home grand prix on a top team and leading the World Drivers' Championship. In 2007 the young driver could never have imagined that in 2020, for the first time in the history of this storied raceway, the straight he was flying down would be named the Hamilton Straight. That honor is more than a decade from Hamilton's first F1 race at Silverstone, but the British fans were keen to support their returning hero.

In advance of the 2007 race, Lewis was learning to deal with his new-found fame and all that went with it. This included more access and contact to people and places that had seemed inaccessible. Meeting Pharrell had unlocked this world for the young driver, and none less than Sean "Puffy" Combs made his way to London in advance of Silverstone. Lewis was the toast of the town, and Combs was nothing if not a shrewd talent scout. He clearly perceived that Hamilton was bringing to life a new version of the luxury Black lifestyle the rap mogul had been cultivating for years.

The first attempt by Lewis to take up Combs on his invitation did not quite work out.

> After meeting Pharrell in Indianapolis, I got a chance to meet another music star I had looked up to for a long time— P. Diddy. He was in London and I was invited to meet him. Unfortunately, I was in the middle of such an intense week that it was impossible for me to take up his invitation.[1]

Whew. After numerous allegations of rape, other sex crimes, and assault, it seems the less contact people have had with Puffy and his parties, the better. A short time later, Hamilton showed up at a dinner hosted by Diddy and was seated next to him for the better part of the evening. The event, as he described it, really didn't start until he arrived about an hour after the appointed time.

> What was he like? Well, he was really very down to earth... He was asking me things about racing and it was clear he did not understand too much about a Formula One car... So, basically, I just filled him in on what happens on a race weekend... It did take some getting used to—hanging out with P. Diddy, calling him Sean... There I was, just days away from the biggest race of my life, and I was at a private dinner with P. Diddy and Pharrell Williams.[2]

Combs has demonstrated that he is interested in very little that doesn't benefit him personally. He seems even less interested in anything that requires him to think of someone else as more important than him. So it is important to carefully consider this invitation for Lewis. Combs didn't know the first thing about Formula One, but he does know charisma when he encounters the phenomenon. At this very early stage of his

1. *Lewis Hamilton: My Story*, 161–162.
2. *Lewis Hamilton: My Story*, 163.

career, Lewis was becoming the center of gravity of a new world made up of fashion, music, night life, society, justice and race. And this was his ninth race.

Before the race weekend could begin, there was a legal drama underway that was an extension of the failed sabotage of Ferrari in Monaco. The perpetrator, Nigel Stepney, had apparently been in contact with a McLaren engineer in an attempt to sell technical information he had stolen from Ferrari. McLaren claimed they had no idea what was going on, and the FIA opened an internal investigation. The problem was compounded because this mess became the subject of both criminal and civil litigation in a variety of jurisdictions. This affair would gain momentum in the coming weeks. At this point, the focus on the race to come at Silverstone and the excitement about Lewis's championship run was able to drown out this noise, but that wouldn't last.

Lewis was buoyed by his recent success and the adulation back in Britain and came out guns blazing in the practice rounds. He ended up at the top of the time sheet followed by the two Ferraris. Fernando found himself in a familiar position outside of the top three. The final practice run on Saturday morning in advance of qualifying that afternoon did not follow the form from the previous day's rounds. Räikkönen took the top spot, just a fraction of a tick ahead of the surging Alonso, who had an almost identical time to Ferrari's other driver, Felipe Massa. Lewis's final run with low fuel (reduced weight) was not to be. A Williams driver botched his hot lap, causing a caution flag to be raised, which prevented Hamilton from having a run at the course with the car in its fastest possible trim. Qualifying promised to be intense.

In Q1, a car disrupted the first round by spinning off the track. Fernando showed early form and seemed as if he was going to take control of qualifying. The same went for round two, with Alonso continuing to show pole position form and Lewis now appearing ready to threaten for P1. As Q3 headed for a close, Alonso seemed poised to rain all over Lewis's homecoming parade by denying him pole position. Alonso's final run was faster than his first attempt in Q3, but Kimi's Ferrari was that much faster, putting the Finn on provisional pole while the crowd waited to see what the British rookie could do about his marginal performance so far. Almost out of nowhere, Lewis put together a completely unexpected lap and snatched the pole away from Ferrari. Hamilton was the only driver to dip under one minute and twenty seconds. Kimi remained second, and Fernando was a disappointed and dejected third on the grid.

The post-qualifying press conference was dedicated to fleshing out what Lewis was thinking now that it seemed that the conventional wisdom indicated he was headed for a world championship. At the same time his teammate put on an optimistic face for the race.

Q: Fernando, fastest in Q2 which is the ultimate speed. That must have been very satisfying.

FERNANDO ALONSO: Yeah, all day in P3, Q1, Q2 being fastest. Also, I was quite happy with the car. Regarding yesterday, we had a couple of problems with the balance of the car. I was not totally happy and overnight we made some changes and today I felt much more confident. For the race, it's looking good, it's looking quite good for us and hopefully I can make up some places immediately after the start of the race and around the pit stop area.

The interview turned back to Lewis and questions about the media frenzy—of which they were part.

Q: There is obviously fantastic support for you this weekend. You've talked a lot about this but how are you dealing with going from relative anonymity to globally recognized sportsman and how does it feel to receive so many plaudits from people in F1? People like Sir Frank Williams who described you as superhuman.

LEWIS HAMILTON: Well, it's overwhelming to hear such good things from people like Sir Frank Williams and a lot of people in the Formula One world. Obviously, I came here to do a solid job, there has been a lot of pressure on from day one and there has not been that many negative comments made so I have been able to keep all this positive energy and it's definitely comforting to hear such nice things. But having my world turned upside-down is... I'm very lucky I have very good balance and sense of awareness so even though it's turned upside-down I can still get on with my life. But it's been really tough obviously walking on the streets and people coming up to you. It is strange. Taken from my past experience when I used to go up to Formula One drivers, I wanted to be slightly different. I wanted for people to be able to approach me and to try and give them as much time as possible. That's what some Formula One drivers didn't do when I was younger.

Q: Lewis, the feelings you are experiencing right now... How does it compare to your first win in Canada? And secondly you were disappointed with your start in France last week with Kimi behind you there. Are you confident that you are going to nail it tomorrow?

LEWIS HAMILTON: Yes, I feel confident. We have worked hard this weekend to improve our starts and I think being on the clean side definitely helps. And my feelings? It definitely feels... I think qualifying is always exciting. Even for you to watch but when you are in the car and you know you are on the last lap, the slightest mistake and you lose it... and you put it all together while you are sitting on a knife edge all the way round. You come round and you see that you did the time... it's a phenomenal feeling, it really is.[3]

———

WHEN THE LIGHTS WENT OFF ON SATURDAY AT LAST AFTER A DELAY when Felipe Massa's engine stalled on the grid and forced a second

3. "British GP: Post Qualifying Press Conference," Pitpass.com, July 7, 2007, https://www.pitpass.com/public/print_article.php?fes_art_id=32047.

formation lap, Lewis had maintained his first-place position for the first sixteen laps. Lewis pitted, and while taking on fuel made his first costly mistake of the season. Thinking that he was signaled to get going, Lewis put the car in gear and jerked forward before realizing his error. This cost him valuable time and track position. He rejoined the race in fifth place. He would never recover the lead and finished a disappointing third place behind Kimi's first place for Ferrari and his rejuvenated teammate. Fernando made it clear to anyone who would listen that this was again(!) the beginning of the end of Lewis's dominance. He told the Spanish press that he intended to rapidly close the points gap to his teammate by staying a step above him on the podium for the rest of the season.

A segment of the public was necessarily concerned that the klieg lights had begun to blind Lewis to what his job happened to be: racing rather than jet-setting and selling sponsored products. The transcendent nature of Lewis's participation in the sport became apparent in the direction that the questions went after the race. One line of questioning from the assembled media after they opened the floor is revealing.

Q: (SEAN MCGREEVY—MOTORING AND LEISURE)
Congratulations on another podium finish, Lewis. How are you dealing with being a role model and the responsibilities that come with that? And who is your role model?

HAMILTON: I don't particularly have a role model anymore because I'm 22 years old. But my brother inspires me because he has always got a smile on his face no matter what. I think you can learn a lot from that. As I always say, whatever he does—he can't play football like the rest of us, he can't play any type of sport like the rest of us—he still gives it 110% even though it is that tough. I think you can learn so much from that so he inspires me.[4]

---

4. "British GP 2007 Sunday Press Conference," Grandprix.com, July 8, 2007, https://www.grandprix.com/races/british-gp-2007-sunday-press-conference.html.

Being a role model is new ground for Lewis, and it was a crucial moment in his growing understanding of his place in world culture both inside and outside of sports. In his book, in a chapter entitled "Dream," Lewis offers nuance to his understanding of what a role model is and what it means to him. Lewis's answer explains that he feels that he has grown up, pointedly ignoring the question of how he is dealing with being a role model, much less the stuff that comes with it.[5]

Lewis's reflections are far from a Charles Barkley moment. NBA fans will recall the incident from the 1993 season when the power forward attempted to spit in the face of a racist heckler and instead hit a little girl sitting courtside. The league fined him $10,000, and the cause of the incident disappeared (racist heckling) and was replaced with the question of the obligation of professional athletes to be better than everyone else at everything else, including ignoring racism or being more accurate spitters.

Barkley asserted, "I am not paid to be a role model. I'm paid to wreak havoc on the basketball court. Parents should be role models. Just because I dunk a basketball doesn't mean I should raise your kids."[6] Nike, to address waning sales among young people, made the quote into a commercial that remains controversial to this day. Lewis arrived on the scene when sports and athletes have had their role in society defined by athletes like Barkley who are unrepentant and frankly unconcerned what the public thinks about them. Lewis had gone from a young man making his way toward a dream to what the reporter understands as a role model with responsibilities beyond being the best driver he could be.

In answering this question Lewis is trying to ensure that a single attribute or even fault cannot be allowed to stand for all you understand, positively or negatively, about a person. He certainly looked up to his father and throughout his career has never wavered in crediting it all to Anthony's determination and disciplined approach for and with his son. Some

5. *Lewis Hamilton: My Story*, 82.
6. "Nike Air Commercial Charles Barkley—I Am Not a Role Model," posted August 30, 2012, by Antonio Yague, YouTube, https://youtu.be/NNOdFJAG3pE.

of that has pushed some of what we classically understand as modern parenting to the side but both father and son seem to have made peace with that reality.

What seems important, especially at this very precarious moment in Lewis's career, when the sudden pressure of fame could have derailed everything or resulted in him being content with what he had achieved so far and parlaying that into a ride that would last as long as it could, is that he proves to want none of the fallback positions. The driver's focus on Muhammad Ali, the athlete–activist whose courage reached beyond the boxing ring, is also important. Ali's influence as an athlete and activist created the notion of the GOAT, the Greatest of All Time, which cannot be contained by the confines of a sport. To be the greatest takes more than excellence within a sport, and Lewis's lack of a role model creates the possibility of him establishing exactly what a role model means in a world that is changing.

Pharrell and P. Diddy and all that came with their environment didn't faze Lewis. He was neither starstruck nor enthralled and was standing on business. This moment of self-supported courage, when he was already considered an example for others, is in some ways predictable. There is no one inside of Formula One who could serve as an exemplar for Lewis. He would have to make this all up and figure it all out as he went along.

CHAPTER 11

THINGS FALL APART

LEWIS AND HIS FANS WERE DISAPPOINTED WITH HIS SHOWING AT SIL-
verstone, but as a practical matter the season was going better than most
could have imagined. Lewis was now twelve points up on Alonso. The
next race was scheduled in Germany at the Nürburgring, which was
called the European Grand Prix because of a branding issue between
F1 and the event promoters. In the time between Silverstone and the
German race, the corporate espionage affair that had been simmering
was coming to a boil. The McLaren team announced that they would be
called to account for their part in the fiasco a few days after the Grand
Prix, all the while asserting their complete innocence.

As Lewis's fame created additional pressure, he found himself with a
calendar full of sponsor events before the race, and the looming hearing
in front of the FIA made matters that much more complicated. At this
point, according to his memoir and contemporaneous interviews, he was
convinced that the team had nothing to do with this and would be found
innocent.

One of the things that had been cropping up again and again
by that stage of the season was a lot of questions about the
McLaren team—about the Ferrari controversy. It had started

before Silverstone and I had to put it out of my mind. I really knew nothing about it at all, though later in the season it was clear that it really mattered a whole lot and had a huge effect on our championship hopes…I felt confident about myself, my driving, and the integrity of the team and so I felt that I had nothing to worry about.[1]

Lewis arrived in Germany with a virus, fatigued from racing and the pressure of his sponsorship duties, and qualifying was an unmitigated disaster. The first two rounds of the session were without incident, but Q3 saw Lewis in a terrible high-speed crash that sent him to the hospital. During the pit stop before his final qualifying run, a lug gun malfunctioned and Lewis went out onto the track with a tire that was improperly mounted, which was not conducive to driving 150 miles per hour. Lewis barely escaped serious injury, saying, "It was really one of the most painful crashes I have ever had…It was a bad one and it is difficult to describe."[2]

Lewis was obviously not able to continue when the red flag his crash caused was lifted, and even his participation in the race was in question pending some serious considerations of his physical status after the wreck. He was ultimately cleared by the medical staff but was relegated to his worst starting position in his Formula One career, far from the front in tenth position. Also, driving with the injuries he sustained from his wreck did not bode well for maintaining the lead he had over his rivals for the championship. Kimi Räikkönen had taken the pole, Fernando seemed to be living up to the challenge he had set for himself leaving Silverstone and was lining up in second position, splitting the Ferraris, with Massa lurking in P3.

Race day was encumbered with torrential rain. Lewis's woes continued to cascade like the water on the track. He made a dramatic move at the opening of the race, gaining four positions on the first lap before the rain began to get worse and led to a chaotic situation as drivers struggled with grip all over the course. Some drivers dove into the pits immediately, which was a good choice, but there was a lot of confusion about which tires were best under these conditions. Some put on intermediate tires, and others went for full wets. A few drivers played weather guessers and tried to stay on racing tires, which was a disaster. The rain came down even harder and the track was basically under standing water, and cars were scattered everywhere.

Lewis had spun off the track. Again. He was able to keep the engine running, and at the time of this incident, to the extent it was possible, drivers could receive outside help to get back in the track. Lewis had gone off near a crane and the operator got him back on the track and on his way. This kind of intervention is no longer allowed. Even with this assist Lewis never recovered from this misfortune and ended up in a non-scoring ninth position when all was said and done.

Fernando had excelled in the wet and took the checkered flag by more than eight seconds over the surging Massa. The ten-point win slashed his teammate's lead to two points. Lewis's teammate was predictably ecstatic during the post-race conference, the first one all season that was Hamilton-Free.

Q: Fernando, how do you rate this as one of your race victories? You looked ecstatic on the podium.

FA: Yeah, absolutely. I enjoyed the race so much because I like the different conditions, the different weather conditions. I always enjoy these types of races and at one point, when I was second, I said maybe it's not the right time to rain, because I was happy with second place. Lewis was out of the points and Kimi as well, so for me eight points were good enough. But then, obviously now with the final result, I like the rain, there's no doubt. Always when it rains, I'm quite happy and I have some fun. On the podium I was so happy because the race was quite exciting, as I said.[3]

3. "Post-Race Press Conference—European GP—Pt. 1," Crash, July 22, 2007, https://www.crash.net/f1/feature/59380/1/post-race-press-conference-european-gp-pt-1.

Lewis was wounded: physically and mentally. The next race in Hungary would prove to be the end of even the pretense of a civil relationship between the McLaren drivers.

————

In addition to the animosity between Hamilton and Alonso, the stench of the stolen technical data scandal haunted the McLaren team and the sport. As is the practice, even outside of the United States, it was not long before the appellation "-gate" was added and spoke to the severity of the problem engulfing the sport. "Spygate," as it came to be known, would be only one headline-grabbing scandal that came out of the Hungarian Grand Prix.

The actual race, unfortunately, was relatively boring compared to the crazy qualifying round. This is important because Hungary was a very narrow track with very little room for overtaking. Lewis started on the pole, a position he was awarded after his teammate was slammed with a devastating five-place grid penalty because of his antics during Q3, a series of events labeled as "Pitlanegate."

During this era of Formula One, cars were still refueling during the race; they were far less efficient than the current environmentally conscious cars driven today. Just like the race, qualifying had to consider fuel loads, and this led to a series of tactics that were meant to give drivers the best opportunity to have their best run with the lowest possible fuel load/weight. At some circuits, cars would be fueled up for multiple high-speed runs, which required that some laps were used for "fuel burning." This gave the driver with the extra fuel the ability to run a lap or so longer. In this instance there had been an agreement at McLaren that on the early Q3 laps, Hamilton would let Alonso through to give him track space. Lewis's version of the story is that he was willing to do it, but because Kimi would have taken advantage of it and in the process blocked his track space, he didn't do it. Needless to say, Fernando was pissed.

It didn't take long for the Spaniard to seek revenge and an advantage for Sunday. As time wound down, McLaren radioed the drivers with a plan for them to both put on fresh tires for the last moments of Q3.

Before pitting, Lewis was on provisional pole, but there was plenty of time left for this gambit to give both drivers another opportunity with the cars in their best trim. The team stacked the McLarens in the pits, and as fate would have it, Fernando was first up for new tires.

The crew changed his tires as efficiently as ever, and Fernando sat there. The signal came to leave the pits so Lewis could get his car worked on with one minute and forty-eight seconds left in Q3; plenty of time for both drivers to make one more run. But Fernando just sat there. He gestured and continued to sit, blocking Lewis. He pointed and sat some more while the mechanics seemed confused. For an agonizing ten seconds Fernando gestured before speeding onto the raceway, leaving his teammate with very little time to change tires and get around the track for an outlap to get a last hot lap. Fernando made it around and put up the fastest lap of the session. Lewis was not so lucky. Fernando had effectively scuttled his teammate's qualifying session, seized the vital pole, and set himself up for a second victory in as many grand prix. For now.

The team principal, Ron Dennis, went ballistic and was sighted snatching the headphones off the head of Alonso's personal trainer to make sure he heard everything he had to say. The post-qualifying press conference was predictably tense, no matter how hard the two-time world champion tried to pretend nothing was going on.

Alonso went first as was his right since he was the pole sitter.

Q. And also a bit of a delay given that the seconds count down with the front right tyre warmer at the beginning of your first run.

FA: Yes, I think the blanket of the tyre had a problem and it stayed inside the wheel, between the wheel and the car and you know, a little bit delayed there. The mechanics pushed very hard at the blanket and I don't know if it breaks or whatever, but the car was fine.[4]

---

4. "Hungary GP Post-Qualifying Press Conference," Pitpass.com, August 4, 2007, https://www.pitpass.com/32354/Hungary-GP-Post-Qualifying-press-conference.

This is complete nonsense. The delay had nothing to do with tire warmers not being removed, and his claims implied that the blame should go to the incompetence of the pit mechanics. The questions then turn to the second qualifier, Lewis, who takes as high a road as was available under the current circumstances, thanking the people at the team for the one-two result. He is pressed by the interviewer to respond to what happened during Q3 and turns it back to Fernando and the notion that they will debrief to deal with it. After talking to Nick Heidfeld of BMW Sauber, the third-place finisher, they return to Fernando to press him on the qualifying fiasco.

Q. (CARLOS MIQUEL—*Diario AS*) We have a question for
Fernando. With the blanket, the extra lap goes to Hamilton, no?

FA: No, I think there was no time to do an extra fuel burning
lap for both drivers, so you know when I had my first pit stop I
knew already that it was not possible. So we pitted one lap earlier
to strip the first set of tyres. So at that point to have the blanket
problem and lose another ten seconds or any more was not really an
important thing for the extra lap, we cancelled it already.

Q. (MICHAEL SCHMIDT—*Auto Motor und Sport*) Fernando,
at the first stop before the blanket problems started you seemed
to wait very long and have a discussion with the pit wall. What
happened there?

FA: No, we changed the front wing, because I had a little bit too
much understeer in my car in the burning fuel lap. So we tried to
adjust the car and as I said because we started at the front of the
grid at the end of the pit lane. We were doing not the extra fuel
burning lap, so I had the extra 45 seconds in the pit stop waiting.[5]

---

5. "Hungary GP Post-Qualifying Press Conference."

Clearly here, Fernando is making the unethical move to place the blame on the faceless mechanics rather than take responsibility for his actions. Lewis, who even at this earliest stage of his career is conscious of the importance and dignity of these workers, won't allow it.

Q. (ANDREW FRANKL—*Forza*) Two weeks ago at the Nürburgring it was amateur theatrics at the tyre change, today they couldn't get the tyre warmer off. Is all the political pressure getting to the team members do you think? Because it really looks like Formula Three or Formula Ford.

LH: No, I don't think you should really be so hard on the team. They do what they are told and I think that is an important thing. They do what they are told. I doubt very much that there was a problem with the tyre blanket because it is quite easy to pull off. The team, as I have said, always do a fantastic job, my group of guys do a great job and during the races they just put so much work in. I don't think people really give them the amount of respect and appreciation they deserve.

Q. (SIMON ARRON—*Motorsport News*) Lewis, we have had four weeks of Stepneygate and we have now had half an hour of Pitlanegate. How do you blank out all the political machinations and focus on the main job?

LH: I guess that is a skill that I have developed over the years. It's what I said from day one, I enjoy it, I love the job. This is something that I've always wanted to do and I still enjoy it. I get in the car and I always have a smile on my face. It is easy for me to overcome any problems I have in the team or outside of the car and get in and do my job the best way I can.

Q. (PETER WINDSOR—SPEED TV) Lewis, a few minutes ago

you said, "I don't know why the team held me up, you need to ask them." But in fact Fernando said the team held him up. Was that a Freudian slip or do you think that the team actually held you up?

LH: No, as Fernando said, he was told to stop and wait. His wheels were on, his blankets were off and he was told to wait. I imagine that I probably lost half-a-minute I would say from my in-lap coming in to waiting behind Fernando. At least 30 seconds, so it definitely needs a good explanation.[6]

The reporters have rooted out the obvious absurdity of Fernando's explanation and return to the pole sitter with more pointed questions.

Q. (PETER WINDSOR—SPEED TV) Fernando, has that ever happened before where the team has held you up to get a gap?

FA: Every qualifying. We stop and we wait, sometimes ten seconds, sometimes five, sometimes 45, as with the first stop today.

The tennis-match-like Q&A goes back to Lewis, who is seated right next to his teammate as is the practice for all of these press conferences.

Q. (ED GORMAN—*The Times*) Lewis, would you say you are more angry about this than you were about what happened in Monaco?

LH: As I said you can see I'm not angry. I'm curious to know what has gone on and I find it quite interesting and amusing. But the good thing is that we had the pace. We did a great job we have got a great car. I was very, very comfortable and I am very comfortable with my strategy for tomorrow, so I am not really mad to be honest.[7]

---

6. "Hungary GP Post-Qualifying Press Conference."
7. "Hungary GP Post-Qualifying Press Conference."

The race stewards were likewise unconvinced by the clownish excuses, and after a meeting with the affected parties, decided to punish the team and Alonso. Moving Lewis to the pole is significant for several reasons. First, as mentioned, pole at this race is often definitive, plus lumping Alonso and the team together for punishment creates an interesting dynamic. One is to imagine that Lewis has been isolated and is in this season alone. The other, and the way the situation seems to have evolved is that Alonso becomes the first albatross around the neck of team McLaren and its new standard bearer, Lewis.

Qualifying at Hungary is of utmost importance. So a probable explanation is that Fernando wanted to keep Lewis from P1. The obvious point is that it is better to be on the pole than not. Alonso also had a legitimate reason to be angry about Lewis defying the instructions to let him through, Lewis's explanation about Kimi coming through as well notwithstanding. The situation with Kimi would have been worth discussing among the team, and as we have seen, it did not preclude Fernando from having the opportunity for a clean run at the pole. The decision Alonso made, to lash out and obstruct his teammate—literally cheating—created a problem for the stewards and eroded his reputation as a competitor.

If a McLaren driver had, for instance, purposefully held up a Ferrari in the pits, the punishment is straightforward. The driver would be punished, and unless there was evidence that the team had ordered the athlete to do so, it is hard to imagine that the team would have been excluded from point scoring because of an individual driver's bad decision. In this situation, because this was an intra-team issue, the FIA was clearly finding itself in a position to make it clear to McLaren that their driver, Alonso in this instance, needed to get his act in alignment with the standards of sportsmanship that most involved at least pretended to care about. One thing is clear. Fernando had come to the conclusion that there was not going to be a way for the team to take care of him again like they had in Monaco. It was already obvious that Lewis had little if any interest in assisting his teammate by sacrificing his own status. The most damning part of Alonso's stunt is that it was a clear admission that he was incapable of competing with Lewis driver to driver; and the Spaniard and his fans didn't like it.

———

As the European Grand Prix continued, Lewis picked up five more points on his teammate, but Ferrari gained in the constructors' title race. If only this had been the limit of the McLarens' woes, the weekend would have been a success. Though Pitlanegate was resolved, at least as far as the consequences were concerned, Spygate threatened the very integrity of the sport itself.

Fernando, over the previous weeks, had routinely taken to Spanish sports radio to complain about his perceived plight at McLaren. One can imagine that in the world that existed before the explosion of social media, Alonso might have thought that the language barrier might give him some privacy for his public outrage. It didn't. The Formula One media had spotted this and was reporting on it. The seeds of an ugly environment for Hamilton were planted by Fernando.

Bizarrely, Alonso even used the opportunity to do something for charity to take shots at his teammate that are at best juvenile and at worst racist. *F1 Racing* is a British magazine that calls itself "The World's Best Selling Grand Prix Magazine." The publication, for its August 2007 issue, asked each of the drivers to draw a caricature of their teammates that would be auctioned off for charity. The magazine was surprised that all twenty of the drivers agreed to participate and actually received the "art" early enough to be included in the August issue.

There are various results, as one might expect, but even the organizers of the philanthropic effort took note of Alonso's drawing of Lewis. In the caption above Fernando's offering, the editors wrote, "Notice the word 'boy' scrawled by Fernando on Lewis's shoulder..."[8] The ellipsis belongs to the editor, inviting the viewer to fill in this massive and controversial space opened by Fernando's artistic imagination. The editors seem to

———

8. *F1 Racing*, August 22, 2007.

grasp how problematic this happens to be but don't press forward on fer-
reting out what exactly is going on with the two-time champion and his
teammate. This wink and a nod at Fernando's perceived casual racism
would lead to a catastrophe for Formula One in the very near future. In
situations such as this there are all kinds of ways to erase the implications
of this kind of slight. One way is to propose that a native Spanish speaker
like Fernando might not have the cultural awareness of how this might
be perceived. Several things seem clear. As you will note from the image,
Fernando is careful to reproduce the sponsor logos on Lewis's driver's
uniform. Obviously, nowhere on his top is the word "boy," so Fernando's
addition was meant to signal what he thought of his teammate—at best
to infantilize him and at worst making a racialized stereotype through
that same language. To be clear, Lewis was a rookie, but in 2007 he was
twenty-two years old, and the Spaniard was only four years his senior;
not exactly a generational divide.

This drawing, in combination with Fernando's ever more unhinged
commentary about the nationality of the team and the driver, creates a
hard-to-avoid narrative that Alonso is deeply invested in blaming circumstances, performance, or non-performance on identity. Lewis, the
"boy" in his mind, was beating him, and it couldn't be because he was a
better driver. This toxicity led to the demise of Fernando's relationship
with McLaren and would haunt him to this day in his dealings with
Hamilton; and the Stepney problem still was coming down the track.

————

IN THE SAME ISSUE THAT CONTAINED THE CARICATURES, *F1 RACING*
covers the moving catastrophe in a short piece with the title: "Will
McLaren's 2007 Be Razed?" The article quoted the following from a
press release from the FIA.

> The team's representatives have been called to answer a charge
> that between March and July 2007, in breach of Article 151c
> of the International Sporting Code, Vodaphone McLaren

> Mercedes had unauthorized possession of documents and con-
> fidential information belonging to Scuderia Ferrari Marlboro,
> including information that could be used to design, engineer,
> build, check, test, develop, and/or run a 2007 Ferrari Formula
> 1 car.[9]

The short answer is that the season would in fact be destroyed in large measure. Nigel Stepney, the central figure in this controversy, was a well-regarded figure in Formula One as an essential member of the success that Michael Schumacher had experienced at Ferrari before his retirement in 2006. Apparently, Stepney had sent his wife to reproduce the stolen documents at a local copy shop where a committed Ferrari fan spotted the importance of the documents and turned the whole bunch of them in to the FIA. McLaren's problems are inextricably related to the dissatisfaction of Fernando. A 2023 article on the Racing News 365 website, "F1's Biggest Scandals: McLaren Fined $100 Million for 'Spygate,'" reveals how bad things had become between Alonso and the team in the aftermath of the controversy in Hungary. Nichols reports in the article that:

> Alonso was docked five places on the grid, while McLaren's
> Constructors' points were wiped out for the race but an argu-
> ment between Alonso and Dennis reignited Spygate, during
> which Alonso threatened Dennis with revealing new informa-
> tion about Spygate to the FIA, also making a demand.
>
> For more than a decade, what transpired was known only
> to a select few, but was revealed by *BBC Sport* in 2018, with
> Alonso demanding McLaren ensure Hamilton ran out of fuel
> in the race.[10]

---

9. "Will McLaren's 2007 Season Be Razed?" *F1 Racing*, August 22, 2007, 22.
10. Jake Nichol, "F1's Biggest Scandals: McLaren fined $100 million for 'Spygate,'" RN365, December 27, 2023, https://racingnews365.com/f1s-biggest-scandals

Just to be clear, in the aftermath of blocking his teammate from having a chance at the pole, Fernando Alonso then demanded that the team sabotage his teammate's car, so he would literally come to a stop during the race because the mechanics were to be ordered to improperly fuel Hamilton's car. In the face of Fernando's threats, Ron Dennis went directly to the FIA, who naturally reopened the investigation, causing the unprecedented fine and the removal of the entire team from the constructors' race. Fernando, the story proposes, realized that Dennis had gone to the FIA, and before the race on Sunday in Hungary, said he no longer wanted Lewis's car sabotaged and also figured he didn't want to give the FIA any more information.

It is hard to imagine how the relationship between the players in this controversy could be repaired. A $40 million fine is also a special note on the balance sheet of a corporation that is hard to explain to shareholders who are interested in selling luxury, not the ins and outs of racing. Fernando was in a difficult position. No driver, particularly a double world champion, wants to be challenged by a teammate, least of all an unproven rookie. Fernando's caricature of his teammate that labeled him a "boy" indicates an explicit disrespect for Lewis that is complicated by race. The problem was that the Spaniard, in his mind, was being dominated by someone who was there to learn and make a gesture at diversity, not make him look bad, and the season still had six races to go.

-mclaren-fined-100-million-for-spygate#:~:text=So%2C%20the%202007%20espionage%20crisis,of%20confidential%20Ferrari%20technical%20information.

CHAPTER 12

THREE RACES

In a 2024 interview posted on the Mercedes team site, Lewis was asked what single race he would want to have changed the outcome of, and he offered three.[1] The interviewers likely wanted the focus to be on a fiasco in Abu Dhabi in 2021. Lewis did not disappoint. He included that one on the list, but the first race he mentioned was from his rookie season: the Chinese Grand Prix of 2007. The second was Malaysia 2016, and then the Abu Dhabi race in 2021. In closing out the analysis of Hamilton's rookie season, the Chinese Grand Prix is instructive, informative, and formative of everything that follows in Lewis's career. This is why, seventeen years later, it still preoccupies his attention.

After the internal controversy of Hungary, the 2007 season was down to six races, and the rookie was holding on to a seven-point lead over Alonso. Immediately after the Hungarian Grand Prix the teams met in Turkey, where a late-race puncture dropped Lewis to a fifth-place finish. Felipe Massa continued his surge for the Ferrari team, winning the race, with his teammate grabbing second place and Alonso filling out the podium in third. Lewis's lead over his teammate was now down to five points with five races remaining.

1. @mercedesamgf1motorsport, Instagram, May 11, 2024, https://www.instagram .com/p/C61YhW6tzYx/?igsh=Nzh3OTRvazN1M2c1&img_index=1.

At the iconic Italian Grand Prix at Monza, Fernando outqualified Lewis for the pole and finished first with Lewis clinging to second. Now the lead was only three points.

Round fourteen was run at the Circuit de Spa-Francochamps, the Belgian Grand Prix. The Ferraris locked out the front row in qualifying, Kimi on pole and Felipe P2. Fernando outqualified Lewis again, and they filled out the third and fourth places on the second row. At the start, the order held, but not without drama. Alonso fought off one of Lewis's early race surges by forcing him off the raceway. At the checkered flag, the race ended as it started, with Lewis off the podium—and only two points ahead of Alonso.

The championship was now headed to the Far East for the fifteenth round: sixty-seven laps of the Fuju Speedway at Ogama, Shizuoka, in Japan, the first time the Japanese Grand Prix had been held away from Suzuka since the late 1970s. None of the drivers had even the most cursory experience at this track in a F1 car. The Japanese Grand Prix, wherever it is held, has a chance to be plagued with weather. Early rain squalls stopped by the time qualifying started, but the track was still soaked, prompting the teams to send the drivers out on wet weather tires. Lewis came into his own and led the qualifying, with Fernando in second. The Ferraris were not far behind in P3 and P4.

The rain may have spared qualifying, but it returned for the race. It rained in such quantities that the race stewards dispensed with the traditional start and sent the cars off behind the safety car. This went on for an excruciating nineteen laps, and the Ferraris both came into the pits to put on "extreme" wet rubber.

The safety car got out of the way on the twentieth lap, and the Ferraris, because of stopping to change tires, found themselves taking up the last two places. The race predictably featured several crashes as drivers struggled with grip. In fact, Fernando Alonso fell victim to a crash that retired his car. In what amounted to a war of attrition, Lewis ended up scoring a win and sharing the podium with Heikki Kovalainen of Renault and Ferrari's Räikkönen. Most important, Hamilton extended his lead to twelve

Lewis Hamilton and Max Verstappen collide at the
Italian Grand Prix in 2021, days before the Met Gala.
Zak Mauger / Getty Images

Lewis and guests at the 2021 Met Gala in New York City.
Dimitrios Kambouris / Getty Images

Lewis celebrates his 2011 Formula One World Championship
with the team and his partner at the time, Nicole Scherzinger.
Clive Mason / Getty Images

Lewis and other drivers protest racist policing.
Mark Sutton / Getty Images

Lewis protests the killing of Breonna Taylor by police.
Getty Images

Lewis and his mother, Carmen Larbalestier, after being knighted in 2021.
Andrew Matthews / Getty Images

Lewis at the 2024 Met Gala.
Dia Dipasupil / Getty Images

Lewis and his father, Anthony Hamilton, have an emotional
celebration after his 2024 victory at Silverstone.
Mario Renzi / Getty Images

points over his teammate with only two races remaining. Lewis seemed poised to achieve the impossible, a world championship in his rookie season, but then there was China—one of the three races Lewis would one day wish he could change.

————

THE GRUELING NATURE OF A FORMULA ONE SEASON IS WEARING ON everyone. But in 2007, Lewis seemed to have gotten a second wind from the squalls in Japan and headed to China riding a wave of positive momentum. The math was on Hamilton's side. After Fernando's disastrous crash in Japan, only Kimi Räikkönen and his Ferrari, trailing by seventeen points, could possibly challenge for the title.

Kimi served notice that he was not going away in the first two rounds of qualifying by putting up session-leading times. Lewis pulled together an epic lap when he needed it in Q3 and inched out Kimi to the pole with Massa in third and Fernando adrift in P4.

A typhoon on the east coast of China served up another wet race. Conditions were not as poor as they had been in Japan, so the race went off normally, with all the drivers on intermediate tires. The rain stopped, and the track dried rapidly. The order of the top four starting places remained the same. McLaren designed a strategy before the race and was hell-bent on sticking to it. The strategy left Hamilton out with tires that were terribly worn. Lewis ran wide at a curve, and Kimi took advantage of the lapse and grabbed the lead.

At this point, it was clear to everyone that Hamilton could not continue on these tires, and so long as he held on to the second position, he would still leave China leading the Drivers' Championship. Then disaster struck.

Entering the pits at this course required drivers to make a sharp left. The condition of Hamilton's tires would not allow it, and he ended up in the gravel. Permanently. Lewis's first retirement of the season came at the most inopportune time, throwing the door back open to other drivers who had formerly been mathematically excluded from the championship.

Räikkönen held on to win the grand prix. Alonso surged to second, and Felipe Massa took the third step on the podium. Lewis left China leading the championship by four points over Alonso and seven over Räikkönen.

The strategic lapse—the failure to be decisive as the conditions changed on the track—is the reason this race haunts Hamilton to this day.

———————

THE FINAL ROUND REQUIRED THE TEAMS TO MAKE THEIR WAY TO BRAzil, where the race result would decide the driver's crown. All Hamilton needed to do was finish in the top four, no matter what other drivers might accomplish, to grab the world championship.

Lewis showed himself to be in solid form, qualifying second behind Felipe Massa, at the same time securing the record for the most front-row starts for a rookie driver. Räikkönen and Alonso filled out the second row, which put three drivers in a position to win the title.

Hamilton made a name for himself in the opening race in Australia, when his expectations for himself exceeded those of the public, by taking advantage of an opportunity at the first corner to improve his position. Lewis's start in the last race of the season was poor. This was hard to explain after he had started the season as an inexperienced driver making bold and decisive moves that set him up for great finishes. At the last and decisive race, Lewis's start was tentative, one that would have been expected in his first grand prix, not the season finale. Lewis gave position to both Ferraris immediately, and not far into the first lap he was passed by Alonso. During the episode he locked up his tires and fell to a devastating eighth place before the first lap was over. The title was slipping away.

Several laps later, as Hamilton fought to recover position, his gearbox malfunctioned. For an agonizing half minute or more, cars blazed past Hamilton while he struggled to get his car working again. When the computer finally reset itself and fired up the car, he found himself in eighteenth place.

The Ferraris sped into the distance, and the championship was gone.

At the end of it all, after dozens of laps in which he tried to claw his way back to fourth place, Lewis ended up in seventh, losing the championship to the ecstatic Kimi Räikkönen by a razor-thin single point. Ferrari had succeeded in winning both the drivers' and constructors' titles because of McLaren finding themselves booted from the team running.

Lewis had announced himself as a star in Formula One despite having lost the championship. But there were questions. Lewis had made major mistakes when the pressure was at its highest, and the question of whether he had what it took to win a title would have to wait until the 2008 season, because based upon the close of the 2007, the answer was "no." The question was whether that was "not yet" or "no" with a period after it.

As up in the air as Hamilton's future seemed to be, the fate of Fernando Alonso was as grounded as a car stuck in the gravel. The Spaniard had had his fill of Lewis and McLaren and terminated his contract. Alonso headed back to one of his former teams, Renault. Whether or not this change would alleviate the animosity between Lewis and Fernando remained to be seen. The start of the 2008 season was only a few months away. No one could have guessed what was coming.

CHAPTER 13

SAYING THE QUIET PART OUT LOUD

SECOND SEASONS ARE ABOUT THE QUESTIONS THAT REMAIN UNANswered from the first season. The most important question for an athlete is to prove that the first season wasn't a fluke—that the success didn't go to their head and they hadn't given up on the hard work that brought rookie success. For Lewis in particular, the failure to close out the championship left him open to the critique that he was not able to meet the pressure of big moments. These could and would be solved on the track.

Formula One, the institution, had things to resolve as well. What many may have thought would amount to a feel-good demonstration that the sport was diverse ended up being much more than that. Lewis had become the face of Formula One, and in so doing had humiliated one of its former champions. The question as to whether Formula One would capitalize on that success and promote Lewis in ways that would be discomfiting to people with antiquated ideas would remain to be seen. There was an untapped audience, and F1 had to decide if and how they wanted to bring them into the sport. While Lewis remade the landscape of motorsports, one of its most storied teams was mired in scandal; could it recover? At the end of the day, the real question was whether F1 was flexible enough to accommodate Hamilton. Could he "fit in"?

The final question is one that Hamilton references to this day, always asserting that he just didn't fit in. This is, to be clear, a euphemism for what having a Black person in Formula One who is also, unquestionably, showing signs of dominance of the sport, means. Lewis and his father make constant and veiled reference to the negative reaction they received throughout their journey to Formula One. It would be naïve to presume that crossing into the top of the sport would suddenly resolve the feeling of not fitting in without confronting it directly.

The caricature by Alonso that appeared in *F1 Racing* when he scrawled "boy" was never directly confronted. Whatever Fernando meant or didn't mean by it, there are those who, upon seeing such things, have their worst inclinations about race served. Fernando Alonso, the two-time world champion, made the move to McLaren and was run off by a rookie. He returned to Williams in the aftermath of the stunt he pulled in Hungary to block his teammate's qualifying run as well as what has been discovered in recent years about his demand that the team under-fuel Lewis's car. This all goes along with his clumsy attempt to blackmail the team. None of it worked. His fans were eager to see Lewis, whom they believed to be the author of his demise at McLaren, humiliated.

The 2008 season was set up to be exciting and potentially controversial. The F1 season begins with the teams showing up for preseason testing, where the cars and the drivers get a chance to see how ready they are to compete after the break. The 2008 testing was taking place in Fernando Alonso's backyard on the track in Barcelona where he had underperformed in 2007. *The Guardian* covered the events that unfolded there in unvarnished fashion. The headlines chronicled the happenings at testing simply and provocatively: "Spanish Racists Vent Hate for Hamilton." It reads in part:

> At pre-season testing in Barcelona in February he was confronted by a group of Spanish fans who blacked up their faces,

donned wigs and t-shirts emblazoned with the words "Hamilton's Family". They booed the British driver and called him a "black shit".[1]

The "fans" were captured on film, and the FIA was forced to respond to this unprecedented situation by ultimately launching an anti-racism campaign similar to the one that is promoted by world class soccer/football. The organization called "Every Race" issued a terse condemnation of the fiasco at the track in Barcelona, saying, "Discrimination and prejudice can have no place in sport or society. Everyone in our sport will join us in condemning these abusive and hateful comments."[2] The everyone, unfortunately, was not inclusive of Fernando Alonso.

ESPN's racing site covered the incident, posting an AP article on February 20, 2008, under the title "Alonso Brushes Off Racism Claims Following Incidents against Hamilton." Fernando is quoted as saying:

> "This is not a racist country. This was an isolated thing and the less it is talked about, the better. There were people enjoying Carnival and look what happened. They called me a dog and no one comes to my defense...I don't think we need an anti-racism campaign like FIA wants to organize for the Grand Prix at Barcelona."[3]

Alonso's quotation is troubling for several reasons. These were clearly racist attacks, but he wants to minimize them by understanding them as

1. Matthew Taylor, Richard Wray, and Giles Tremlett, "Spanish Racists Vent Hate for Hamilton," *The Guardian*, October 31, 2008, https://www.theguardian.com/sport/2008/nov/01/lewis-hamilton-spain#:~:text=In%20Spain%2C%20however%2C%20the%2023,the%20words%20%22Hamilton's%20family%22.
2. "FIA Announces 'Everyrace' Campaign in Barcelona," ESPN.com, April 24, 2008, https://www.espn.com/racing/racing/f1/news/story?id=3364645.
3. Associated Press, "Alonso Brushes Off Racism Claims Following Incidents Against Hamilton," ESPN.com, February 8, 2008, https://www.espn.com/racing/news/story?id=3255381&seriesId=6.

isolated incidents. Apparently, according to Fernando and other apologists, Spain has racists, but it isn't a racist country. Second, he attempts to make it about him and some incident when someone called him a "dog," with little further explanation or context except it seems to be in the realm of what drunken college students refer to as a "party foul" in his mind. Finally, one must wonder what harm an anti-racism campaign could do. Fernando wants only silence on the issue as if he assumes that it won't happen again, but if it does it's an isolated incident. He seems to be saying, "Who cares?"

Despite Alonso's assertion, Spain was in crisis regarding Lewis Hamilton. The Spanish fans' disdain for Hamilton seems to have gone beyond being heartbroken that the Brit had soundly beaten the Spaniard and causing Alonso to flee McLaren. The crisis, according to the people who showed up to hurl racist insults at Hamilton, was because he was Black. Coincident with the events at the testing track, one local Spanish website called for fans to stick nails and pins into an image of the circuit to have spirits harm Hamilton's car. Another website domiciled in Spain was, like the racist fans at the testing track, concerned with Hamilton's parentage and called him a "half-breed" before its New York–based parent shut it down.

Lewis, in continuation of the practice developed by Anthony, admitted that he was bothered by the incident but had "moved on." When you think about the tactic that his father advocated, "Do your talking on the track," it becomes clear that it probably wasn't useful in actually doing anything about racism. Lewis had certainly spoken loudly and emphatically on the track. His skill was unquestioned. The problem with "talking on the track" is that the response to his excellence was a series of racist attacks. This would not be the last time that Fernando would find himself as a principal or somehow related to racism in Formula One, which, despite his argument to the contrary, has a problem with racism that has lasted for years.

———

Flashing forward a decade or so from 2008, Lewis had a record of taking up anti-racism globally, as a personal activist and as a social

justice project. In due course, we will look closely at what is arguably the defining rivalry of Lewis's career—with the Dutchman, Max
Verstappen—but as we consider racism in Formula One, it is appropriate
to briefly discuss a specific aspect of the complexity between them.

Through association, Max Verstappen has become close to Nelson
Piquet Sr. Nelson's daughter, Kelly, has been in a serious relationship
with the Dutch driver for some time. Understanding this, Nelson Sr. was
firmly on the side of his daughter's partner during the hard-fought campaign in 2021. In November that year, Nelson Sr. was giving an interview on a podcast in Brazil about the controversial crash at Silverstone
that opens this book. The Brazilian took Lewis to task for the wreck and
during his diatribe uses the term *neguinho* to refer to Hamilton. That
word can be benignly translated as "little black guy" with the more dire
implication and context being "nigger."[4]

When the interview surfaced, Formula One, Mercedes, and the FIA,
according to a June 29, 2022, report by Matias Grez, "condemned Piquet
for using the racial slur."[5] Hamilton responded to Piquet's comments in a
series of posts on Twitter (now X), writing: Vamos focar em mudar a men-
talidade, translated from the Portuguese as "Let's focus on changing the
mindset." Lewis went further, saying:

> [the] time has come for action on racism. It's more than lan-
> guage. These are archaic mindsets [that] need to change and
> have no place in our sport...I've been surrounded by these
> attitudes and targeted my whole life. There has been plenty of
> time to learn. Time has come for action.[6]

4. "Nelson Piquet Calls Lewis Hamilton the Little N Word in Interview Footage—
Translation Included," posted June 28, 2022, by yazzfetto, YouTube, https://youtu.be
/CCcAEjTQmcg?si=xUIbbbwafnejv6OQ.
5. Matias Grez, "Nelson Piquet Says Racial Slur Aimed at Lewis Hamilton Had
No Racist Intent," CNN.com, June 29, 2022, https://www.cnn.com/2022/06/29
/motorsport/nelson-piquet-apologizes-lewis-hamilton-racist-slur-spt-intl/index.html.
6. Jerome Pugmire, "Hamilton Says 'Archaic Mindsets' About Color Must Change,"

This is the opposite of letting his talking happen on the track and hoping that it will get better. The environment within Formula One had also evolved beyond Fernando's ideas from the 2008 season. Australian driver Daniel Ricciardo was perhaps the most articulate in responding both to the racist incident, and to Lewis's example. He was quoted in Grez's CNN piece from his Instagram post.

> Discrimination and racism has no place in this sport or our society. Those who still choose to spread this hate and use these words are no friends of mine.
>
> I want to acknowledge Lewis and all the work he has done both on and off the track to not only spread messages of equality but combat that hate.
>
> I've never dealt with any racially motivated actions, but he has for his entire life. Yet each time his response to hate is motivated by maturity, positivity and educating the world on how we should act. I stand with him and will do whatever I can to follow and support.[7]

All this furor encouraged people to look further into Nelson Piquet Sr. As we have said, Piquet had a history of offensive commentary, choosing to style himself as a prankster. Predictably, he had made other bigoted statements about Lewis. In 2016, when Lewis lost the title in a grueling season to his teammate Nico Rosberg, Piquet proposed in an interview that if Lewis had not been having sex with men, he would have been victorious.[8]

Associated Press, June 28, 2022, https://apnews.com/article/entertainment-sports-race-and-ethnicity-racial-injustice-formula-one-c02ada62e4b441d0b8785f75df66ae75.
7. Grez, "Nelson Piquet Says Racial Slur Aimed at Lewis Hamilton Had No Racist Intent."
8. Eléonore Hughes, "Piquet Fined for Racist, Homophobic Comments About Hamilton," Associated Press, March 25, 2023, https://apnews.com/article/hamilton-f1-piquet-racism-1b2c2e5a90d0047f483c5d9802028744.

Brazil's National LGBTI+ Alliance filed charges against the bigoted driver that resulted in him being fined $950,000 for "moral damage" for his comments about Hamilton. The support that Lewis earned through his example comes not just from his fellow drivers and the structures of Formula One but also from human rights organizations who see him as worthy of protection just like others.

The response by the F1 community also improved itself from its response to what occurred when Lewis was still struggling with how he managed his understanding of his Blackness in 2011 during the Monaco Grand Prix. At that race, Lewis continued a hard-to-imagine streak of investigations and visits to be admonished by the stewards. When asked about it, he responded to the question by saying, "Maybe it's because I'm Black. That's what Ali G says, I don't know." The backlash was fierce and exactly the opposite of the response to Nelson Piquet Sr.'s racism a decade later. *The Bleacher Report* ran an article under the headline "Lewis Hamilton Plays the Race Card After His Monaco Grand Prix Penalties." The article, written by Barry Rosenberg, took Hamilton to task, emphasizing that the driver had apologized to the stewards for his "bad joke" and that "[t]his observer would like to know, from Hamilton, what would have been the right time to say, 'Maybe it's because I'm black.' I'd like to know what part of it is funny. Lewis Hamilton has the same feeling of entitlement that Ayrton Senna had—as if God was on his side. I hope he doesn't end his career the same way Senna did." These final two sentences of this article are astonishing for several reasons. The first is that there is no evidence of Lewis Hamilton proclaiming a sense of divine entitlement but that he is luridly referencing the Brazilian's death in Italy in 1994.[9]

This is to be expected. The same writer, in the same publication just two days before, derided Hamilton and finished his attack by proposing "but as a man, a person, he's a blight on intelligent society. If he would just shut up,

---

9. Barry Rosenberg, "Lewis Hamilton Plays the Race Card After his Monaco Grand Prix Penalties," Bleacher Report, May 29, 2011, https://bleacherreport.com/articles/716576-lewis-hamilton-plays-the-race-card-after-his-monaco-grand-prix-penalties.

he'd gain respect." Rosenberg was pushing the same notion that Fernando had proposed in response to the racists in Barcelona: just be quiet. Hamilton was evolving into an athlete who was not going to be told to "shut up and drive."

Ironically, at the 2024 Miami Grand Prix, another race-related response was given to the press, this time by Fernando Alonso, now driving for Aston Martin. The Spaniard was penalized for his driving while his perennial nemesis, Lewis, was not. Alonso had collided with his Aston Martin teammate before also crashing into Hamilton. Fernando blamed Lewis and went on to argue that he was being penalized because he was Spanish. The controversial statements were reported by Lawrence Edmondson, the F1 editor at ESPN.

> "I have to open the gap because Hamilton was coming from the inside without control of the car, so if I do that for sure I get the penalty," Alonso said.
>
> But speaking directly after the sprint race, the Spaniard added that he did not expect Hamilton to be penalized.
>
> "I guess they won't decide anything because he's not Spanish. But I think he ruined the race for a few people."
>
> Asked later in the day if he truly felt nationality influenced stewards' decisions, he added: "I do feel that nationality matters, and I will speak with Mohammed [Ben Sulayem, FIA president], with the FIA, whatever.
>
> "I need to make sure there is not anything wrong with my nationality or anything that can influence any decision, not only for me also for the future generation of the Spanish drivers they need to be protected."[10]

So much for Fernando's insistence that the proper course was silence

---

10. Laurence Edmondson, "Alonso Accuses F1 Stewards of Bias Following Miami GP Sprint Incident," ESPN.com, May 4, 2024, https://www.espn.com/f1/story/_/id/40083838/alonso-accuses-f1-stewards-bias-following-miami-gp-sprint-incident.

in the face of acts of racism, real or, in this case, imagined. There is no evidence that he was being penalized because of his nationality, but he thought he deserved a meeting with the president of the FIA. At its most basic level, this is another of Fernando's poorly concealed attacks on Hamilton that is at least implicitly racist. In this instance, he is saying that Lewis won't be penalized because he is Black. Unlike the demand for an apology from Lewis's "joke" in Monaco in 2011, Alonso apparently met with the FIA, but there is no information available about that meeting. There is also no apology, clarification, or evidence forthcoming. Lewis has had an interesting effect on the culture of Formula One. He has created the space for Alonso to allege that he is the victim of bigotry, when the status quo had been a demand for silence.

All of this personal experience with a variety of "isms" and phobias can't be discounted when thinking about Lewis's social justice efforts both inside and outside of Formula One. It is important to note that Hamilton's concerns extend beyond race, in the same manner that they outdistance Formula One. People like Piquet Sr. apparently take Lewis's concern for the LGBTQ+ rights (as evidenced by his display of the rainbow flag) as proof that he is a member of that community, an accusation that he has never dignified with a response. Second, in addition to minority and LGBTQ+ rights, Hamilton is equally concerned with gender equality and opportunity. He has institutionalized this with his Mission 44 initiative.

CHAPTER 14

GOAT?

No conversation about any sport will go on for very long before the question "Who is the greatest of all time?" gets raised. "Who is the GOAT?" Most people will tell you that it was Muhammad Ali, who proclaimed himself the Greatest of All Time in 1964, that forever cemented this question within the foundation of sports conversations. Ali never tired of (re)asserting this claim, in good times and bad, throughout his life. Had Parkinson's disease not tragically silenced him, there is no reason to believe that he would have ever stopped saying it. That tells us the GOAT verdict is not a "what have you done for me lately?" question. To even be considered the greatest of all time, athletes in this conversation, in whatever sport, have put such distance between themselves and the rest that there is very little need for additional space atop this mountain. Sports fans have a perpetual need to interrogate the careers of athletes who are great in one way or another. And so we find ourselves asking, "Who is the greatest of all time in Formula One?"

First, we should establish what the term means. The GOAT question quickly becomes complex by stringing together a series of absolutes. It's the difference between "this is the best pizza I've had this year," and "this is the best pizza *anyone* has ever had *anywhere, any time.*" GOAT arguments trend toward the latter rather than the former. It's not just the greatest performance you have ever seen with whatever brackets you might choose to place around it: This Olympics. This season. By a person under six feet seven inches, etc. Claiming someone is the GOAT is meant to assert that there is no chance there is a performer in whatever circumstances you can imagine who has done the thing better. This is the "of all time" part that supercharges the greatest.

In the world of Formula One, the GOAT debate centers on three candidates: Juan Manuel Fangio, Michael Schumacher, and Lewis Hamilton. But there are several credentials required before a driver can summit this Mount Rushmore. Let's take a look at a few of them.

———

To be taken seriously, an athlete must have won multiple championships. No matter what the apparent skill level of a driver happens to be, if they have not won multiple titles there is no chance of making the cut. In addition to the question of how many championships a driver wins, there is additional nuance when they come in a row. (Think about the Chicago Bulls' two three-peats as an example.) Championships being spread across eras of competition is another important consideration. In Formula One, winning championships is not just a question of the competitive environment but also the way a driver is able to master technical changes in the sport year to year. All of this speaks to longevity, another essential credential of GOAT aspirants.

Determining the F1 GOAT would be much simpler if the competition were bracketed by eras but again, the "of all time" makes that impossible. This is difficult in all sports, but the technical changes in what we understand as a "car" complicate the discussion for F1. For instance, Fangio could not have imagined what an open-wheel race car would be capable of in modern times from his era, smack in the middle of the twentieth century. As a practical matter, the same goes for the evolution of the car from Schumacher to Hamilton. This means determining who is the greatest across eras requires that there are qualities about an athlete that assert that they would be able to be dominant in whatever era they happened to find themselves. This rarely works in reverse, meaning that most people would wonder if Fangio could keep up in the twenty-first century as opposed to wondering if Lewis could have been a champion in the 1950s. So what are these intangibles?

First, there is the will to win. Professional athletes want to win. The average professional athlete almost certainly has a greater desire to win than most of the general public. Winning is not trying really hard, doing the best that they could, or having a "meaningful experience." Winning means *winning*, without qualification. This is what creates the distance between the best and the rest. Those who become a candidate for the GOAT do not back down when everyone is a winner. The will to win shows itself in what might charitably be described as pathological behavior: an athlete is willing to make extreme sacrifices to win even when other professionals might be wondering why they aren't content with the x number of championships. Personal relationships, physical pain, mental anguish are no barrier to pushing to win. Anything and anyone can be sacrificed at the altar of winning, and it can happen repeatedly.

Once there is separation of the great from the good, the decision about who is the GOAT becomes even more difficult.

Now that only the "greatest" of the great are in the arena, it is helpful to go back to where we started. The first calculations and measures of greatness are a sheer numbers game. Most, fastest, most consecutive, shortest, longest. After this crass calculation of wins and losses, the conversation necessarily returns to the intangibles. The next such intangible is what an athlete accomplishes under less-than-ideal conditions. Factors like recovery from injury, bad luck, substandard equipment, or, unfortunately, cheating. At the bottom of the ledger is what we might label with the catchall of "sportsmanship," the gender of the term notwithstanding. So what about these three—Fangio, Schumacher, and Hamilton?

Juan Manuel Fangio was born on June 24, 1911, in Balcarce, Argentina, and died in 1995. He won five Formula One world championships: 1951, 1954, 1955, 1956, and 1957. The F1 official website maintains a hall of fame and is clear about their opinion of Fangio's career.

Many consider him to be the greatest driver of all time. In seven full Formula One seasons (he missed one recovering from a nearly fatal injury) he was World Champion five times (with four different teams) and runner-up twice. In his 51 championship Grands Prix he started from the front row 48 times (including 29 pole positions) and set 23 fastest race laps en route to 35 podium finishes, 24 of them victories. His superlative track record was achieved by some of the greatest displays of skill and daring ever seen. Fangio did it all with style, grace, nobility and a sense of honour never seen before or since.[1]

The numbers speak for themselves. But then we arrive at the difficulty of grappling with exactly the way we would understand Fangio's career across all the eras of the sport. The last sentences in the F1 website's memorial of Fangio speak to the nuances that get beyond and behind the numbers. This is the type of information that implies that Fangio was a competitor who would have been dominant in any era.

The proposal that Fangio's record on the track was "achieved by some of the greatest displays of driving ever seen" is provocative.[2] This is all the foundation of the argument that Fangio could make it happen in the 2020s just as he did in the 1950s. In that vein, it is revealing to watch video of Fangio during that era. The cars are obviously much slower and resemble something one might piece together out of a metal garbage can and bicycle tires. There is a video on YouTube of Fangio testing a Maserati in 1957. One is immediately struck by the physical exposure of the drivers and the lack of protective clothing. Fangio looks like he is about to mow his lawn rather than test a race car, casually dressed in a T-shirt and dungarees with a light helmet and goggles. There is absolutely no safety equipment on the car. In fact, it is clear that if there is a safety belt, he doesn't bother to put

---

1. "Juan Manuel Fangio," Formula1.com, July 18, 2024, https://www.formula1.com/en /information/drivers-hall-of-fame-juan-manuel-fangio.6SSng3B5E6j6pxPNbyqQIv.
2. "Juan Manuel Fangio."

it on before he takes off on a few hot laps. It is unclear how these cameras are mounted, but the video gives a great representation of a fast lap in what was arguably the most technologically advanced and fastest car in the world at the time. The look and feel of the video have a distinctive Buck Rogers movie from the 1950s vibe. Despite the huge difference in absolute pace between this vehicle and what we see today, the genius and skill of Fangio are apparent, as well as the sheer danger. If a rock so much as gets thrown up it could have killed him. A crash would have been catastrophic. The cars are as basic as one could imagine, but the speed is real, and the competitive nature of the drivers obviates the need to imagine that the races of that era are less competitive than later times.[3]

What is most intriguing is the attention paid to Fangio's character, his "sportsmanship." In the bio presented by Formula One, the quality of the driver's character elevates him to GOAT status above and beyond the numbers.

> He was a true gentleman in every sense of the word, proving the exception to the supposed rule that nice guys finish last. His generosity of spirit, sense of fair play, invariable courtesy, surprising humility and sheer humanity were universally praised and appreciated, especially by his peers.[4]

This is in stark contrast to the next driver for consideration here, the German, Michael Schumacher, who broke Fangio's record of five world championships on his way to the sport's current summit of seven. The introduction of Schumacher on the F1 site is revealing:

> Since the Formula One World Drivers' Championship began in 1950 the title has been won by 32 different drivers, 15 of whom won more than one championship. Of the multiple

---

3. "Onboard with Juan Manuel Fangio Testing a Maserati," posted October 18, 2012, by Duke Video, YouTube, https://youtu.be/5Xg4Fr9SY04?si=dgtyA7Qgg081S6Z-.
4. "Juan Manuel Fangio."

champions the most prolific was Juan Manuel Fangio, whose record of five titles stood for five decades until it was eclipsed by the most successful driver in the sport's history. Seven times a champion, Michael Schumacher also holds nearly every scoring record in the book by a considerable margin. Though his ethics were sometimes questioned, as was his decision to make a comeback after retiring, his sheer dominance when in his prime is beyond doubt...

These questions about his character immediately put into crisis the possibility of Schumacher being considered the GOAT. The numbers game speaks for itself. Seven world titles (1994, 1995, 2000, 2001, 2002, 2003, and 2004). Out of 306 starts, Schumacher earned 91 wins, an amazing 155 podiums, 68 pole positions, and 77 fastest laps. But, it is important to deal with the ethical lapses that trouble his candidacy for the GOAT.

During the 1994 season, Schumacher was driving for Benneton, and there were serious allegations that his car used unauthorized equipment. Ayrton Senna said that Benneton was employing illegal traction control that granted Schumacher an advantage over his competitors.[5] This was never proven, but what was validated was the use of an unauthorized refueling system that cut vital time off pit stops. Setting aside this record of cheating for a moment, we must also consider Schumacher's history of purposefully colliding with opponents for competitive advantage.

Schumacher's 1994 championship, his first, was decided in the final race in Australia. Damon Hill and Schumacher came into the race separated by a single point with the German ahead with a total of ninety-two points. On lap 35, Schumacher brushed the wall and lightly damaged his car, giving Hill the opportunity to pass him and snatch the championship. Schumacher aggressively turned into Hill, and both cars were knocked out of the race, handing the title to Schumacher. This was not a one-off.

---

5. Charles Bradley, "How Senna's Early Pacific GP Exit Raised His Benetton Suspicions," *Motorsport*, April 17, 2024, https://us.motorsport.com/f1/news/ayrton-senna-pacific-1994-benetton-doubts/4781549/.

In 1997, Schumacher had left Benneton and was in his second season with Ferrari. During the European Grand Prix, Schumacher collided with Jacques Villeneuve, further damaging his reputation (in addition to the cars). *Motor Sport* magazine revisited the incident in an October 26, 2020, story by Jake Williams-Smith titled "Michael Schumacher's Moment of Madness at Jena, 1997." Despite having a substandard car, Schumacher came into the race leading the championship, and so long as he finished ahead of Villeneuve, he would be world champion. On lap 48 Villeneuve saw an opportunity to overtake Schumacher. What the Canadian got instead of the lead was a collision that shook loose some of the electronics in his Ferrari, though his car was still raceable. Schumacher was not so lucky, and ended up with his car trapped in a gravel pit. An investigation after the race by the FIA went poorly for Schumacher, who was stripped of his championship points as punishment for his blatant attempt to take his rival out. Again.

Ironically, the third strike against Schumacher's character involves fellow cheat Fernando Alonso. During the final qualifying round at Monaco in 2006, Schumacher stopped his car at the Rascasse corner to prevent Alonso from taking pole position. For this stunt, which Schumacher implausibly insisted was driver's error, he was demoted to the back of the grid for Saturday's race, promoting Alonso to the pole. Alonso won the race and the 2006 Drivers' Championship. This is just another example of the ways that Schumacher's skills were employed in a "win at all costs" strategy that in my estimation places him behind Fangio.

And then there is Lewis.

Hamilton's first season established him as a great driver. Let's deal with the numbers before getting into the decisive intangibles. As of this writing, Hamilton has won seven world titles. Out of 339 starts he has 103 wins, 197 podium finishes, 104 pole positions, and 65 fastest laps.

What the world learned from Lewis's first season was that he was a driver who knew how to win. His one-point loss in 2007 was redeemed by a one-point win in 2008. The 2008 season, like the previous one, came down to the final race and in this case the last corner of the Brazilian

Grand Prix. As of this writing, that championship is under scrutiny. Felipe Massa filed a lawsuit that is unrelated to any action by Hamilton. During the 2008 Singapore Grand Prix, Nelson Piquet Jr., the son of the disgraced racist, apparently purposefully crashed to allow fellow Renault teammate Fernando Alonso to win the race. Alonso expected Lewis to provide similar support when they both raced for McLaren. After Piquet Jr. was dumped from the Renault team in 2009, the Brazilian admitted the terms of what has come to be known as "Crashgate."

Felipe Massa, the runner-up to Hamilton in the Drivers' Championship in 2008, filed a lawsuit in 2023 to have the result of that race overturned, which would make him the world champion. Lewis has remained relatively silent on this case, but after winning his first title, another six seasons elapsed before he would win a second title.

Now we must turn to the intangibles. Hamilton, like Fangio, has no blemishes on his record that indicate that he lacks principles and sportsmanship. In fact, Australian driver Daniel Ricciardo's response to the racist display in 2008 demonstrates how Lewis is viewed as a leader and role model to a great number of his competitors. "I stand with [Hamilton]," Ricciardo said, "and will do whatever I can to follow and support."

When Hamilton proved the naysayers wrong in 2008, those who proposed that he would "choke" in the final moments necessary to secure a championship, the question became, "How many will he win?" The concept of an "Era of Hamilton" had begun.

F1 Racing magazine put Hamilton on the cover of its January 2008 issue with the cover promising to deliver "Lewis: The Whole Truth." The question the interviewer Stuart Codling wants to answer is "…how ready is [Lewis] to lead development of the new car then dominate the 2008 season?" These are the first rumblings of the GOAT debate because the author doesn't want to know if the second-year driver can reverse a one-point deficit but rather if he can "dominate."[6]

The article spends very little time on the technical question of whether

6. Steven Codling, "Destiny's Child," *F1 Racing*, January 2008, 31.

he can become the number one driver and provide the essential feedback necessary to produce a winning car. Lewis also makes sure readers know he's ready by asserting that he has already done it.

> "I think I can bring a lot to the team...this year (2007) event though I was the second driver, inexperienced compared to some others, I believed I had a huge impact." [7]

There would be no excuses, and the mistakes like those that cost him the 2007 title would not be chalked up to inexperience. The question was whether Lewis could handle the pressure prior to the 2008 season, and after winning a championship, how he would meet expectations from himself and others. In that vein, Codling's article spends the bulk of its coverage examining what can best be called Hamilton's cultural effect, what the author calls "Lewismania," an affliction that activated a new or dormant fan base.

> More interesting still was the demographic. There were so many families: men in their thirties who hadn't been to a GP in 10 years, bringing their wives and kids. In most cases it was those very wives and children who'd insisted on going, because they wanted to see Lewis race, too. So here was a long-dormant F1 audience, re-enthused, standing alongside a new one—and both here to see one man in action. [8]

What is curious about the writer's analysis of Hamilton's cultural reach is the complete absence of the fact, positive or negative, of Lewis's race, outside of an oblique reference to Black culture in the title of the article inside the pages: "Destiny's Child." Yet there are no fewer than nine photographs of Hamilton in the magazine. This absence of a discussion of Lewis's race is arguably one of the intangibles of the GOAT competition.

7. Codling, "Destiny's Child," 38.
8. Codling, "Destiny's Child," 34.

It is referenced in the many articles that appear about the British driver's effect on the sport around this time. That intangible element is what an athlete's performance and identity do to broaden the appeal of a sport to people who ordinarily didn't care. Lewis, from the earliest moments of his F1 career, is both inspirational and aspirational. In the *F1 Racing* article Lewis makes a similarly oblique reference.

> I want to at least make a difference. Whether it's to an 80-year-old man or, even better, a young kid—to touch them and to make them work a little harder, or to have a goal in life. Because if you don't have a goal, that's when you get lost— and, even if you don't make it, at least by having a goal you can steer yourself, steer your life in a certain way.[9]

This is the young Lewis demonstrating an understanding of his position as a role model beyond Formula One, a more evolved position than his answer to a similar question during his first season when he said he didn't particularly have role models any longer except for his brother. Lewis, like Fangio, maintained a commendable level of kindness among their rivals while still competing with vigor and fairness. That attribute, in my thinking, leaves these two head and shoulders above the incredible numbers of Schumacher's career. That leaves me to conclude that Hamilton—despite the closed nature of Formula One *until* he arrived— cripples the competition in other eras because there was simply no possibility that every driver, from anywhere, would have an opportunity to compete. It is the excellence of Hamilton and the way he conducts himself both in good times and in bad that separates Lewis from other drivers with similar won/loss records.

This is not to diminish Schumacher's achievements. But to call someone the Greatest of All Time, and in no small way to pay homage to the towering figure who coined the term, must be more than merely a

9. Codling, "Destiny's Child," 35.

calculation of wins and losses or even record. What endures across eras of competition that can make a sport unrecognizable to itself are the effects the athlete has on the culture inside and outside of the sport. Calling someone the GOAT is perhaps more about what the athlete does when things aren't going their way, how they get up when they have fallen down, or even in the case of Simone Biles, walking away when everyone says you should stay. That move at the 2020 Tokyo Olympic Games Biles called her "biggest win."[10] Biles, like Ali, had transcended the sport by showing the world that there were things more important than competition. Simone told the world that it is okay to not be okay and to embrace that as a win.

In the case of Lewis Hamilton, he will endure a lack of success before he becomes more than a great driver and at the same time focuses his attention away from the track to will the world to be a place that is better for everyone.

The first two seasons of Hamilton's career had been nothing short of miraculous. But two seasons do not a GOAT make. By establishing what it means to be a candidate for that honor, the trajectory of his career after his first title can be interrogated with that question in mind, but first, he has to get through a rough patch.

10. Sara Tardiff, "Simone Biles Called Dropping Out of the Tokyo Olympics Her 'Biggest Win,'" *Teen Vogue*, July 18, 2024, https://www.teenvogue.com/story/simone -biles-called-dropping-out-of-the-tokyo-olympics-her-biggest-win#:~:text =During%20the%202020%20Tokyo%20Olympics,was%20a%20win%20in%20itself.

CHAPTER 15

THE DOWN YEARS

Formula 1 Grande Prêmio de Brasil 2008
Autódromo José Carlos Pace
São Paulo, Brazil
November 2, 2008

The 2008 season ended with a championship but not without drama. The race in Brazil was the final round of an arduous season. Lewis was leading the championship over Felipe Massa by 7 points, 94 to 87. If Massa were able to win, Lewis could finish no lower than sixth to win the title. Lewis came into the race with the stench of a terrible race at Japan where he gave away precious points with a dismal twelfth-place finish. The British press and others took him to task for what they deemed as needlessly aggressive driving, and for the most part Lewis owned his mistakes. Many were afraid that, like 2007, the pressure to finally grab hold of the championship was too great, and Hamilton would fall short again. The gap between Hamilton and Massa was two points following Japan, and Lewis picked up five more points on his nearest rival with a win in China in the penultimate race. Everything would be resolved in Brazil.

Felipe demonstrated that he was not prepared to make things easy for Lewis by qualifying on the pole, leaving Lewis in a distant fourth. This meant Lewis would have to line up next to Felipe's Ferrari teammate, Räikkönen, who was in perfect position to assist him. The weather refused to cooperate. The start was delayed because of rain. Once it began, the usual chaos reigned with retirements and crashes.

The track dried early, but it didn't stay that way. With only eight laps remaining, Hamilton was in a battle with Sebastian Vettel for fourth place. When the two came in with five laps remaining to put on intermediate tires, it appeared that Lewis would be able to hold on to position and win the championship. With two laps remaining, the clouds opened again, and Lewis missed the racing line on a curve and dropped to fifth place behind Vettel, who took advantage of Hamilton's troubles. Felipe took the checkered flag, and a celebration erupted in the Ferrari garage. Team Ferrari presumed Felipe would be victorious over the struggling Hamilton. But, in the final curve of the grand prix, Lewis secured fifth place and his first world title, becoming the sport's youngest champion. Lewis was ecstatic, and Felipe was laudably gracious in defeat. Former British world champion Damon Hill pronounced Lewis "one of the greatest drivers we have had in this country."[1] The Era of Lewis was underway. Sort of.

Great drivers need great cars to put them in a position to contend for world championships. From 2009 to 2012, McLaren was simply not up to the competition technologically. The superiority of the Red Bulls and Ferraris was overwhelming. Lewis continued to win grand prix and podium finishes during this period but was never honestly in a position to win a championship. The closest he came was in 2010, when the final race at Abu Dhabi saw Lewis among four drivers mathematically in contention. Hamilton, Fernando, Mark Webber, and Sebastian Vettel all had hope. At the end of it all, Vettel won his first world title, displacing Hamilton as the sport's youngest champion by 166 days, the first of four

<hr>

1. "Hamilton Claims Title Glory in Remarkable Finish," *The Guardian*, November 2, 2008, https://www.theguardian.com/sport/2008/nov/02/formulaone-lewishamilton1.

consecutive titles for the German driver: 2010, 2011, 2012, and 2013. If there was an era that came after Lewis's 2008 championship, it was Vettel and Red Bulls'. From Hamilton's perspective, as the dry years piled up, he knew something had to change.

———

ANTHONY HAMILTON REMAINED THE MOST IMPORTANT FIGURE IN HIS son's personal and professional life. The difficulty for Anthony and Lewis was always the way the roles of dad and manager were not clearly separate. Lewis mentioned years before that he really wanted and needed his dad.[2] He could find another manager. Lewis's tattoo with his dad just being his dad illustrated what he wanted. In 2010, he fired his manager and at the same time at least suspended his father. For most of his life, racing had been the space that father and son occupied together. By Lewis staying in racing while pushing his dad out of it, the task of re-establishing the relationship would not be obvious. Years after the fact, Lewis unveiled the details of the 2010 dismissal of his manager, who in reality was never formally hired in the traditional sense of interviewing a list of qualified professionals to pick the best for the situation. He and his dad did racing together, so the parenting at the racing events was also the managing. Further, Lewis was always both sensitive to and grateful for the sacrifices his family and particularly his father made to support his racing so then saying, "Thanks for that, but your role is done" must have been a very difficult decision for everyone involved and tragic in its inevitability. Lewis had to chart his own course.

In the almost hypnotic serenity of the *On Purpose* podcast with Jay Shetty, Lewis addresses the relationship. As usual, Lewis first makes sure to say how grateful he remains for all his parents—especially his dad— had done for him. He indexes his father as his role model and mentor. Lewis makes clear that when he experienced the hurt and humiliation of racial slurs, it was his dad who understood what it felt like. He received

2. "Lewis Hamilton Breaks Down His Tattoos," posted May 17, 2018, by GQ, You-Tube, https://youtu.be/—5-4WPEs6Y?si=RO-cqEs3xd25wV9S.

love from his mother in the aftermath of these tragic circumstances, but his dad was the rock he held on to.

The complexity of their relationship made it difficult for his dad to just give him a hug. Based upon what he tells Jay Shetty, part of the rift was also purely professional. Anthony worked like a demon to get his son to Formula One, but in reality, he knew close to nothing about the off-track responsibilities of the manager of a worldwide superstar. How could he? It is one thing to manage a first-rate driver and what is required to interact with the team so he is in position to win. There are a lot of skilled drivers on the grid, and they have professional, competent management. It has to be acknowledged that no driver in the history of the sport had been in a similar position as Lewis both professionally and culturally.[3]

Anthony did the best he could. The tension between athlete and manager/son and father was the overlap between what happened on the track and what happened in the outside world. The racist incident during testing in Barcelona underscores the limits of Anthony's management ethos: be the best driver you can be. But Lewis also desired to be the best *world citizen* he could be. The latter aspiration required more of him than winning races. Athletics as a platform for activism was not in Mr. Hamilton's DNA. It wasn't in the corporate knowledge of the sport either.

Now that his son had become "the first Black driver in Formula One," the public relations efforts had to meet the challenge of an athlete as worldwide social activist while at the same time dominating the sport. Lewis expounded on the tension with Shetty.

> I think for me and my dad, we were really bumping heads at one stage. It's like I really just want you to be my dad so we can...let's go and have fun and let's go and have a laugh. But we hadn't had that for a long time and so eventually I decided to part ways from my dad and I was going to start

3. "Lewis Hamilton: Everything You've Been Taught About Success Is a Lie," posted January 23, 2023, by Jay Shetty Podcast, YouTube, https://youtu.be/Ayi WKXTd9aY?si=WHUukXmQA26U2-1S.

making some of the decisions for myself and some of the
mistakes that I'm gonna need to make and there was definitely a period of time when we spoke less...But we both
have worked so hard to come back together and we have one
of the greatest relationships. You know, he's the first person I
want to call when I finish a race...[4]

This was a terribly traumatic period for the young driver as he tried
to navigate a way forward in the context of his unique challenges and
possibilities. Anthony's perfectly reasonable notion that Lewis could do
his talking—which meant avoiding anything controversial—on the track
would have created a much different career for his son. There is no reason to believe that Lewis would have been less of a driver, but there is
every reason to believe he would be less of a cultural icon and activist. For
Lewis, continuing to embrace his father's management style would have
been following the path of least resistance. But the athlete and manager,
father and son, had valid yet completely incompatible ideas about ways of
being Lewis Hamilton.

The expulsion of his dad from his inner circle happened at the same
time that Lewis experienced what we might call his first mature relationship. Lewis had been involved with people before, specifically his college relationship with Jodia Ma. But this was a different world for him,
shouldering the weight of worldwide fame. Sometime in 2007, Lewis
began a relationship with pop star Nicole Scherzinger of the Pussycat
Dolls, whom he met at an MTV awards show. The eight-year, some-
what on-again/off-again intimacy between the two seems to be the first
and last of his serious relationships as we understand these things. Scherzinger became a fixture in the paddock and was there to celebrate with
Lewis and his team and family. As the lean years came, ultimately seeing
the dismissal of Anthony from his management job, some went so far as
to blame the Pussycat Doll for the rift.

4. "Lewis Hamilton: Everything You've Been Taught About Success Is a Lie."

This has largely been debunked. The Lady MacBeth trope is tiresome and sexist, and Lewis has taken full responsibility for his actions. This is not to say, as Lewis has himself said, that he was taking charge of his personal and professional life. The question for him was what role Nicole, or anyone, for that matter, would fit into in what he was intending to accomplish on the track and off.

Years later he reflected on the difficulties of the period, telling *Vanity Fair* that as with most rocky periods in life he also learned a great deal.

> I learned the hard way...I really wanted to go through a growth process of getting myself to the point where I'm happy on my own, comfortable in my space. So that if I ever do meet someone, it's an addition, rather than I need you in my life.[5]

Part of what the driver learned is that he prefers to keep his private life private. It is notoriously difficult to pin down who the driver has been involved with after his time with Nicole Scherzinger. Broadly, Lewis is often seen "in the company" of people, like singer Shakira, who was seen in the paddock and out with the driver. Lewis, as is his practice, either refuses to confirm a relationship or asserts that the person in question is "just a friend."

Whatever the case, Lewis has enjoyed the company of famous and quasi-famous women like Gigi Hadid, Kendall Jenner, Rihanna, Rita Ora, Barbara Palvin, Winnie Harlow, Sofia Richie, Nicki Minaj, and Camila Kendra, according to a February 2024 *People* magazine article.[6]

It is worth speculating that the fleeting nature of Hamilton's

5. Divyansh Priyadarshi, "'I Learned the Hard Way...': Lewis Hamilton Reveals Tragic Repercussion After Long-Term Relationship with Nicole Scherzinger," Essentially Sports, August 10, 2022, https://www.essentiallysports.com/f1-news-i-learned-the-hard-way-lewis-hamilton-reveals-tragic-repercussion-after-long-term-relationship-with-nicole-scherzinger/.
6. Alex Gurley, "Lewis Hamilton's Dating History: Every Star the F1 Driver Has Been Linked To," *People*, February 26, 2024, https://people.com/lewis-hamilton-complete-dating-history-8598559.

relationships might have something to do with the fact that his publicly and seemingly exclusive relationship with Nicole Scherzinger happened to overlap with a very unproductive professional period. *Hello!* writer Jenni McKnight quoted him as saying, "In general for athletes, having the right mindset and trying to find the right balance of how dedicated you are as opposed to resting back and enjoying your quality time, it's different for everyone."[7]

Breaking up with Nicole at this time was one thing, his father another. But the most radical professional break was perhaps the end of his long-term professional relationship with McLaren.

There had been some instability at the team on the ownership side of things with various corporate interests as well as the sovereign fund of Bahrain making investments that led to Ron Dennis stepping down as CEO in 2009. At the same time, the car was simply not competitive.

As one might imagine, changing teams in Formula One is not a minor feat, particularly at the highest level of the sport. It is often a stretch to imagine that there are four teams in the sport with the mix of car, driver, and team that can compete for a world title. That means there are eight seats that make sense, and a driver who occupies one of them is going to hold on to it like grim death. This is also situation dependent, meaning the mix of drivers on a team can go anywhere from positive to the debacle at McLaren in 2007.

AFTER ALONSO'S DEPARTURE FOLLOWING THE 2007 SEASON, RON DENnis and the McLaren team took a huge risk with their long-term support of Lewis as a driver. It paid off for both, but over the course of the down years it became clear that something had to give, and Hamilton decided it was time for him to take a risk and leave the team that brought him into the game. In a sense, Lewis was a hot commodity. World champions are

---

7. Jenni McKnight, "Why Did Lewis Hamilton and Nicole Scherzinger Split Up? Inside Their On/Off Romance," *Hello!* November 18, 2023, https://www.hellomagazine.com/brides/507736/why-did-lewis-hamilton-nicole-scherzinger-break-up/.

not a dime a dozen. But the teams that could provide the type of support Lewis needed were well staffed. Plus, Formula One teams generally shake out into one of several categories. There are teams that are associated with automobile manufacturers: obviously Ferrari, Renault, McLaren, etc. Then there are teams that are part of entirely different industries that, for whatever marketing and affinity reasons of the executives, want to be in the sport. Clothing company Benneton comes immediately to mind, as does the successful Red Bull team, a team that Lewis maligned as an energy drink company that wouldn't accomplish much in F1.

McLaren had a relationship with Mercedes-Benz, so when Lewis began looking for a team, the German car manufacturer was an obvious choice. Michael Schumacher had come out of retirement to join Mercedes, a team that was rejoining Formula One after departing the sport in 1955. The legend Schumacher did not accomplish much during his years at Mercedes, and it was clear to most that it was time for him to hang up his driving boots. This opened the door for Lewis, who signed a three-year deal to join the team. Lewis joined his childhood/karting friend Nico Rosberg at Mercedes. His thinking was reported by the BBC's chief Formula One writer Andrew Benson in September 2012.

> "It is now time for me to take on a fresh challenge and I am very excited to begin a new chapter," said 2008 world champion Hamilton, who will partner Nico Rosberg at Mercedes. "Mercedes-Benz has such an incredible heritage in motorsport, along with a passion for winning which I share. Together, we can grow and rise to this new challenge. I believe that I can help steer the Silver Arrows to the top and achieve our joint ambitions of winning the world championships."[8]

Mercedes had spent the previous three seasons figuring out the sport, and Lewis seemed convinced that this was an upward rather than lateral

8. Andrew Benson, "Lewis Hamilton to Leave McLaren After Signing Mercedes Contract," BBC Sport, September 28, 2012, https://www.bbc.com/sport/formula1/19755236.

move that would yield results immediately. Things, however, did not get off to the best start for Lewis. First the team principal, Ross Brawn, had apparently learned not to recreate the chaos of the Alonso/Hamilton pairing that was caused by a lack of clarity as to how the competitive relationship between drivers would function. Brawn made it clear immediately that there would be no hierarchy between Lewis and Nico. This was not a bad thing, per se, but if Lewis expected to arrive at Mercedes as a world champion and have the team focused on his next one at the expense of his teammate, that would not be the case, officially.

After some initial growing pains in preseason testing where Lewis crashed the car and Nico had reliability issues, the season began with Lewis finishing fifth in Australia. This was obviously not as good as his first race with McLaren, but he remained optimistic even as it became clear Rosberg had every intention of making himself the de facto number one at Mercedes by beating his rival on the track rather than in contract negotiations.

Lewis spent the first several months of the season frustrated by his own performance and being outperformed by his teammate, who scored a huge win at Monaco before sticking it to Lewis with a first-place win at Silverstone, while Lewis finished a humiliating fourth place in front of his demanding home crowd. It was not until July, in Hungary, that Hamilton won what would turn out to be his lone victory that season. Sebastian Vettel continued his dominance and won his fourth consecutive Drivers' Championship while Lewis finished a distant fourth but eighteen points ahead of his teammate.

Lewis continued to work at getting his feet under him with the new team. He headed into 2014 with renewed optimism. But Vettel and Rosberg would present Lewis with real challenges during this period. His struggles were far from over.

CHAPTER 16

SEB, NICO, AND LEWIS

GREAT COMPETITORS REQUIRE GREAT COMPETITION, AND LEWIS Hamilton's career and argument for GOAT status would not be fairly examined without attention to drivers who challenged him at various stages of his career. Fernando Alonso and Felipe Massa fit this category for much different reasons during the early stage of Hamilton's F1 career, but there are three other drivers, Sebastian Vettel, Nico Rosberg, and Max Verstappen, who define the contours of the latter part of his career. Verstappen is in a different category than the first two and will be examined separately.

Sebastian Vettel is a fiercely competitive and skilled driver from a humble upbringing in Germany. His first title stripped the record of youngest world champion from Lewis. The numbers Seb produced put him, without question, in the category of great drivers in the sport. Yet Seb is never seriously considered in the GOAT-stakes for reasons that will be obvious.

In 299 starts, Vettel has 53 wins, 122 podiums, 57 poles, and 38 fastest laps on his way to a stunning four consecutive world titles in 2010, 2011, 2012, and 2013. Lewis began his karting career early, but Vettel did it earlier. He was apparently a quick study at three years old and joined the Red Bull Junior Team at the age of eleven. Starting his career at such an early age and proving to be a highly skilled driver in spite of his age is why Vettel holds the record for both the youngest pole sitter and youngest world champion in the history of the sport. Seb was signed by the BMW Sauber Formula One team, and when he made his driving debut at the Hungarian Grand Prix in 2006, Vettel set the record for the youngest to participate in a grand prix—a record since broken by Verstappen.

In 2007, Vettel returned to the Red Bull team that had signed him at eleven years old with the energy drink company's Scuderia Torro Rosso. Note that the "Scuderia" name is because the engines were provided by Ferrari at the time. Vettel's series of notably uneven and perhaps even reckless incidents was overshadowed by the rookie season of Hamilton. But in the 2008 season, after a fitful start, Seb won his first grand prix in Italy, becoming the youngest to do so. At this point, the inevitable comparisons to Michael Schumacher started to become more serious. The moniker "Baby Schumi" began to show up in various places, and in 2009 he moved to Red Bull Racing, where he scored the team's first ever win at the Chinese Grand Prix, beating his much more experienced teammate, Mark Webber, by almost eleven seconds.

That was only the start of a Baby Schumi–like run of victories at Silverstone, Japan, and the first ever night race at Abu Dhabi. The German finished the 2009 season in second place, nine points adrift of Jenson Button. This set him up to take the crown in 2010, again becoming the youngest to do so. It was the beginning of an incredible four titles in a row, a feat only matched by Fangio and Schumacher. So what happened? Why isn't the German driver the fourth member of the GOAT debate?

It is clear that during this period of dramatic changes in the FIA regulations regarding the construction of cars, Red Bull simply nailed it. This is an important issue to consider. There is no evidence that there has been a car so dominant that a substandard driver could win a Formula One title in it. Great drivers deserve great cars, and the sport is better for it. Periodically, a driver and team will become dominant to the point that a season seems uncompetitive. During the 2014 season, when Vettel and Red Bull were untouchable, Seb won an unprecedented nine grand prix in a row. There were more than a few occasions when he was roundly booed by the fans, a situation that Vettel said at the time troubled him. "It's very difficult for me personally, to receive boos, even though you haven't done anything wrong."[1]

It is reasonable to imagine that among these boo-birds there were those who believed that Formula One should put every driver in the same car and see what comes of it. This would presumably even the technical field and provide a clear run at evaluating the driver without a substantial amount of technical mediation. But for many fans of the sport, this is an awful idea. Formula One is an incubator and laboratory for automotive innovation in all aspects of a car. Sebastian was a great driver with a great car, and he made the most of it.

So it is not because he benefited from unfair technical advantage that he is not in consideration for the greatest of all time. The "problem," if you are inclined to view it in that way, is what happened after he left Red Bull in 2014.

The 2014 season was frustrating for Seb, and the bloom was off the Red Bull technical advantage rose. Throughout the season, Vettel struggled with the car's handling, and it suffered reliability issues. After Vettel became only the second defending world champion to fail to win a single race the following season, Red Bull Racing announced that Vettel's incredible run with the team and the company was over. He was headed to Ferrari. All good things must come to an end, and Vettel seemed ready for a change of scenery that would revitalize his career and fulfill what he announced to the press and was reported in *The Mirror* as a childhood dream to drive for the Scuderia.

1. Andrew Benson, "Sebastian Vettel Says He Feels 'Hurt' After Being Booed by Fans," BBC Sport, October 28, 2013, https://www.bbc.com/sport/formula1/24707809.

"The next stage of my Formula 1 career will be spent with Scuderia Ferrari and for me that means the dream of a lifetime has come true. When I was a kid, Michael Schumacher in the red car was my greatest idol and now it's an incredible honour to finally get the chance to drive a Ferrari. I already got a small taste of what the Ferrari spirit means, when I took my first win at Monza in 2008, with an engine from the Prancing Horse built in Maranello. The Scuderia has a great tradition in this sport and I am extremely motivated to help the team get back to the top. I will put my heart and soul into making it happen."[2]

This proved not to be the case. It is impossible to imagine Formula One without Ferrari. It is perhaps more difficult to swallow the inability of the team to put together a championship season during Vettel's tenure from 2015 to 2020.

To be clear, there were flashes of brilliance for both driver and manufacturer/team during Vettel's seasons with Ferrari, but they were insufficient to the task of winning a driver's or manufacturer's championship. Vettel followed up a third-place finish in the season opener with the first victory in two years for the Scuderia in Malaysia. At the season midpoint, the rejuvenated Hamilton was leading the championship series over Vettel by forty-two points. What Vettel called "a miracle season" came to an end with the German driver in third place behind the championship defense by Hamilton and another second-place finish for Lewis's teammate Nico Rosberg.

In some ways, Seb's struggles can be attributed to the ebb and flow of the fortunes and technical dominance of the various teams. The mantle had clearly passed from Red Bull to Mercedes, from Seb to Lewis, but

2. Aaron Flanagan, "Sebastian Vettel Honoured to Michael Schumacher's Footsteps at Ferrari in 2015," *The Mirror*, November 20, 2014, https://www.mirror.co.uk/sport /formula-1/sebastian-vettel-honoured-follow-michael-4660714.

the frustration of the competitive context did not bring out the best in Vettel.

During the 2016 season, Vettel did not win any races and had several on-track incidents of what can best be described as rage. A notorious expletive-laden rant over the radio against the beloved race director Charlie Whiting and a young Max Verstappen exemplifies the problem. The FIA's press release read:

> At the recent Mexican Grand Prix, the Ferrari driver Sebastian Vettel made comments over team radio using repeated foul language directed at both the FIA Formula 1 race director Charlie Whiting and a fellow competitor which were retransmitted during the live broadcast of the event.
>
> Immediately following this incident, Sebastian Vettel spontaneously sought out Charlie Whiting to express his regrets for his behaviour in person. He then, again on his own initiative, sent letters to each of the FIA president Jean Todt and Charlie Whiting, in which he apologised profusely for his actions. He also indicated that he would likewise be contacting Max Verstappen and vowed that such an incident would never occur again.
>
> In the light of this sincere apology and strong commitment, the FIA president has decided, on an exceptional basis, not to take disciplinary action against Mr Vettel by bringing this matter before the FIA international tribunal.[3]

Each incident promised more and much worse ahead. During the 2017 season, Vettel returned to elements of his form, finishing second to Hamilton in the Drivers' Championship, but his efforts included more frankly

3. Giles Richards, "Five Things We Know with Two Races Remaining in F1 Title Race," *The Guardian*, October 31, 2016, https://www.theguardian.com/sport/2016/oct/31/f1-sebastian-vettel-lewis-hamilton-nico-hulkenberg-mexican-grand-prix.

strange cases of lapses in judgment. This was most pronounced in an incident between Hamilton and Vettel in Azerbaijan.

Around lap nineteen, Lewis came on the radio repeatedly complaining about the slow pace of the safety car that had been necessary because of a Torro Rosso stranded on the course. Out of nowhere, Vettel ran into the back of Hamilton, causing damage to both cars, claiming that Hamilton had "brake tested" him. Out of frustration, still under the safety car, Seb pulled next to Hamilton and turned into him, purposely ramming the Mercedes driver. An investigation by the race stewards of the telemetry data from Lewis's car showed that he had never touched his brakes during the time that Vettel said Lewis had slammed them in order to cause Vettel to run into his rear. Reuters reported on the incident under the embarrassing headline "Vettel Escapes Further Sanction for Baku 'Road Rage'" in an article by Alan Baldwin that read:

> The German, four times world champion, had been given a 10-second stop-and-go penalty during the race for angrily banging wheels with his Mercedes rival while they were behind the safety car. He had risked a heavy fine, disqualification from the Baku results or even a race ban after the International Automobile Federation decided last week to review the causes of the incident.
>
> Vettel, who turned 30 on Monday, attended a meeting at the FIA's Paris headquarters with Ferrari team boss Maurizio Arrivabene. The driver admitted full responsibility, pledged to make a public apology and also "committed to devote personal time over the next 12 months to educational activities across a variety of FIA championships and events."[4]

---

4. Alan Baldwin, "Vettel Escapes Further Sanction for Baku 'Road Rage,'" July 3, 2017, https://www.reuters.com/article/motor-f1-ferrari-vettel/vettel-escapes -further-sanction-for-baku-road-rage-idINKBN19O26V/.

Lewis was not amused and called Seb a "disgrace." He was quoted in the BBC by Andrew Benson upping the ante, saying:

> "He was obviously sleeping and driving alongside and deliberately driving into a driver and coming away scot-free is a disgrace. He disgraced himself. If he wants to prove he's a man, we should do it out of the car face-to-face. Driving dangerously in any way can put another driver at risk. Luckily we were going slow. If we were going fast it could have been a lot worse. Imagine all the kids watching Formula 1 today and seeing that kind of behaviour from a four-time world champion. It says it all."[5]

Despite having led the championship during the 2017 season, Vettel lost it to Hamilton, setting up the 2018 campaign, which featured the first occasion of two four-time champions competing against each other for a fifth title. Vettel came out swinging. It was not until the eighth round in France that Vettel lost the lead to Hamilton, who ultimately won his fifth Drivers' Championship. Hamilton won by eighty-eight points, and Vettel's disappointing second-place finish was exacerbated by fans claiming that a series of on-track gaffes, including an unforced car crash at his home grand prix, cost him the title.

The 2019 season was another major disappointment for Seb, mostly because preseason spin assured fans that Ferrari's car was the one to beat and that Vettel would finally grab his fifth world championship. This proved to be as wrong as it could possibly be: Vettel finished a distant fifth as Hamilton secured his sixth world title and Seb found himself outscored by his teammate, the young and skilled Charles Leclerc. But the season was not without another bizarre encounter between Hamilton and Vettel. During the Canadian Grand Prix, Vettel lost control and returned to the track in what the stewards deemed an unsafe manner, forcing

Lewis off the track. For the incident, Vettel was given a time penalty that secured the victory for Lewis. In another act of rage, the four-time world champion parked his car at the pit lane entry rather than in the spot reserved for the second-place finisher and swapped the first-place sign in front of Hamilton's car with the second-place placard that was in front of his empty parking space. Ferrari announced that 2020 would be the frustrated German's last year with the team. The 2020 COVID season, the year of Lewis's seventh world title, included Ferrari's worst team result in forty years and just thirty-three total points for Vettel, the low water mark of his career. Vettel was signed by Aston Martin and spent a difficult two years there before announcing his retirement in the middle of the 2022 season with his first ever social media post. It is long but worth reading to mark the evolution of Vettel's character. A transcript of his Instagram video read:

> I hereby announce my retirement from Formula 1 by the end of the 2022 season. Probably I should start with a long list of people to thank now, but I feel it is more important to explain the reasons behind my decision. I love this sport, it has been central to my life since I can remember. But as much as there's life on track, there's my life off track too. Being a racing driver has never been my sole identity. I very much believe in identity by who we are and how we treat others, rather than what we do.
>
> Who am I? I am Sebastian, father of three children and husband to a wonderful woman. I am curious and easily fascinated by passionate or skilled people. I am obsessed with perfection.
>
> I am tolerant and feel we all have the same rights to live no matter what we look like, where we come from and who we love.
>
> I love being outside and love nature and its wonders. I'm stubborn and impatient. I can be really annoying.

I like to make people laugh, I like chocolate and the smell of fresh bread. My favourite colour is blue. I believe in change and progress, and that every little bit makes a difference. I am an optimist and I believe that people are good.

Next to racing, I have grown a family and I love being around them. I have grown other interests outside Formula 1. My passion for racing and Formula 1 comes with lots of time spent away from them, and takes a lot of energy.

Committing to my passion the way I did and the way I think is right, no longer goes side-by-side with my wish to be a great father and husband. The energy it takes to become one with the car and the team, to chase perfection, takes focus and commitment. My goals have shifted from winning races and fighting for championships to seeing my children grow, passing on my values, helping them up when they fall, listening to them when they need me, not having to say goodbye, and most importantly being able to learn from them and let them inspire me.

Children are our future, further I feel there is so much to explore and learn about life and about myself.

Speaking of the future, I feel we live in very decisive times and how we all shape these next years will determine our lives. My passion comes with certain aspects that I've learned to dislike. They might be solved in the future, but the will to apply that change has to grow much stronger and has to be leading to action today. Talk is not enough and we cannot afford to wait. There is no alternative, the race is under way.

I look forward to racing down unknown tracks and I will be finding new challenges

My best race is still to come, I believe in moving forwards and moving on. Time is a one-way street and I want to grow with the times. Looking back is only going to slow you down. I look forward to racing down unknown tracks and I will be finding new challenges. The marks I left on track will stay until time and rain will wash them away. New ones will be put down. Tomorrow belongs to those shaping today.

The next corner is in good hands as the new generation has already turned in. I believe there is still a race to win.

Farewell and thank you for letting me share the track with you, I loved every bit of it.[6]

What is most interesting is the explicit commitment to social justice, about which the Hall of Fame narrative says, "Inspired by Lewis Hamilton's crusade, Seb chose to use his high profile to promote positive change in social justice, political and environmental issues."[7] After their on-track hostilities, the two found common ground and real friendship in activism, supporting each other during the most complicated moments of 2020 when Hamilton was pushing forward his various concerns described in Vettel's Hall of Fame narrative. The two became such friends that Seb's farewell dinner was hosted by Lewis.

But what of the other great competitor, Nico Rosberg? Would Lewis and Nico enjoy a similar friendship in retirement?

———

6. "'My Best Race Is Still to Come'—Read Vettel's Retirement Statement in Full as the Four-time Champion Calls Time on His F1 Career," Formula1.com, July 28, 2022, https://www.formula1.com/en/latest/article/my-best-race-is-still-to-come-read-vettels-retirement-statement-in-full-as.PVolZQIJEwV40R3A5gxPF.
7. "Sebastian Vettel," Formula1.com, n.d., https://www.formula1.com/en/information/drivers-hall-of-fame-sebastian-vettel.GBy6vPkxKOKUV89QOhZe5.

THE UNITED STATES GRAND PRIX
CIRCUIT OF THE AMERICAS
AUSTIN, TEXAS
OCTOBER 25, 2015

AFTER A RACE, THE THREE PODIUM FINISHERS ARE REQUIRED TO WEIGH
themselves to ensure that nothing is amiss with the requirement that
drivers and all their personal safety equipment weigh at least eighty kilos.
After that, the podium finishers go into a "cooldown room" to prepare for
the victory ceremony. Typically, they chitchat about the race and catch
up on bits of information that they didn't know about how each of them
ended up on the podium, fully aware that everything they do and say is
on camera.

Lewis was victorious at the United States Grand Prix in 2015, Nico
Rosberg was in a disappointing second, and Seb third. The win secured
Hamilton's third world title, tying the total of his idol Ayrton Senna.
Lewis was naturally ecstatic and Nico furious. Lewis made an aggressive
move at the opening of the grand prix, and Rosberg lost position after
having secured pole position the day before. In the cooldown room, an
ebullient Hamilton greeted Paddy Lowe, the Mercedes technical director, while Rosberg sat in a chair looking like he was waiting in the lobby
of a dentist for a root canal. At the time, tire sponsor Pirelli provided
baseball caps for the podium ceremony with their logo and the finishing
place on the side. Lewis tossed the second place cap to Rosberg, who
waited a beat and flung it back at his teammate while Lowe stared back
in disbelief. Hamilton ignored him and headed out to celebrate his victory. The incident, known as "Capgate," is the stuff of legend. Some argue
that it was a turning point for a new level of competitiveness by Rosberg and the start of real animosity between the teammates. Nico, when
asked about it, said it was meaningless and that the two had been playing
around like that since they were kids.

The two had definitely been at these kinds of hijinks since they were children, having come up in karting together, racing for the same team in 2000 in the Formula A kart series. Lewis typically won, but things never deteriorated into hostility. The two were known for just this type of playing around in spite of much different backgrounds.

Nico was the son of former F1 world champion Keke Rosberg and had grown up in Monaco, managed by his experienced and wealthy father. The two finally ended up together at the top of the racing world when Michael Schumacher retired permanently from Mercedes and Lewis took his seat. In 206 starts, Nico earned twenty-three wins, fifty-seven podiums, thirty pole positions, and one world championship (2016), which is where we will focus our attention. Nico raced with Lewis at Mercedes from 2013 to 2016 and finished second to him twice when Hamilton won championships in 2014 and 2015.

Rosberg decided that 2016 would be a different story and embarked upon a process of mental, physical, and philosophical preparation to win a championship. You may recall that when an interviewer asked Hamilton which race he would alter the results of if he could, he gave three that he would alter; one of them was the Malaysian Grand Prix from 2016.

By the time the 2016 season made it to Malaysia, Rosberg and Hamilton were going back and forth at the top of the standings. Provocatively, on the eve of the season's start, the team principal of Mercedes, Toto Wolff, swapped the lead mechanics for Lewis and Nico. Wolff insisted it was done for the larger interests of the team because the two sides of the garage were splitting into unproductive factions. Rosberg agreed and is quoted on the Autosport website agreeing with the prudence of the swap.

> "We have been fighting for three years, we are fighting for race wins and championship, it is quite natural that a little separation can happen between the two sides of the garage. For

overall team performance that is not a good thing. You want great team spirit, everybody fighting for one direction and working together. And that is why the decision was taken to rotate a little bit."[8]

Lewis was provocatively uncomfortable with the decision and hinted in no uncertain terms that there was something else to the decision, saying to Nico during a joint press conference: "I want to hear the reason you were given. You'll have to buy my book in 10 years' time to find out exactly what happened, it will be an interesting read."[9] As of this writing, we have one more year to wait, and sources close to Hamilton have no additional information to contribute to this book on this point. The unspoken consensus is that there was a desire to give Rosberg a better shot at beating his teammate, and the mechanical side of the garage was one factor in that effort. We will all have to wait for Lewis to tell this story.

With these changes, Rosberg opened the season with four straight wins: Australia, Bahrain, China, and Russia. Hamilton won his first race of the season at Monaco and the following round in Canada. Rosberg interrupted Hamilton's surge with a win at the European Grand Prix before Lewis had his own series of four consecutive wins: Austria, Silverstone, Hungary, and Germany. Rosberg then won the three races preceding the Malaysian Grand Prix that continues to preoccupy Hamilton, taking the checkered flag at Spa, Italy, and Singapore.

Lewis eked out an eight-point lead over Rosberg before coming to Singapore. He had a difficult race with both mechanical snafus and errors on the track that resulted in a third-place performance behind

8. Matt Beer, "Lewis Hamilton Hints at Story Behind Mercedes F1 2016 Crew Swaps," Autosport, November 24, 2016, https://www.autosport.com/f1/news/lewis-hamilton -hints-at-story-behind-mercedes-f1-2016-crew-swaps-5028300/5028300/.
9. Beer, "Lewis Hamilton Hints at Story Behind Mercedes F1 2016 Crew Swaps."

Rosberg's win, a win that put Rosberg ahead in the scoring by two points.

Lewis qualified on the pole at Malaysia ahead of Rosberg in second and Max Verstappen's Red Bull in third. At the race start, somehow Sebastian Vettel ended up colliding with Rosberg from his fifth-place starting position, sending Rosberg into a spin after which he rejoined the race from last place. Forty-one laps into the fifty-six-lap race, Lewis's engine failed, forcing him to retire from the race. Daniel Ricciardo took the checkered flag with Verstappen on the second stair and Nico recovering to third place, now leading the championship over Hamilton by thirteen points.

The championship headed for Japan, where Rosberg won with Hamilton settling for third place. This put Rosberg a devastating thirty-three points ahead of Lewis with only four races remaining. Lewis won the next three races in the US, Mexico, and Brazil and headed to Abu Dhabi trailing Rosberg by twelve points. There were four scenarios that could lead to a fourth consecutive championship for Hamilton and five for Rosberg. Lewis qualified on the pole and at the start left behind a conservative Rosberg, who could not afford a race-ending wreck under any circumstances. Lewis maintained a lead, and in a last-ditch effort to win the title with around fifteen laps left in the race, he began to slow down. He was repeatedly ordered to speed up and pointedly ignored the order. Lewis was trying to force Rosberg into the clutches of his pursuers. The first of the winning scenarios for Hamilton was one in which he won the race and Nico finished fourth or lower. It didn't work, and Rosberg came in second, winning his first and only title by a razor-thin five-point margin.

Some decried Hamilton's tactics, but others could see the point. The post-race press conference was revealing.

Q: Lewis, your 53rd victory in Formula One but I suspect this is a slightly different feeling to some of the others?

LEWIS HAMILTON: Honestly, I feel great. Firstly, I want to say a big thank you to everyone that came out to support us. I've got so many British fans out here this weekend. Thank you so much, I love you guys. Thank you to all my family for all their support and especially to the team for doing such a great job. It's been a real privilege being part of this team and achieving the success we've had this year. I never would have thought when I joined this team that I would have that many wins. I think that's 32 wins with this team so a big thank you to everyone here and back at the factory. And a big congratulations to Nico, of course, his first world championship. Good job, man.

Q: Allow me to get out of the way when you are doing the handshake. Well done, [Nico,] you're nice and wet. I don't want to force anything but maybe you could do the handshake again. There you go, there's the love. Nico, just another day at the office?

NICO ROSBERG: Hell, no! That was definitely not the most enjoyable race I've ever had. With Max in the beginning and then with those guys coming up in the end, really not very enjoyable those last few laps. Very, very glad it's over and unbelievably ecstatic. What do you call it when you give the win to my wife, to you [Vivian], amazing, thank you for all the support and to our daughter Alaïa...

Q: Don't you cry on us, Nico!

NR: Oh, I'll thank everybody else afterwards...unreal.[10]

---

10. "FIA Post-Race Press Conference—Abu Dhabi," Formula1.com, November 27, 2016, https://www.formula1.com/en/latest/headlines/2016/11/fia-post-race-press-conference—-abu-dhabi.html.

Nico would not just cry afterward; he would quit Formula One. The season had drained him, and the effort to beat Hamilton was not something he intended to find himself waking up every day to pursue. His retirement video said this explicitly.

> This season, I tell you, it was so damn tough. I pushed like crazy in every area after the disappointments of the last two years; they fueled my motivation to levels I had never experienced before. And of course that had an impact on the ones I love, too—it was a whole family effort of sacrifice, putting everything behind our target. I cannot find enough words to thank my wife Vivian; she has been incredible. She understood that this year was the big one, our opportunity to do it, and created the space for me to get full recovery between every race, looking after our daughter each night, taking over when things got tough and putting our championship first.[11]

Nico and Lewis's relationship had been strained to the point of breaking, but what Rosberg knew, perhaps better than most anyone else, was that Hamilton was never going to be satisfied. Nico was not prepared to keep leveling up his performance and the sacrifices necessary to compete. So he walked away, joining his father as a world champion and electing to focus his attention on his family and his manifold other interests. Nico left the climb to more and more championships, despite the sacrifices, to people like Lewis.

In the years since, Lewis and Nico have repaired their relationships, and Hamilton, according to Nico, sends a big box of gifts to his daughter every Christmas. Nico Rosberg's perfectly reasonable decision to walk

---

11. "Rosberg Announces His Retirement from F1 Racing," Formula1.com, December 2, 2016, https://www.formula1.com/en/latest/headlines/2016/12/rosberg-announces -his-retirement-from-f1-racing.html#:~:text=%E2%80%9CThrough%20the%20 hard%20work%2C%20the,to%20make%20that%20dream%20happen.%E2%80%9D.

away is a clear indicator that there are great drivers who are not willing to do what is necessary to be the greatest. Lewis is not one of them.

Formula One rivalries are unlike any others in sports. It isn't like the Eagles and the Cowboys in the NFL, who play each other once a year and perhaps again in the playoffs if things work out. Formula One drivers compete against their rivals every event of the season. The extreme familiarity breeds a complex mixture of contempt and admiration.

Wins and losses in the sport are always gauged against the quality of the car and, even more so, the quality of the drivers. The longevity of Hamilton's career is made even more remarkable by his competitive record against excellent competitors like Vettel and Rosberg.

CHAPTER 17

THE CHAMPIONSHIP YEARS

2014, 2015, 2017, 2018, 2019, 2020

THE MOVE TO MERCEDES WAS CONTROVERSIAL AT THE TIME. AT THE same time that Formula One transitioned to new technical regulations for the engines, the automotive behemoth that was Daimler Benz was uniquely situated to capture the moment and deliver the car that Lewis required. The company had been involved with Formula One in one way or another since the 1950s. Prior to the current incarnation of the brand, Mercedes provided the engines that led to the championship Lewis won with McLaren. Success in Formula One is about two sometimes competing virtues: continuity and innovation. Ross Brawn serves as the bridge between the engine success of Mercedes and assembling a team that can win titles.

Brawn was the mastermind behind Michael Schumacher's titles at Honda, and the prospect of winning titles with the German behemoth Mercedes lured Schumacher out of retirement to drive alongside Nico

Rosberg in 2013. Schumacher had un-GOAT-like performances, and his departure back into retirement cleared a space for Lewis to move from the doldrums at McLaren. Around this time, Torger "Toto" Wolff, a former driver in various other series, made a boatload of money through his capital ventures and acquired 30 percent interest in what had become the Mercedes–AMG PETRONAS Formula One Team. The partnership that continues to this day with Hamilton was wildly successful, with the team winning a record seven consecutive double world championships (driver's and manufacturer's) from 2014 to 2020. Toto and his wife, Susie Wolff, have been incredibly supportive of Lewis as a driver and of his efforts at social justice, most particularly in the realm of gender diversity in motorsports. Susie Wolff was a professional driver and is now the managing director of F1 Academy, a woman-owned racing series for women drivers. F1 Academy is of critical importance for the project of diversifying motorsports, especially the premier series.

The move from McLaren to this rich environment situated Lewis to reach the peak of his effectiveness with a company that had the engineering know-how to lead the sport. The 2014 season was the first of the turbo-hybrid engines, an era defined by the relationship between Hamilton and Mercedes.

The season opened in Australia but didn't prove to be the stellar start Lewis was hoping to achieve. He took the pole in a rainy qualifying session, with his teammate Rosberg third behind the Red Bull of Daniel Ricciardo. Lewis blew a cylinder at the start and ended up retiring from the race. Rosberg took the checkered flag, and Lewis had an immediate and disappointing twenty-five-point deficit to his ambitious teammate. But Lewis turned things around in a big way, starting with the Malaysian Grand Prix, which was the first of four consecutive wins, with victories following at Bahrain, China, and Spain. These wins granted him only a three-point lead over the persistent Nico Rosberg. Monaco was friendly to Rosberg, who snatched victory and a four-point lead from Lewis in the championship totals. The dominance of the Mercedes team made for exciting competition between their two drivers, but by this time, only six races into the season, Mercedes led the constructors' race by a stunning 141 points, 240 to Red Bull's 99 points.

The competition moved to Canada. Meanwhile, Lewis moved in the wrong direction, retiring from the race with brake problems while Nico took second behind Ricciardo's Red Bull. Nico was now leading the scoring, 140 to Lewis's 118 championship points. In Austria, Nico magically won the race from a second-row start, and Lewis clawed his way from the ninth grid position to finish second, leaving Montreal twenty-nine points behind Rosberg.

Ricciardo was victorious in the next two grand prix in Hungary and Belgium, with Lewis finishing third to Nico's fourth in the first of these races and retiring at Spa because of a collision with Nico, who remained in the race, taking second, which sent the championship to Monza with Lewis still trailing by twenty-nine points.

There, Lewis took the pole with Nico lined up alongside him. Lewis had a bad electronic setup for the start and found himself in fourth. During this wild race, Lewis ignored orders from the pit to maintain a gap behind Nico and ultimately overtook him, taking the lead, winning the race and cutting into his teammate's lead by seven points.

The win at Monza was the first of five victories in a row for Hamilton, which included Singapore, Japan, Russia, and the US Grand Prix. With the win in Singapore, Lewis wrested back the championship lead and extended it to ten points with a win in Japan, a race that was marred by the horrific crash and subsequent death of much beloved Marussia Ferrari driver Jules Bianchi. This terrible loss, the first Formula One death since Ayrton Senna, resulted in the FIA investigation that invigorated the move to fit the cars with the halo device to close the cockpit.

The series limped to Sochi for the inaugural Russian Grand Prix on the brand-new raceway. Rosberg was again second to his teammate and now seventeen points behind. With only three races left in the season, only Hamilton, Rosberg, and Ricciardo were still mathematically capable of winning the title as they headed to the United States.

At the Circuit of the Americas, Rosberg outqualified Lewis and maintained a lead until the twenty-fourth lap, when Lewis used an aggressive move to overtake the lead. Nico was run off the track and again finished second, falling twenty-four points back with only two races remaining and just the two Mercedes drivers capable of winning the title.

In São Paulo, Rosberg reversed his seemingly endless string of losses to Hamilton and cut the lead to seventeen points with Abu Dhabi remaining.

The FIA had bizarrely decided that the final race of the season would award double points. So, rather than first place offering twenty-five points, there were fifty to play, meaning that Lewis had to finish first or second to win the title. Under the standard system, a gentlemanly sixth place would have done the job. The points bonanza handed Nico six ways to win the title if Lewis failed to finish first or second. Nico then sent a chilling message to the Hamilton fans by outqualifying his teammate and taking the pole. But Lewis quickly answered at the start of the grand prix and increased his lead over his rival. Rosberg had a devastating failure of his engine recovery system (ERS), and there were fears that Lewis's car might suffer a similar fate. It did not, and he won the race, with Rosberg finishing a gutsy fourteenth, even though it would have been perfectly reasonable to retire the car. Both drivers were gracious after the race, and the post-race press conference gave Hamilton a chance to process the positive result of his move to Mercedes.

INTERVIEWER: Lewis, many, many congratulations. You've had a little time there to collect your thoughts after the whirlwind of the race and the podium. It's been a long tough season. You did it in style though, with that sensational start and a victory. How important was that to you today and what was the turning point this year?

LEWIS HAMILTON: It's very hard to soak all this up. When you're going through the race, when you're coming here this weekend, there's so much pressure from around you, you're just trying to ignore it, trying to keep your eye on the ball. Coming in today...Niki was right, I didn't sleep last night. I went to bed at about 1am and woke up at like 5am this morning and I went for a run this morning and a massage and everything and I thought for sure I'm going to be tired when it gets to the race but somehow I felt composed and my family came and surprised me at breakfast, which was really a great thing. I wanted them to be here but I just knew how intense the weekend would be and I didn't know if I was going to have time to give them any time. I didn't want to finish the day or the weekend saying "I wish I did that or I wish I did that." This has been an incredible year. I just cannot believe how amazing this has all been. Coming to this team last year, the decision to come here, when a lot of people said it was the wrong choice. The steps we took last year and then coming into this year, it was just unbelievable and then again, as I said, the fan support has been phenomenal. I never in a million years thought I'd have that kind of support, so as I said before, this is the greatest moment in my life. It's very hard to...it feels very surreal. It feels like an out-of-body experience. I feel like I'm back here watching this going on, it's not really happening. So I'm going to really make sure I give my thanks and count my blessings.

The questioning also allowed Lewis to reflect on what it was like returning to Abu Dhabi with a championship at stake and not having the type of failure that had ruined his title run in 2007.

Q: (SAHER SOUKAR—*Saneou Al Hadath*) Lewis, you told us yesterday that you felt you were a lot wiser coming into this race, as opposed to 2008. How did the emotions compare—and why is this moment the greatest moment of your life or career?

LEWIS HAMILTON: Well, 2007 was a very bad experience, obviously losing the championship I fell to a low that I couldn't control and 2008 came back, fighting in the championship, Felipe won the race, won the championship for a second and then obviously what happened in the last corner, I got it back and for me I'd lost it, won it, lost it and, whilst it was a great experience, my emotions were shot. I don't know, that year, I was just immature. I didn't have the knowledge that I have now. Didn't approach the race the same as I did today. Today I went in . . . normally you go in butterflies in the stomach, a bit nervous, today I was going into the race thinking "I feel extremely calm," which is really weird. Is that a good thing or a bad thing? Obviously it was a really good thing. Last night sitting there thinking, Jeez, tomorrow is the day. We could go into the race, something could happen to the car and that would be the championship done. Naturally just thinking of all the negative things possible, y'know? And working really hard to bring the positives into it. I brought that today. I think really that knowledge and experience got me through the race today. Looking after the car. Battling to the point where I'd got the championship in a good position and then, obviously it helped that Nico's car was not performing properly so, when he fell out of the points, I knew that I could fight with Felipe and . . . yeah . . . that was the most fulfilling experience I have to say.[1]

With this win, the question would naturally be whether Hamilton could do it again and not have the type of dry spell that followed his 2008 championship.

———

1. "Read Transcript from Postrace Abu Dhabi Formula One Press Conference," *Autoweek*, November 23, 2014, https://www.autoweek.com/racing/formula-1/a1911506 /read-transcript-postrace-abu-dhabi-formula-one-press-conference/.

FORMULA 1 ROLEX AUSTRALIAN GRAND PRIX
ALBERT PARK CIRCUIT
MELBOURNE, AUSTRALIA
MARCH 15, 2015

LEWIS HAD QUESTIONS TO ANSWER AFTER HIS FIRST CHAMPIONSHIP with Mercedes and second overall. The most obvious one was whether the success on the track, and the things that come with success off the track, would be enough for Lewis. There is nothing wrong with spending the rest of a life in leisure and luxury as a two-time world champion. He had enjoyed a break that featured worldwide travel and public dates as his relationship with Nicole Scherzinger wound down. His use of social media and a fundamentally new style of celebrity that was at the same time unreachable and all too accessible led fans to question his point of focus. Social media allowed fans to have intimate knowledge of his experiences, which were hopelessly beyond their own reach. This became especially kinetic when he was unable to complete preseason testing because of an illness that critics blamed on his jet-set lifestyle. When the season opened in Australia, Lewis addressed his expectations for the season in the preseason press conference.

INTERVIEWER: Let's start with the defending champion. Lewis, if you're able to successfully defend your title this year you'll be a three-time world champion. Has that always been your career goal? Is that fair to say?

LEWIS HAMILTON: I would say that I always wanted to do what Ayrton did. Ayrton was my favourite driver and I guess as a kid I always wanted to emulate him.

INTERVIEWER: You won here in Australia back in 2008, the year you won your first title, but you haven't won the race since then, despite being on pole a couple of times. Can you talk about how important it is for you this year to start on the front foot, as opposed to last year where you were chasing for a while in the first part of the season?

LEWIS HAMILTON: It's the same. I don't see a particular exaggerated importance [compared] to any other time. Of course you come here and you'd like to start on the right foot, but as I did want to last year, but there is a long, long way to go so it's not the most important start of the year.[2]

Hamilton certainly started off on the right foot by qualifying ahead of his teammate, Nico Rosberg. He went on to win the race with his stablemate finishing second. Mercedes had put on such a dominant performance, with two cars more than thirty seconds ahead of Sebastian Vettel's Ferrari in third place, that drivers and fans voiced concern over whether the season would be competitive. Lewis was focused and unwilling to rest on his two championships, refusing to put the traditional number 1 on his car and opting to stay with number 44 from that moment forward to symbolize each season standing on its own. Forty-four was the number he had used during much of his karting and was meant to pay homage to his father, Anthony, whose license plate when Lewis was growing up was F44. Mr. Hamilton may have been gone from his son's management, but he was still on his mind.

Lewis may not have viewed the 2015 season as a continuation of the successes before, but Nico Rosberg certainly let his failures from the last couple of seasons drive him to the point of real animosity toward his teammate and estranged friend. In 2021, when team principal Toto Wolff visited the *High Performance* podcast, GiveMeSport.com reporter George

---

2. "2015 Australian Grand Prix—Thursday Press Conference," FIA, March 12, 2015, https://www.fia.com/news/2015-australian-grand-prix-thursday-press-conference.

Dagless quoted Toto's troubled reflections on the conflict and the potential it had for derailing the team.

> "In the events of 2014, I felt there was some selfish behaviour. I said, the next time you come close to the other car, you think about the Mercedes brand, you think about single individuals in the team, you think about the CEO of Mercedes. That's going to change the way you act. You're not going to put your teammate into the wall. And I always made clear that if this were to happen regularly then I have no fear in making somebody miss races. So maybe in some ways that period was a really important period for the team because you know, that's a place you don't want to go back to."[3]

Managing the competitive nature of drivers who could be primary competitor on any of the teams on the grid is made even more difficult when, as is clearly the case, there are only a few teams that are capable of delivering the car required to win a title. Fernando Alonso and Lewis clashed at McLaren, and now the competitive animosity between Lewis and his "friend" Nico at Mercedes caused the team principal to threaten them with suspension. Toto put them on notice that the F1 team was a very small part of a large international business. Their squabbles could have consequences for the Mercedes brand, which they needed to understand had been there before they arrived and would be there long after they were gone. And, truth be told, most people driving a Mercedes-Benz don't know or care about the sport of Formula One, much less the drivers. But for those who do, the dominance and technical advantage of the

---

3. "Mercedes Threatened Hamilton and Rosberg with Suspension at Height of Rivalry, Reveals Wolff," April 7, 2021, https://www.formula1.com/en/latest/article/mercedes-threatened-hamilton-and-rosberg-with-suspension-at-height-of.1c0WDqds0SubPhyPGxVK4a.7.

Mercedes Formula One car that year was a positive thing. Unsportsman-like behavior between the drivers was not.

As was reviewed in the last chapter, it was the pressure of the 2015 season that led to the Capgate incident and also pushed whatever buttons were needed to have Nico make the changes in his life and mindset to beat Lewis in the same car. It was that effort that led him to be certain that he would never do it again.

Part of this phenomenon, which sometimes results in counterproductive behavior on the track or self-defeating statements in press conferences, is that once the machine is taken out of the comparison between drivers, these hyper-competitive individuals have to grapple with the notion that on *that* curve, or in *that* stint, during *that* grand prix, or during *that* season, they were simply *not as good* as the other driver. When the team doesn't put its thumb on the scale and imply or assert that the fortune of one driver is to be protected over that of another (team orders), when there was no safe cover about one piece of engineering versus another, and when they couldn't look themselves in the mirror and make a valid argument that the team was helping the other driver, then it comes down to a realization of insufficiency.

Fernando Alonso chose to lash out at the team and his teammate and ultimately quit for another team. He didn't imagine that he could reach beyond what had proven to be his limits in driving with and against Lewis. So he bounced for another team and a teammate who would be ordered to crash to help Alonso win.

Nico, to his credit, looked in the mirror that was held up to him in the 2015 season and saw room for improvement. He could lose a kilo, get stronger, learn to breathe differently, meditate, and abdicate his familial responsibilities. He could also still be almost driven by Lewis into an overtake by other drivers, which would cause another season to disappear in the last race. But he bet it all, and he did it. He had won in 2016. He was driven to it by the mastery of Hamilton in 2015.

Hamilton would win ten grand prix, and eleven poles, and eight fastest laps on his way to a fifty-nine-point win in 2015, a win that was not skewed by double points in the last race and that he didn't leave to the last lap. Nico won half of his six grand prix that season after the championship was already decided, and those empty calories left him ravenous, resulting in the victorious 2016 season—the season that kept Hamilton from his three-peat and what would have been the winning bridge to the trio of championships from 2017 to 2020.

2017 Mexican Grand Prix
Autódromo Hermanos Rodríguez
Mexico City, Mexico
October 29, 2017

The 2016 world champion Nico Rosberg was with his family, and the show went on without him in 2017. There was again no car wearing number 1, and it wasn't because a driver was committed to some other numerals. Nico was replaced at Mercedes by Finnish driver Valtteri Bottas, who Hamilton would ultimately hold up as his greatest teammate—which had nothing to do with the driver's winning ways.

The 2017 season is the point of focus when examining the rivalry between Ferrari driver Sebastian Vettel and Lewis. Vettel had come out swinging, winning the season opener in Australia, and it was not until the twelfth round of the championship series that he gave up the lead to Lewis. By the time the drivers arrived in Mexico City, Lewis had the title firmly in hand, leading Vettel 331 points to 265. There were only a few scenarios that would allow the Ferrari driver to delay the inevitable. Hamilton needed only a fifth place finish to win the title, and Seb needed to outscore him by seventeen to make it to Brazil. The qualifying rounds indicated that there would be a fight, with Vettel on the pole, Max Verstappen next to him, with Lewis and Valtteri in third and fourth positions. At the start, Max bullied his way past Seb, the two coming together before the Ferrari clipped Lewis's rear tire, puncturing it and sending the two championship contenders back to the pits and rejoining the race at the rear.

Ultimately, Vettel clawed his way up to fourth place, and Lewis won the championship from a lead-burying ninth place. The post-race press conference was obviously more about the driver who had barely finished in the points in this race but had accumulated a championship, winning 333 points. Lewis joined the post-race press conference with the members of the podium celebration: Verstappen, Bottas, and Räikkönen.

(BRITISH RACING LEGEND) DAVID COULTHARD: Lewis, you're a four-time world champion?

LEWIS HAMILTON: Viva Mexico!

DAVID COULTHARD: Lewis, we can see some battle scars on your car, you had to fight hard for this one, almost as hard as I'm fighting to get you to say something. Lewis, it wasn't the way you wanted to win the world championship, but you won this world championship. Tell us about the race and tell us about the emotion.

LH: I just want to say a big thank you to everyone that came out to support us. I hope we gave them a great race today. The Mexican fans are, I think, the best I've seen around the world. Honestly, you don't get to see this everywhere. We've got great fans around the world, but this is . . . you guys really create this atmosphere, so big thank you. I did everything I could. I had a good start. I don't really know what happened at Turn 3, but I gave him plenty of room. I tried my hardest to come back. Just a big thank you to my family, to my team—Mercedes have been incredible for the past five years and I'm so proud to be a part of it.

DAVID COULTHARD: You've had time to think about this championship, does it mean more than the previous three, now that you are in an elite club of only five men that have achieved that amazing record?

LH: Honestly, it doesn't feel real, man. Obviously that's not the kind of race that I want, when you're 40 seconds behind or something. But you know, I never gave up and that's really what's important, what's in my heart. I kept going right to the end. I'm grateful for today and I just want to lift it up to my family and to God and, as I said, my team.

DAVID COULTHARD: Congratulations, Lewis Hamilton, our four-time world champion.[4]

———

2018 ABU DHABI GRAND PRIX
YAS MARINA CIRCUIT
ABU DHABI, UNITED ARAB EMIRATES
NOVEMBER 25, 2018

ONE OF THE MOST IMPORTANT SAFETY INNOVATIONS IN THE SPORT WAS introduced in the 2018 season over the objection of many drivers, fans, and pundits. In July 2017, Sky Sports reporters James Galloway and Matt Morlidge covered the various opinions of the drivers. Hamilton's position evolved over time.

———

4. "F1—Mexican Grand Prix Sunday Press Conference Transcript," FIA, October 29, 2017, https://www.fia.com/news/f1-mexican-grand-prix-sunday-press-conference-transcript.

The Mercedes driver says it is hard to ignore the governing body's research, even if he is neither a fan of the look nor weight of the Halo. "There's been talk of it for some time now, so we knew it was coming," said Hamilton. "It's kind of a difficult one because when they told us about it last year they mentioned there was a 17 per cent improvement in our safety and it's difficult to really ignore that. It definitely doesn't look good—we've already said that and we know that. On my side, on the drivers' side, it doesn't look great and also the weight of the car goes up. The car is already way too heavy. We've got these little brakes trying to stop this heavy car, so I just hope they do a better job and bring the weight down so that when they put this thing on it's not actually getting heavier and harder to stop."

Hamilton's position covers the waterfront, and he and Fernando Alonso were in agreement that it was needed, though the Spaniard was much more enthusiastic. Again, Sky Sports quoted him as saying, "This device can help in many of the fatal accidents that we have had in the last 10 or 15 years, that has been proved by the FIA. If we could go back in time and save our colleagues' lives we would be happy. That's the first and only thing we should talk about." Verstappen was against it, proposing that "I think since we introduced the Virtual Safety Car, that reduced a lot of risk when you're speeding under the yellow flag in the race. Also, the wheel tethers are quite strong at the moment so I don't think you will lose a wheel very easily. And when there are parts flying around from the car it's not really going to protect you. I don't really understand why we should need it."

Fans adopted many of these points regarding aesthetics and performance, but there were those who didn't like the device because it increased safety. The website Overtake.gg set up a conversation for fans on this matter at the opening of the 2018 season. A commentator, "Racer67," voiced an opinion that is worth thinking through, writing:

Horrible fluke accidents do happen. Sometimes when we do amazing things with passion there is a cost for that. Thousands of planes circle the globe every day and we accept the risk of failure for the ability to travel quickly around the world. Yet planes crash and kill people even with all the safety and control that we have.

I wonder if F1 is so obsessed with never having any possibility of anyone dying or being injured is that really being realistic? Halo or no halo.

The notion that Formula One is not the same without the risk of drivers being killed is a troubling point of view, but one that is not unique to motor racing. American football grapples with the same undercurrent of bloodlust from fans who feel that the sport would be less interesting with measures taken to reduce the incident of brain trauma or even death. This thinking is a throwback to the days of gladiators in ancient Rome and has no place in modern sports culture. Sports should not be about the potential for athletes being killed for the lurid pleasure of fans who are sitting at home secure from risk. All sports are enhanced by safety, and fans have to embrace that for the good of the athletes. This book opened with an incident that would have certainly proved fatal for Hamilton if it were not for the halo device, and at this point, after these varied concerns, the device has become innocuous to most.

The cars may have been changing, but the drivers who were competing for the championship remained the same, along with the evolving brilliance of Max Verstappen and a re-energized Red Bull team. Sebastian Vettel and Ferrari served notice in Australia that they were prepared to disrupt Lewis's quest for a fifth Drivers' Championship, tying him with Fangio and leaving only Schumacher ahead. Vettel bested Hamilton to the checkered flag in Melbourne, with Lewis a disappointed second place since he had taken pole position on Saturday.

The race was conducted under a pall because, three days before the season began, Charlie Whiting, the Formula One race director, died unexpectedly. Whiting had been a critical player in improving the safety of F1 and endeavoring to maintain a predictable, rules-based regime in the sport. Formula One and its fundamental fairness would suffer from the loss of Whiting as we will see in extreme fashion in the 2021 season. A pre-race press conference on the day of his death set the tone for the weekend.

Q: We're gathered under very sad circumstances, following the news that Charlie Whiting, the FIA's Director of Formula One, died during the early hours of this morning. I'd like to start this press conference by asking each of the drivers present for their thoughts and memories of Charlie. Lewis, could we start with you, please?

LEWIS HAMILTON: I've known Charlie since I started in 2007. I made some comments this morning on my Instagram. It may have not worked, as I think it's down but obviously incredibly shocked this morning to hear the sad news and my thoughts and prayers are with him and his family. What he did for this sport, I mean, his commitment...he really was a pillar, as Toto said, such an iconic figure in the sporting world and he contributed so much for us, so may he rest in peace.

Q: Sebastian?

SEBASTIAN VETTEL: Well I guess I was as shocked as we all are still now, when I heard the news this morning, especially because I spoke to him yesterday and walked the track for the first couple of corners together with him. Difficult to grasp when somebody is just not there anymore. To add to what Lewis said. I've known him for a long time and he's sort of been our man, the driver's man. Obviously there are regulations and all that and then there is us and he was the middleman. He was someone you could ask anything of, anytime. He was open to everyone at any time. His door was always open. He was a racer. He was just a very nice guy. Shocked. I don't think there's that much to add. I think all our thoughts, the whole paddock, the whole circus, the whole family of Formula One; all our thoughts are with him and especially with his family in these difficult circumstances.[5]

The drivers' respect for Whiting and the dignity and clarity with which he performed his job, as Seb said, serving as the judge so to speak, would not be replicated by his successor, Michael Masi. Fortunately, this race was not marred by controversy. The drivers addressed the proceedings in the post-race press conference, conducted by former driver Mark Webber, where Lewis and Vettel set the tone for the season's pitched battle, which would also have to deal with the loss of a towering figure like Whiting, who did his best to keep things level for the drivers.

Q: Sebastian, 48th victory, 100th podium, a couple behind Alain Prost, so run us through it—what a race.

SEBASTIAN VETTEL: Yeah, obviously pretty good. We got a bit lucky with the safety car but yeah, really enjoyed it. A great turnout today, you saw in the grandstands, I really enjoyed the lap back in. And for the race, I mean my start, I was hoping for it to be a little bit better, but it didn't really work, so I had to settle for third. And then, towards the end of that first stint I lost a little bit the connection to Lewis and Kimi ahead. I was struggling a little bit with the tyres. I felt happier with the soft tyres, with the yellow tyres at the end, for the second stint. Obviously I was praying for a safety and there was a car that stopped in Turn 4 and I was like "no, it's not coming out" and then somebody stopped, I

5. Matt Maltby, "Lewis Hamilton Pays Tribute to Charlie Whiting as F1 Race Director Dies, Aged 66," *The Mirror*, March 14, 2019, https://www.mirror.co.uk/sport/formula-1/lewis-hamilton-pays-tribute-charlie-14133824.

think it was a Haas, in Turn 2, and then when I saw it I was full of adrenalin, even though the race is frozen, but still to come into the pits, everything on the limit, trying to get back out, because they told me it was really close with Lewis. And when we got out ahead I knew it was difficult to pass but he kept some pressure on, especially at the beginning of the last stint and then at the end, during the last five laps at least I could enjoy it a little bit more.

Q: Well done. Lewis, God, what a weekend you've had! Give him a round of applause. He's been incredible this weekend, absolutely on fire yesterday in qualifying. You've been on this podium eight times, more than any other driver in history in Australia. I thought you drove phenomenally this weekend, mate, it got away through tactics in the pit lane. Talk us through the race, how was it for you?

LEWIS HAMILTON: It's been an incredible weekend, honestly. To arrive and have the performance we had today. A big congratulations to Sebastian and Ferrari. Today, obviously, they did the better job and we have to go back to the drawing board and work on it. We still have great pace, our qualifying was great, I think through the race I was able to apply some pressure towards the end. This is one awesome circuit but it's so hard to overtake, even with the extra DRS, obviously with the cars being as close as they were. At the end it was really trying to live to fight another day, save the engine and we'll try to regain the point later on. But a big thank you to everyone that has come out this weekend. We've got so many British flags and for the Australians for having us this week.

Q: Sebastian, we meet up again on this podium with (you) victorious. It's a nice meeting point in terms of Ferrari winning, the season starting off on the front foot, last year it was a titanic battle with Lewis, off to Bahrain in a few weeks. How do you see it playing out?

SV: Obviously we were a little bit lucky today. Lewis had a great lap yesterday. He deserved pole position. He drove a very good race; controlled it in the beginning. As I say, we got a bit lucky, but we'll take it. We put a flag up in Maranello for every win and I asked them to do that this morning back in Europe. We're not yet there where we want to be. I'm not yet exactly there with the car, you know. If I don't feel what I need to feel then it's a bit tricky. I think we all know. But I think it gives us a good start, a good wind and fresh motivation for the coming weeks.[6]

The season would also, as Webber had characterized 2017, be a titanic struggle between Hamilton and Vettel with it taking until round four in Azerbaijan before Lewis would take the lead for the first time; a lead he would give back to Vettel several times during a season that was not resolved until the final race in Abu Dhabi.

The fifth title put Lewis in an elite group. The questions regarding seven championships that seemed so out of place when he had joined the sport in 2007 were real. The post-race press conference conducted by David Coulthard was a celebration of the excellence of all of the world champions who were competing that season, as Lewis firmly separated himself from that pack, and it had been announced that Alonso was retiring.

Q: Lewis, incredible end to the season.

LEWIS HAMILTON: I'm so happy right now. Thank you guys so much for all the support this year.

---

6. "Australian GP: Post-Race Press Conference," Motorsport, March 25, 2018, https://us.motorsport.com/f1/news/australian-gp-post-race-press-conference-1018949/1398291/.

Q: Actually, Seb, stay here, stay here. You guys have made this season epic. So, a little words; we don't often get to hear you talking together. How much has it meant to be battling out there wheel-to-wheel?

LH: It's been a real honour and a privilege racing against Sebastian. I've known him since Formula 3 days and he's always been an honest, hardworking racing driver and he has always raced his heart out. He did a fantastic job this whole season. There's so much pressure on us all, so don't ever look at our shortcomings as anything less than us giving our best and Sebastian did. I know next year he's going to come back strong, so I've got to make sure I come back with him, but I'm really grateful for the time.

Q: Seb, for you, racing wheel-to-wheel with Lewis?

SEBASTIAN VETTEL: Well he's the champion and he deserves to be the champion. Yeah, it's been a tough year. I tried everything until the last lap, also today, I really enjoyed. Catching a little bit, a little bit, but I think he controlled the pace at the front. I would have liked it to be a little more wheel-to-wheel but yeah, a long year, a lot of races. Congrats, and as he said I will try, we will try, I think our whole team will try to come back stronger to make sure we give him a harder run into next year. But the final word: I think also well done to Fernando. I think the last years have been very tough for him, we've been missing him and we will miss him, so well done on his career.

Q: Maybe the three of you all together, because this is multiple world championships between Lewis Hamilton, Sebastian Vettel and Fernando. Fernando, we wish you well in your retirement. You'll be coming back to visit Formula 1 though?

FERNANDO ALONSO: Yeah, as long as I'm not commentating, you know like some of the ex-Formula 1 drivers! But yeah, it has been a pleasure racing with these champions. I feel very privileged, with you too obviously. Thanks for everything. Thanks Formula 1. I will always be a fan of this show.

Q: OK, Fernando, you've been a true legend, enjoy the journey home. Lewis, you won the race, it's been an incredible season, but there was a slightly uncomfortable moment there where you pitted on lap six, you came out in traffic. We heard you on the radio saying "hey guys, did you know I was going to come out behind this traffic?"

LH: Well, firstly just let me . . . as you already spoken of Fernando, he's a true legend. It's been a real honour and a privilege to race in a period of time where he has been racing. Before I even got to Formula 1 I was already watching him and admiring what he had achieved. I was asked all weekend "will you miss him" and naturally I don't really quite feel like I miss another driver ever, but the sport will miss him, we will miss him and I will definitely will miss him being in the sport.

Today, well, my engineers always talk about stopping super early. They're way too chilled behind the wall! And I was like "yeah, I've got a long way to go and this doesn't feel too good right now." But it lasted long, once again they were calculated and correct and that's why we have to put so much trust in those guys. A big, big thank you to Mercedes and all of the team, all of the sporting partners. We wouldn't have had this championship without them. The championship wouldn't be the same without the fans, these guys that are travelling around the world, thank you so much for coming, appreciate it.[7]

7. "FIA Post-Race Press Conference—Abu Dhabi," Formula1.com, November 25, 2018, https://www.formula1.com/en/latest/article/fia-post-race-press-conference-abu-dhabi-2018.TmdI9io0WQyOuCqiYEiQ6.

Alonso would leave the scene, for now, and Lewis had firmly planted the flag that signaled the arrival, finally, of the Hamilton Era in Formula One. The Spaniard graciously exited the stage with what must have been the realization that maybe it wasn't so bad after all that Hamilton had driven him to cheating in the first season. Lewis was just better, and his run of championships put Alonso in the category of athletes whose careers are stymied by running into a competitor who defines a sport. Michael Jordan did this in basketball. The number of great players who were never able to win a championship during his era is staggering and invariably frustrating to those who couldn't solve the problem he represented. Lewis represented the same kind of obstruction, along with Vettel, for Alonso, but Hamilton having eclipsed his teammate at McLaren from day one was hard on the two-time champion.

The seventh championship obviously couldn't come without securing the sixth, and Max Verstappen and Red Bull were demonstrating that they were ready to compete for a world title.

———

2019 UNITED STATES GRAND PRIX
CIRCUIT OF THE AMERICAS
AUSTIN, TEXAS
NOVEMBER 3, 2019

MERCEDES DOMINATED THE 2019 SEASON FROM THE VERY START. VALTteri Bottas had come into his own and led his teammate during the season before Hamilton was able to surpass him and secure his sixth championship in Austin. The season, as predicted, saw Max Verstappen finish third in the championship standings, setting up the next few years as being primarily about Max and Lewis.

Formula One also had to deal with the death of the legendary Niki Lauda in 2019. He had joined Mercedes in what can best be described as a mentorship position where he and Lewis had become close. Lauda had been in the hospital for kidney dialysis and passed peacefully in his sleep just before the Monaco Grand Prix. Teams and drivers memorialized the loss to the sport. As noted earlier, few drivers defined the fearlessness of Formula One drivers and the need to protect them as much as possible as Lauda.

Bottas's competitiveness was something that Lewis had not experienced since the retirement of Nico Rosberg. Valtteri notched four victories and was an almost permanent fixture on the podium. Lewis manifested a type of consistency that had even some of the most poignant critics of his off-track activities calling him one of the greatest drivers the sport has ever seen. Just as in the 2018 season, outsiders said Lewis was not a serious competitor and was using the platform of Formula One to spend his time with famous people in America, hanging out at fashion shows, and talking about making music.

Lewis did not change his lifestyle, and his on-track performance was without parallel. He won eleven of the twenty-one races and was only off the podium four times, scoring 413 championship points to his teammate's 326. In the post-race press conference, Lewis could barely enjoy this championship before it was time, inevitably, to think about number seven. Former F1 driver Martin Brundle conducted the post-race press conference, first pausing to chat with Valtteri, who had won the grand prix.

Q: Valtteri Bottas, pole position to victory and you've just beaten one of the greatest drivers of all time in Formula 1 history. You must be so satisfied with that victory?

VALTTERI BOTTAS: Yeah, it's a nice win. Feels good. It just felt very good since yesterday, the car, and yeah, we had a strong pace so we were able to get the win. It was the only thing I could really focus on and do this weekend in terms of the championship, but obviously it was not enough and Lewis got the title...

Q: You weren't lucky with the traffic. Was there a point where you thought "I might not win this now"? You really had to come back at Lewis and his pace was amazing.

VB: Yeah, I wasn't quite sure which strategy was going to be ending up the better one, but luckily my pace was good so I could make even that two-stop happen, which was not planned initially. Yeah, we both had some traffic here and there.

Q: Have you got a quick word about Lewis and for Lewis?

VB: Yeah, obviously big congrats to him. I personally failed on my target this year, but there's always next season. But he deserves it. He had some season.

Q: OK, we're going to talk to the six-time world champion. He had a great second place today as well. Lewis Hamilton, congratulations, six times a world champion. You're one clear of the great Fangio and you're one behind Michael Schumacher, bless him. How does that feel? What's going through your head?

LEWIS HAMILTON: It's just overwhelming if I'm really honest. It was such a tough race today. Yesterday was really a difficult day for us. Valtteri did a fantastic job, so huge congratulations to him. Today I really just wanted to recover and deliver the one-two for the team. I didn't think the one-stop was going to be possible but I worked as hard as I could. I'm just filled with so much emotion. I have my whole team here, everyone back at the factory. I've got my mum and my dad, my stepmum and my stepdad here, my uncle George and my aunt from Trinidad, and all the family back home obviously. It's just an honour to be up here with those greats.

Q: Great start: you went around the Ferraris, so now you've put yourself into nice championship position. You could have put your feet up, but you just never give up do you?

LH: My dad told me when I was like six or seven years old to never give up and that's kind of the family motto, so no. I was pushing as hard as I could. I was hopeful that I might be able to win today but it didn't have it in the tyres unfortunately.

Q: How far can you go? How many championships? Just where can this end?

LH: I don't know about championships but as an athlete I feel fresh as can be right now, so I'm ready for these next races, we won't let up, we'll keep pushing. I've got to say a big, big thank you to all team LH around the world, everyone that has come out here this weekend to really make this event what it is, and also to all the Brits and people with the UK flags supporting me this weekend. Thank you so much from the bottom of my heart.[8]

The 2020 season would be unlike any other. The global pandemic and police violence in the United States would threaten to upend the world as we knew it.

8. "FIA Post-Race Press Conference—United States," Formula1.com, November 3, 2019, https://www.formula1.com/en/latest/article/fia-post-race-press-conference-united-states-2019.4Z2SRXMyxsFsWWRwlU28z5.

CHAPTER 18

CHAMPIONSHIP NUMBER SEVEN

2020

THERE IS NO EVIDENCE THAT BREONNA TAYLOR HAD EVER HEARD OF Lewis Hamilton. Unfortunately, Lewis Hamilton and millions around the world would hear of her and "Say Her Name." On March 13, 2020, Breonna and her partner, Kenneth Walker, were surprised by at least seven police officers serving a "no knock" warrant, killing Taylor. According to a 2022 CNN investigative report by Theresa Waldrop, Eliot C. Mclaughlin, Sonia Moghe, and Hannah Rabinowitz, the police were looking for Jamarcus Glover, Taylor's ex-boyfriend, who was accused and has since been convicted of narcotics trafficking.[1] The important term here is "ex-boyfriend." Breonna Taylor had nothing to do with Glover's drug dealing and was not

1. Theresa Waldrop, Eliott C. McLaughlin, Sonia Moghe, Hannah Rabinowitz, "Breonna Taylor Killing: A Timeline of the Police Raid and Its Aftermath," *CNN US*, August 4, 2022, https://www.cnn.com/2022/08/04/us/no-knock-raid-breonna -taylor-timeline/index.html.

dating him. During the course of the federal trial, necessary because the authorities in Kentucky declined to prosecute the officers, it came to light that officers had filed a false affidavit to authorize the warrant at Breonna Taylor's residence, claiming that a postal inspector had evidence that packages containing illegal narcotics had been delivered there.

The police broke down the door while Breonna Taylor and her actual partner, Kenneth Walker, were in bed. Walker and Taylor naturally assumed they were being robbed, and Kenneth fired at the officers with his legally owned firearm. The police fired thirty-six times, killing Breonna Taylor. Walker was charged with attempted murder of a police officer and first-degree assault, charges that were later dropped. Evidence that should have been readily available to the authorities and the public in the form of police body-cam footage was not because the officers all had their cameras turned off. And for months, the authorities did nothing.

There is no evidence that George Floyd had ever heard of Lewis Hamilton, but in the wake of worldwide outrage at the video of Floyd being murdered by a police officer with his knee on Floyd's neck, Lewis and millions of others have heard of him. As the global pandemic raged and threatened to collapse the world as we knew it, activists all over the United States took up the cry that Black Lives Matter, the slogan that emerged after the killing of Michael Brown in Ferguson, Missouri; and Lewis Hamilton joined in.

The impact of police violence on Black athletes is hard to understand without seriously considering Colin Kaepernick. His silent protests on the sidelines of football games during the national anthem captured the minds of athletes who wanted to make their voices heard, even if that sound was silence. Kaepernick was participating in a long line of athletic protests of injustice against Black people. These protests go back as far as Jesse Owens's humiliation of the concept of white supremacy at the Nazi-run 1936 Olympic Games in Berlin, the silent protest of Peter Norman, Tommie Smith, and John Carlos at the 1968 Games in Mexico City, and pretty much everything that Muhammad Ali did or said. Kaepernick revitalized the use of sports as a platform for demonstrations against various forms of bigotry that had been largely ineffective at garnering attention, much less substantive change, since the 1960s. The efforts of athletes like NBA guards Mahmoud Abdul-Rauf and Craig Hodges in the 1990s are notable for examples of the context in which Kaepernick launched his protest against police violence.

Abdul-Rauf, while playing for the Denver Nuggets in 1996, decided that he would refuse to stand for the national anthem because, as he told Mail Online in 2023, "he has no regrets about his protest or his condemnation of the United States as a symbol of oppression."[2] The NBA front office got involved and fined the guard $30,000 per incident, a penalty that forced him to compromise by standing and looking down or having his eyes closed. This protest is understood as the thing that ended his career because there was nothing about his performance on the court that indicated his career should be over.

Craig Hodges used the visit to the White House after the Chicago Bulls' second championship to bring his concerns about the state of the Black community to the attention of George Bush (the elder) by handing a letter to the press secretary that read in part, as reported in the *Chicago Tribune*:

Mr. President,

The athletes from the Chicago Bulls, number 12, 10 of who are the descendants of African slaves, I've taken on the responsibility to speak on behalf of those who are not able to be heard from where they are.

We have a sector of our population that is being described as an "endangered species" i.e. the young black man.

The question must be asked why is the condition of the inner cities

2. Alex, Raskin, "Before There Was Kaepernick: In 1996 Mahmoud Abdul-Rauf Refused to Stand for the Anthem, Sparking Outrage and His Exile from the NBA...but the 53-Year-Old Says He Has NO REGRETS About His Activism As He Becomes the Focus of a Documentary Film," *Daily Mail*, February 4, 2023, https://www.daily mail.co.uk/sport/nba/article-11706707/Kaepernicks-predecessor-Mahmoud-Abdul-Rauf -opens-national-anthem-controversy-new-film.html.

around the country in a state of emergency because of wanton violence, lack of jobs, or drugs.

It is very important that the citizens of this great nation make a determination on what side of the history we will be on in this most critical hour...

The purpose of this notice is to speak on behalf of poor people, Native Americans, homeless and most specifically, African-Americans who are not able to come to this great edifice... Being a descendant of African slaves, I feel it is very important our plight be put on the list of priorities... It must be clear... that the African-American community is unlike any other. We have a sector of our population that is being described as an endangered species, that is the young black man, and the inner cities are in a state of emergency because of the violence we inflict on one another. In studying this condition, we must look at low self-esteem, which is often due to lack of jobs and not understanding who we are... This letter is not begging the government for anything... but 300 years of free labor has left the African-American community destroyed. It is time for a comprehensive plan for change. Hopefully this letter will help become a boost in the unification of inner-city youth and these issues will be brought to the forefront of the domestic agenda.[3]

It is impossible to read this letter as anything but measured and respectful, and the delivery to the press secretary was designed to follow the proper protocol and also not to disrupt the proceedings. None of this measured response to a country in crisis solved anything. This was in the aftermath of the riots in Los Angeles caused by the lack of accountability for the savage beating of Rodney King. Hodges's career was also ended by this protest. Notably, Michael Jordan was not at this meeting, choosing to skip it as he

3. Murray Crnogaj, "Craig Hodges Delivered an Activist Letter to President George H.W. Bush," Basketball Network, October 10, 2023, https://www.basketballnetwork.net/off-the-court/craig-hodges-delivered-an-activist-letter-to-president-george-h-w-bush.

had in 1991. That was a statement as well, but there was no chance that the greatest player in the history of the game was going to suffer the same fate as Abdul-Rauf or Hodges. (Not that Michael Jordan would ever have taken a stance like this. But that is another story.) What we know without any doubt is that the common thread here, from Owens letting his performance do the talking to the Nazis, to the White House visit after a jury failed to hold officers accountable for the savage beating of Rodney King, is state-supported and perpetrated violence against Black people.

In 2015 Colin Kaepernick's career was on the decline from its peak in 2012 when he led the San Francisco 49ers to the Super Bowl. He lost his starting job and was hobbled by a series of surgeries, and when the 2016 season began he was doing his quarterbacking from a seat on the bench. The summer before the 2016 season, Kaepernick had begun to demonstrate concern about a series of violent incidents by police all over the United States. Alton Sterling, Philando Castile, and Charles Kinsey were all shot by the police in the month of July. When asked about why he was sitting during the national anthem after the third preseason game, Kaepernick did not mince words, stating as reported by Steve Wyche that "I am not going to stand up to show pride in a flag for a country that oppresses black people and people of color. To me, this is bigger than football and it would be selfish on my part to look the other way. There are bodies in the street and people getting paid leave and getting away with murder."[4]

If there was any gas left in Kaepernick's tank to play in the National Football League, we would never find out. He was run out of the league and ultimately agreed to a settlement with the cartel over his lawsuit claiming that owners had colluded with the assistance of the league to keep him from finding a job.

None of these athletes ever disrupted the actual sports they were there to play, but fans and the people who run the respective organizations

4. Steve Wyche, "Colin Kaepernick Explains Why He Sat During National Anthem," NFL.com, August 27, 2016, https://www.nfl.com/news/colin-kaepernick-explains-why-he-sat-during-national-anthem-0ap3000000691077.

certainly acted as if they had. Lewis knew all about what had been going on in the United States and had been struggling to find his voice. He was not comfortable sitting this out. The difference is that, unlike Abdul-Rauf, Hodges, and Kaepernick, Hamilton was both at the very top of his sport and in possession of an international platform that was observing the madness in the United States from a position of empathetic distance. He was a superstar athlete, but he had also experienced the same types of bigotry and cared to have it stop.

As far as Lewis Hamilton was concerned, 2020 was plagued with both a global pandemic and the seemingly unsolvable problem of bigotry that ends up with people being killed by the police. Lewis would begin his campaign for a record-tying seventh world title under the most bizarre conditions. The season was meant to begin in March and consist of twenty-two races but it, like the rest of the world, was thrown into uncertainty by the pandemic and did not begin until July with a pieced-together, eighteen-race campaign. The first eight races of the season were run in empty venues with the only sound being the deafening roar of the cars.

———

2020 AUSTRIAN GRAND PRIX
RED BULL RING
SPIELBERG, STYRIA, AUSTRIA
JULY 5, 2020

VALTTERI BOTTAS WON THE RACE, AND LEWIS WAS FOURTH AFTER being demoted from second because of a five-second penalty. Charles Leclerc was second for Ferrari, and Lando Norris filled out the podium for McLaren.

The Monday after the race, journalist Matias Grez published an article on CNN Sports with the title "Formula One Drivers Divided as Several

Choose Not to Kneel in Support of Black Lives Matter Movement."
Before taking up the notion of there being some division between drivers,
Lewis makes an important linkage to the evolution of Black protest cov-
ered here. Grez writes:

> After the race, Hamilton told reporters he had previously tried
> to take a public stand against racism after being inspired by
> the kneeling protests of former NFL star Colin Kaepernick.
>
> However, the 35-year-old said he was talked out of it,
> though he didn't specifically say by whom. "I thought that was
> a very powerful statement," Hamilton said. "Then he lost his
> job and he was a great athlete. I spoke to him a couple of years
> ago shortly after that for the [2017] US Grand Prix.
>
> "I had a helmet made in red for his top with his number on
> but back then I was kind of silenced. I was told to back down
> and 'Don't support it,' which I regret. So it is important for me
> that during this time I did my part."
>
> After qualifying on Saturday, Hamilton said he was disap-
> pointed that some drivers hadn't used their platforms to speak
> out against racism. However, the Briton said he didn't ask any
> driver to kneel alongside him on the start line.
>
> "I said: 'I will be doing it but you do what you feel is right,'"
> he told reporters. "I am really grateful for those who did kneel
> along with me. I think it is a powerful message, but it won't
> change the world.
>
> "It's a much, much bigger issue across the world; everyone
> had the right to their own choice and for me it felt right to do.
> Everything we do is not enough; we all need to do more. There
> has been awareness for a few weeks and what we don't need is
> for it to die a silent death and disappear."[5]

5. Matias Grez, "Formula One Drivers Divided as Several Choose Not to Kneel in
Support of Black Lives Matter Movement," CNN.com, July 6, 2020, https://www

The chaos of 2020 broke the limits that Lewis had once placed around his activism. The title of the article speaks of division, which I'm not certain is exactly the right term. It would be hard to imagine that Lewis, after his own decision to moderate his activism, would begrudge others to have the same time and space to decide how they would best react. What he did have disappointment with is F1 racing and the FIA. The organization had just launched its "We Race as One" initiative, which the F1 site describes with the following:

> In 2020 we launched the #WeRaceAsOne initiative, a platform aimed at tackling the biggest issues facing our sport and global communities, underpinning the Formula 1 strategy to make a tangible difference in the world in which we race. In 2020, the campaign was centred around two main issues: the COVID-19 pandemic, and inequality. And now, with #WeRaceAsOne being adopted as the official Environment, Social and Corporate Governance (ESG) platform for Formula 1, the focus will shift to the three new key pillars: Sustainability, Diversity and inclusion, and Community.[6]

Lewis cares deeply about all of these things, but it is the specificity of police violence against Black people that is missing from this declaration and that forced him to push further. What he didn't know at the time is that the demonstration (kneeling)—"protest" is not the right term here—was only shown briefly on the broadcast, which cut away to show celebratory skydivers. Recall that there was no in-person audience for this event, so the only way that the public could be aware of what the drivers were up to and the choices that were being made in real time was through

.cnn.com/2020/07/05/motorsport/f1-austrian-grand-prix-drivers-kneel-and-stand-hamilton-bottas-spt-intl/index.html.
6. "Formula 1 Launches #WeRaceAsOne Initiative to Fight Challenges of COVID-19 and Global Inequality," Formula1.com, June 22, 2020, https://www.formula1.com/en/latest/article/formula-1-launches-we-race-as-one-initiative.3s2AhNDApNDzrCoQDc1RY8.

the broadcast, and that opportunity was lost. None of this stopped the Formula One establishment from voicing opinions. Fox Sports caught up with former world champion Jenson Button, who joined Lewis's call to action:

> "I think we as Formula One have to be proactive in pushing forward and ending racism and we race as one. It can't go quiet, we need to mention it every race, we need to not only be mentioning it, we need to be proactive in making change. I still don't know how we go about that to help diversity in our sport as well. It's something we all need to sit down and discuss and make change."[7]

To be frank, what Formula One can do about police violence is next to nothing. This doesn't mean that these demonstrations are not a vital component of ending that scourge. What F1 *can* do something about is diversity. Prior to this, Lewis announced the formation of the Hamilton Commission, which was designed to address diversity in motorsports. Some, like Button, embraced the concept, but others were not interested or didn't care. One of the most disappointing (yet frankly predictable) comments came from the former head of the sport Bernie Ecclestone, who you might recall was allegedly involved in the cover-up of the Piquet Jr. crash to rig a race back in 2008.

In addition to covering up a conspiracy to change the outcome of sporting events, in 2009 Ecclestone had publicly lauded Hitler's ability to "command a lot of people [and] get things done." In October 2023, in addition to several other allegations of fraud and bribery, Ecclestone was convicted of fraud and ordered to pay 653 million pounds in back taxes and fees and sentenced to a suspended seventeen-month prison sentence.

---

7. "F1 Under Fire for Protest Cutaway as Drivers Urged to 'Get It Together,'" Fox Sports, July 13, 2020, https://www.foxsports.com.au/motorsport/formula-one/f1-2020 -lewis-hamilton-protest-black-lives-matter-prerace-kneel-cut-away-during-tv-coverage /news-story/8add3e01a0c83dbe2ecf1e8e90d2010f.

All of that being said in response to Hamilton's establishment of a commission to promote diversity, Ecclestone said, as reported by CNN:

> "I don't think it's going to do anything bad or good for Formula 1," he said.
>
> "It'll just make people think which is more important. I think that's the same for everybody. People ought to think a little bit and think: 'Well, what the hell. Somebody's not the same as White people and Black people should think the same about White people.'
>
> "In lots of cases, Black people are more racist than what White people are."

Lewis blasted Ecclestone on his Instagram page, writing,

> Damn, I just don't even know where to start with this one.
>
> Bernie is out of the sport and a different generation but this is exactly what is wrong—ignorant and uneducated comments which show us how far we as a society need to go before real equality can happen.
>
> It makes complete sense to me now that nothing was said or done to make our sport more diverse or to address the racial abuse I received throughout my career.
>
> If someone who has run the sport for decades has such a lack of understanding of the deep routed issues we as black people deal with every day, how can we expect all the people who work under him to understand. It starts at the top.
>
> Now the time has come for change. I will not stop pushing to create an inclusive future for our sport with equal opportunity for all.

To create a world that provides equal opportunity for minorities. I will continue to use my voice to represent those who don't have one, and to speak for those who are underrepresented to provide an opportunity to have a chance in our sport.[8]

Formula One was equally outraged, sending out a press release that stated, "At a time when unity is needed to tackle racism and inequality, we completely disagree with Bernie Ecclestone's comments that have no place in Formula 1 or society."

Lewis refused to see the lack of equity in sports or anywhere else as a separate concern from police violence. While managing his activism around police violence and navigating a global pandemic as he traveled the world, Hamilton had a seventh world championship to win, and at that point he still hadn't heard of Breonna Taylor.

2020 TUSCAN GRAND PRIX
AUTODROMO INTERNAZIONALE DEL MUGELLO
SCARPERIA E SAN PIERO, TUSCANY, ITALY
SEPTEMBER 13, 2020

LEWIS CAME TO THE TUSCAN GRAND PRIX WITH 164 CHAMPIONSHIP points, 47 points ahead of his teammate, with eight of the revised eighteen-race schedule complete. Breonna Taylor had been dead since March, and nothing had been done about it. The officers involved in the killing had not been charged, and the news that there was no movement

---

8. "Hamilton says Ecclestone Comments Show 'How Far We Need to Go,'" Formula1.com, June 27, 2020, https://www.formula1.com/en/latest/article /hamilton-says-ecclestone-comments-show-how-far-we-need-to-go.2UUyqtayl taClIxgCmHx9U. https://www.formula1.com/en/latest/article/hamilton-says -ecclestone-comments-show-how-far-we-need-to-go.2UUyqtayltaClIxgCmHx9U.

to bring them to justice finally traveled across the Atlantic and into Hamilton's awareness. Three days before this race, Li Cohen published an article for CBS News with the sobering title: "Police in the U.S. Killed 164 Black People in the First 8 Months of 2020. These Are Their Names."[9] Breonna Taylor is one name of many that cannot all fit on a shirt, much less be remembered. She is bigger than herself.

It took until the end of May for the investigation of the killing to be turned over to the attorney general of Kentucky, the Black Republican Daniel Cameron, and the FBI. It was clear that something had gone wrong with the raid when all of the charges against Kenneth Walker were dropped two days after the referral to state and federal authorities. Protests began on May 28, 2020, against Cameron's handling of the case and against the lack of accountability for the officers involved in Taylor's death. On July 14, two days after Lewis's first victory of the season at the Styrian Grand Prix, eighty-seven people were arrested after a protest held on the front lawn of Cameron's residence. Cameron seemed determined to protect the police from accountability in the death of Breonna Taylor.

John Nichols wrote in May 2023 about the role Cameron played in the international outrage regarding the lack of accountability on the part of these officers in an article for *The Nation* entitled "The Man Who Called Breonna Taylor's Killing 'Justified' Could Be Kentucky's Next Governor":

> In Kentucky, conservative Republican Attorney General Daniel Cameron was in control of the inquiry. Cameron concluded in the fall of 2020 that the use of force by the Louisville Metro Police Department officers that led to Taylor's death was "justified" under Kentucky law. No charges would be brought against the officer whose shots were determined to have killed Taylor. Indeed, the only charges recommended that fall to a grand jury

9. Li Cohen, "Police in the U.S. Killed 164 Black People in the First 8 Months of 2020. These Are Their Names," CBS News, September 10, 2020, https://www.cbsnews.com/pictures/black-people-killed-by-police-in-the-us-in-2020-part-2/.

by Cameron were against an officer who was accused of endangering Taylor's *neighbors*.[10]

While the authorities in Kentucky were finally realizing they would have to convene a grand jury, Lewis led qualifying in Tuscany, taking P1 with Bottas beside him with the Red Bulls of Verstappen and Alex Albon in third and fourth. The race in Italy was marred by a series of crashes that caused two red flags (full stoppage of the race), which meant there were three standing starts in the race. Lewis won the on-again, off-again competition with Valtteri second and Albon third from Red Bull. Hamilton extended his lead over Valtteri, now leading the race 190–135.

Lewis appeared on the podium in a black shirt emblazoned with the slogan "Arrest the Cops Who Killed Breonna Taylor" which he emphasized with an Instagram post that read, It's been 6 months since Breonna Taylor was murdered by policemen, in her own home. Still no justice has been served. We won't stay silent.[11] Who was silent were the state prosecutors. They were not in the business of justice for Breonna Taylor. Lewis Hamilton credited tennis phenom Naomi Osaka with making him aware of this catastrophe. According to CNN sports, "Ahead of Monday's opening round US Open match, Osaka entered the court wearing a face mask bearing Breonna Taylor's name."[12] Lewis explained his thinking in response to a post-race question about the shirt.

Q: (ALAN BALDWIN—REUTERS) Question to Lewis.
Congratulations for the win. About the t-shirt that you wore at the

---

10. John Nichols, "The Man Who Called Breonna Taylor's Killing 'Justified' Could Be Kentucky's Next Governor," *The Nation*, March 18, 2020, https://www.thenation.com/article/politics/daniel-cameron-governor-kentucky/.

11. Lewis Hamilton, Facebook, posted September 13, 2020, https://www.facebook.com/LewisHamilton/posts/its-been-6-months-since-breonna-taylor-was-murdered-by-policemen-in-her-own-home/3715593718521929/.

12. Jill Martin, "Naomi Osaka Wears Mask Honoring Breonna Taylor Before Winning US Open Match," CNN.com, September 1, 2020, https://www.cnn.com/2020/09/01/us/naomi-osaka-breonna-taylor-mask-us-open-trnd/index.html.

start and at the end obviously, the Breonna Taylor t-shirt. Is this a change in the anti-racism campaign? It was always Black Lives Matter up until now. Is this an individual change—rather like Naomi Osaka's face masks at the US Open?

LH: Not much of a change, it's still fighting the same thing. It's just…it took me a long time to get that shirt and I've been wanting to wear that and bring awareness to the fact that there's people that have been killed on the street and there's someone that got killed in her own house, and they're in the wrong house, and those guys are still walking free and we can't rest, we can't…we have to continue to raise awareness with it and Naomi has been doing amazing, so huge congratulations to her, and I think she's an incredible inspiration with what she's done with her platform. I think we just have to continue to push on the issue.[13]

Ten days later, Attorney General Cameron announced that the killing was justified. The NAACP Legal Defense Fund website covered the fact that, despite all of the international pressure, Cameron had not bothered to present any possibility of charging the officers with crimes. It was not until 2022 that the US Department of Justice stepped into the breach in the search for justice, a breach created by the efforts of Cameron to shield the officers from charges. According to a press release by the Department of Justice, the federal government had "charged four current and former Louisville police officers with federal civil rights violations, including lying to obtain a search warrant for the raid on Taylor's apartment."[14]

As Formula One headed to Russia for the Grand Prix at the Sochi Autodrom, news of Cameron's obstruction had spread, and athletes all

---

13. "F1—2020 Tuscan Grand Prix—Sunday Press Conference," FIA, September 13, 2020, https://www.fia.com/news/f1-2020-tuscan-grand-prix-sunday-press-conference.

14. "Current and Former Louisville, Kentucky Police Officers Charged with Federal Crimes Related to the Death of Breonna Taylor," Office of Public Affairs, US Department of Justice, August 4, 2022, https://www.justice.gov/opa/pr/current-and-former-louisville-kentucky-police-officers-charged-federal-crimes-related-death.

over the world joined in voicing outrage. BBC Sport ran a story titled, "Breonna Taylor: Sport Stars React to Decision Not to Charge Police with Black Woman's Death." The article opens, "Sport stars including LeBron James, Lewis Hamilton, Megan Rapinoe and Colin Kaepernick have expressed their disappointment at a decision not to charge any police officers with the killing of Breonna Taylor." Lewis's Instagram was quoted in the article:

> "I'm so sad but not surprised at this outcome. Police continue to get away with murder every single day and it needs to stop! She was innocent and did not deserve to be shot and killed. Where is the justice, this clearly isn't it.

> "It hurts to know somebody was killed and nobody was held accountable. Imagine that was your mum, your brother or sister or friend, her life mattered but the system which was meant to protect her failed her all because of her skin colour. So mad."[15]

The rhetoric from Lewis and other celebrities is notable because it does not bother to soften the blow with predicates like "police have a difficult job to do," or "there are bad apples in every profession" and the ubiquitous "we haven't heard both sides yet." Lewis is unequivocal in his critique of policing: "Police continue to get away with murder every single day and it needs to stop!"

What also couldn't be stopped was Lewis's drive to his record-tying seventh world title. After a third-place finish in Russia, Lewis posted consecutive victories in Portugal, back in Italy at the Emilia Romagna Grand Prix, and finally secured his seventh in Turkey, where, iconically, he called for children to follow their dreams wherever they might lead. In the post-race press conference, Lewis was predictably joyful.

---

15. "Breonna Taylor: Sport Stars React to Decision Not to Charge Police with Black Woman's Death," BBC Sport, September 24, 2020, https://www.bbc.com/sport /54278797. 24 September 2020.

Q: Lewis, the mark of a great sport sporting champion is to win on the days when you are maybe not the fastest or the strongest or don't have the best equipment. You've come through the pack today to become a seven-time world champion with a true champion's drive.

LEWIS HAMILTON: Thank you, I'm a bit lost for words. Naturally, I have to start with saying such a huge thank you to all the guys here and all the guys back at the factory, both our factories, and all our partners for enabling us and giving us this opportunity. I wouldn't be able to do this if I didn't join this team and the journey we have been on has been monumental. I'm so proud of them. I want to also say a big thank you to team LH for sticking with me all these years and uh... then to my family you know. We dreamed of this when we're young, when I was young, when we were watching the grands prix and this is way, way beyond our dreams. It's so important for kids out there to hopefully see this and know that... don't listen to anybody that tells you you can't achieve something. Dream the impossible and speak it into existence. You've got to work for it. You've got to chase it and you've got to never give up and never doubt yourself.

Q: You have equalled the great Michael Schumacher with seven world titles. That was a drive Michael Schumacher or any of the truly great drivers in our 70-year history would have been proud of.

LH: Thank you. We knew coming here it was already such a difficult weekend. We weren't massively disappointed with our qualifying position. We knew that we were kind of on the back foot and we did the best we could. But then we learned a lot. This is what we do as a team. There is no blame game. We hash it out. We do hash it out. We continue to try to improve our communication so that we can make moves forwards. We don't always get everything perfect. We had that small moment at the beginning of the race with the new tyres and then I couldn't get past Seb for a while. At that point I could see Albon pulling away and I thought "Jesus, this race is falling through my fingers." But I just kept my head down and kept believing that I would eventually just pick up pace of some sort at some stage. And that's what I did.

Q: A few laps in you were over a pit stop behind the leaders, you were nowhere. At which point did you think: "I could win this"?

LH: There was a point at which Seb was pulling away from me and I couldn't figure out at the time what it was. I was checking my temperatures. I didn't know if it was because the tyres were overheating or they were too cold. They went through a drier patch. I went through the real rough phase of the graining on the tyres and then it started to come back, the grip started to come back. The track was drying in some areas and I was improving my driving lines the whole way through the race and I started to pick up pace. And then Seb pitted and for me I knew that wasn't the right choice personally and so I decided to stay out and as the tyres got more and more slick that's exactly what you needed. Fortunately that intermediate tyre holds temperature. If I went out on new slicks I wouldn't have made it round.

Q: Your tyres are completely slick, they are naked, they are bald. You overruled the team in the end, you didn't fancy splashing down a wet pit lane. You thought you could get it to the end.

LH: Well, you remember I lost the world championship in the pit lane and I learned my lesson from 2007 that's for sure. I felt like I really had it under control and the grip was feeling good and I was going to deal with the rain if it dropped...oh wow.[16]

---

16. "FIA Post-Race Press Conference—Turkey," FIA, November 15, 2020, https://

Wow is right. Thirteen years after his interview at the end of his GP-2 career, when Lewis was in awe of the seven world titles of Michael Schumacher and dared to wonder if he could even win one. Now he stood next to the legendary Schumacher as the greatest champion of the sport and perhaps the greatest of all time, and Great Britain took notice. He had taken a big commercial risk as well. Taking a stance against social injustice can turn sponsors off, but none of that concern seemed to trouble Lewis's desire to make his voice heard.

In a perfect world, when the world celebrated Lewis's seventh title, Breonna Taylor would have heard about it. She would have been preparing to leave her apartment in Louisville for another week as a paramedic, finally feeling like she had her career and personal life in balance, and gone about her business. The best part of all of that would have been that seven-time world champion Lewis Hamilton would never have said her name.

www.formula1.com/en/latest/article/fia-post-race-press-conference-turkey .EzAcqP8BdMRLcLIXS5fkd.

CHAPTER 19

I'M NOT A BUSINESSMAN, I'M A BUSINESS...MAN

FORMULA ONE IS, AT THE END OF THE DAY, A BUSINESS, AND LEWIS Hamilton, especially after matching Schumacher's record, is the face of the sport, and that comes with staggering financial awards. With that in mind, it is important to put in financial context the risk that Lewis's activism represents. One may recall that Muhammad Ali sacrificed prime years of his career and a great deal of money in protest of the Vietnam War. Meanwhile, athletes like Michael Jordan have been reluctant to take political positions for fear of their pay suffering. Anyone who thinks that winning is always more important than other elements of public perception need only examine the blackballing of Colin Kaepernick by NFL owners. Lewis, in many ways unlike any other athlete, has figured out how to enjoy financial success and have his voice be heard.

———

JAY-Z JOINS KANYE WEST ON THE REMIX OF HIS 2005 "DIAMONDS FROM Sierra Leone" and he rhymes, "I'm not a businessman, I'm a business...

man. Now let me handle my business, damn!" The same could be said of Lewis Hamilton, who isn't a businessman per se, he is a Formula One driver, but he is a business, man. According to the website Spotrac .com,[1] Hamilton's first contract in 2007 was for a (surely at the time) mind-blowing $4 million for one year. After his breakout rookie campaign, Spotrac reports that he signed another contract for his second year, this time for $5 million, and announced he was headed to Switzerland to get away from the paparazzi and the even more intrusive British taxing authorities. That was the last of Hamilton's seven-figure contracts. Lewis is not just about money. He is about the platform that his skill, luck, and tenacity have brought him, and the money that attends it is one way of many our culture is able to keep score.

In 2009 he was paid $18 million. In 2010 that increased to $21 million, and in 2013, Lewis signed a three-year, $82.8 million deal with Mercedes-Benz upon his departure from McLaren, all of which goes into his bulging pockets, because he left Switzerland years before for the tax haven and more exciting night life of Monte Carlo. In 2019, after his sixth championship. Lewis signed a two-year extension with Mercedes worth $133 million. As of 2024, as Lewis prepares to leave Mercedes for what will likely be the last phase of his career, his total on-track earnings are more than $550 million, but there is much more.

Lewis is a cultural icon, and companies all over the world have teamed up with him to represent their products. According to Sportskeeda, Hamilton's endorsements include, but are not limited to, luxury watch manufacturer IWC, a design deal with Tommy Hilfiger, Bose, Electronic Arts, Mercedes-Benz, INEOS (oil and gas company), Puma, Police eyewear, and Monster Energy drinks.[2] In keeping with his global lifestyle, Lewis is also the brand ambassador for luggage manufacturer Rimowa

1. "Lewis Hamilton: Contract Details," spotrac.com, https://www.spotrac.com/formula1/player/_/id/47369/lewis-hamilton. Accessed September 16, 2024.
2. "Lewis Hamilton Net Worth," Sportskeeda.com, January 26, 2024, https://www.sportskeeda.com/f1/lewis-hamilton-net-worth.

and quenches his thirst, soberly, with his own brand of non-alcoholic blue agave spirits, Almave.

High water floats all boats, and the rise of Formula One and Lewis are not unrelated. Formula One had always been popular in Europe, but when Lewis Hamilton became a star to American audiences the value of the sport and everything around it skyrocketed. Part of this frenzy is due to the Netflix Series *Drive to Survive*, which debuted in March 2019. What is interesting about the cultural impact of the first three seasons of the show (2019, 2020, and 2021) is that they are covering the 2018, 2019, and 2020 Formula One Seasons. Lewis Hamilton declined to participate in those seasons of the documentary. So, in years when he won the championship, the show proceeds like he isn't there.

This would be the equivalent of a documentary on the great Bulls NBA championship teams without Michael Jordan. This causes a segment of the American public that is introduced to the sport through the show to view Lewis Hamilton as some kind of absentee force that has to first be located and then defeated. The show summaries for season one, the 2018 season, one in which two quadruple world champions are competing against each other for the first time, must leave the battle between Lewis and Seb a victim to legal rights agreements.

Episode one from season one is called "All to Play For," and according to the Netflix summary, it allows viewers to look on while "Driver Daniel Ricciardo looks to make a statement on the track while the teams prepare for the first race of the season at the Australian Grand Prix." The lead story of that weekend was that Vettel finished first with Lewis second. This goes on all season. In the real world, Lewis clinches his Fangio-tying fifth title at the Mexican Grand Prix; in the world of Netflix that race doesn't get an episode. Red Bull joins early, and by the time Lewis has won his seventh title and is competing for his eighth, the animosity from the energy drink's principal, Christian Horner, has turned into an us vs. them narrative.

The 2021 season and Lewis's quest to surpass Schumacher was complicated by the absence of the great German driver. Tragically, Schumacher has not been heard from since a skiing accident in the French Alps that left him severely incapacitated, absent from the sight of the public, and silent. The silence of Michael Schumacher creates multiple empty spaces that must be filled. Typically, when a record is about to be broken and the current record holder is alive, there is the gracious "records are made to be broken" statement that authorizes the sport to move on. If the record holder is deceased, then the sport that has been searching for a new standard bearer has found one. In this instance, Schumacher is still alive yet sadly unable to participate, and some have taken it as an afront that Lewis might displace him. Notably, the controversial former CEO of the sport, Bernie Ecclestone, stated that he is "'surprised' that Lewis Hamilton has not retired out of respect for Michael Schumacher's record tally of Formula 1 world titles,"[3] which is an improvisation on the adage that reads something like "some records are not to be broken by some people."

THE EXPANSION OF VIEWERSHIP INTO A MARKET LIKE THE UNITED States and the drama that accompanied the ascendence of Verstappen to the top tier to do combat with Lewis raised the value of the sport to staggering levels. In November 2023, CNBC aired a documentary called *The Business of Formula One* that details the current state of play.

Liberty Media announced that it was acquiring the sport of F1 on September 7, 2016. Teams are often sold in every league all over the world, and major sponsors and media deals happen all of the time. What does not often happen is for a major sport to be purchased in total and revamped. Bernie Ecclestone owned Formula One for the better part of four decades until Liberty Media, a huge media and sports conglomerate in the United States, walked up to the cash register. An acquisition of this size is a complicated transaction with cash, stock, and debt components that have to be worked out among the parties. Let it suffice to say that,

---

3. Jack Rathborn, "Bernie Ecclestone 'Surprised' Lewis Hamilton Wants to Beat Michael Schumacher Title Record," *The Independent*, December 3, 2021, https://www.independent.co.uk/f1/bernie-ecclestone-lewis-hamilton-michael-schumacher-b1969183.html.

when the ink was dry and all the moving parts had been marked to the market, the enterprise value of Formula One was around $8.8 billion. The president and CEO announced the transaction on the company's website.

> Greg Maffei, President and Chief Executive Officer of Liberty Media, said: "We are excited to become part of Formula One. We think our long-term perspective and expertise with media and sports assets will allow us to be good stewards of Formula One and benefit fans, teams and our shareholders. We look forward to working closely with Chase Carey and Bernie Ecclestone to support the next phase of growth for this hugely popular global sport."[4]

Sara Eisen, a financial reporter on CNBC's *Squawk on the Street* produced the *Business of Formula One* documentary and had a chance to sit down with Maffei to understand the strategy they charted for what he said was a "fully priced" acquisition of the sport. First, he told Eisen that the intent from the very start was to focus on developing the US market. That he did. In fact, in an interview regarding the making of the documentary, Eisen said that the inspiration for the project came from her kids, who are five and seven years old and Formula One fanatics. The excitement that the reporter's children grabbed on to was a product of the media focus of Liberty that intended to, according to Maffei, "give the drivers personalities." This is not to say that there had not been interesting characters in the sport before but rather that the revolution in media delivery—streaming, social media, etc.—had not been a part of a cohesive strategy on the part of F1, and they changed that in a major way. Maffei tells Eisen that when he bought F1, Lewis hardly "tweeted" at all prior to the Liberty acquisition, but at the point of filming the documentary, he had three times as many followers as NFL quarterback Tom Brady.

---

4. "Liberty Media Corporation Agrees to Acquire Formula One," Liberty Media Press Releases, September 7, 2016, https://www.libertymedia.com/investors/news-events /press-releases/detail/139/liberty-media-corporation-agrees-to-acquire-formula-one.

This is the context for the Netflix special, directed at the American audience, that told the story behind the race: the trials and tribulations of drivers in the middle and even back of the pack who work to keep a seat and maybe pick up points while the top teams and drivers fight it out for world championships. The absence of the top drivers to some extent during the first season created curiosity about what was really going on. America loves an underdog, but what it loves even more than that is a winner.

Drive to Survive was a tremendous success. When COVID-19 locked the world indoors, bingeing Formula One became an escape for new fans, who developed their own notion of heroes, villains, and brand loyalty. By the time Lewis had won his seventh world title in the winter of 2020, the world, including a new American fan base, was poised and ready to watch the 2021 season unfold in real time and then have the opportunity to binge the back stories when Netflix had the season of their show ready to go.

———————

Lewis's representation of products, because of his stature in F1, is the entry point to full participation in the business of sports. The next step—one that few athletes take, much less imagine—is ownership. Hamilton has picked up the things that go along with being a rich person and savvy investor: a worldwide luxury real estate portfolio and a legendary car collection. The move to become an owner in the global ecosystem is a complicated venture, and Lewis found a mentor in businesswoman Mellody Hobson.

Lewis met Mellody and her husband, George Lucas, in 2007 at the Monaco Grand Prix, when Lucas told his wife that "a rookie Black driver had just broken into the top ranks for the first time in the sport's 70-year history."[5] Mellody and Lewis developed a close relationship, one that was characterized in the *Jedi News* in this way: "Hamilton considers Hobson

———————

5. James Burns, "Lewis Hamilton and His Close Friendship with Mellody Hobson and George Lucas," Jedi News, August 9, 2022, https://www.jedinews.com/film-music-tv

a big sister, a mentor, and, generally, 'one of the most inspiring women I've ever met in my life.' Part of what they share is the experience of what he describes as being 'the first and only one' to achieve what they've achieved."[6]

In 2020, Mellody was named one of the 100 Most Powerful Women in the World and was recently named the chairwoman of Starbucks International as well as continuing as president and co-CEO of Ariel Investments. In 2017, Hobson was a Horatio Alger Award recipient. The announcement quoted her as saying, "It's important that young people learn to be brave and take risks,"[7] an ethos that she and Lewis both share and that has led them both to achieve what would seem to have been impossible. Mellody's Horatio Alger narrative describes her upbringing.

Mellody Hobson, the youngest of six children by nine years, was born in 1969, in Chicago, Illinois. She was raised by a single mother, who renovated apartments and condos in old, and sometimes abandoned, buildings. "My mother believed anything was possible," says Hobson. "She was shy, quiet, religious, and 100 percent a dreamer. She had tremendous faith in the future, and she had the ability to see what a derelict place could be with a little work. Unfortunately her vision and dreams did not really ever amount to financial success."

Hobson's mother was often denied bank loans due to racial segregation, which prevented her from renovating some buildings. That forced the family to move to Chicago's rougher South Side. "We moved often," says Hobson. "There was always a lot of drama surrounding our living situation.

/articles/lewis-hamilton-and-his-close-friendship-with-mellody-hobson-and-george -lucas/.

6. Burns, "Lewis Hamilton and His Close Friendship."

7. "Mellody Hobson," Alger Association, https://horatioalger.org/members/detail /mellody-hobson/#:~:text=Mellody%20Hobson%2C%20the%20youngest%20 of,was%20possible%2C%22%20says%20Hobson. Accessed 17 December 2023.

At times, my mother couldn't pay her bills and our electricity would be cut off, and we would have to heat water for our baths. We also had our phone cut off at times. We were even evicted a few times and had our car repossessed. But it wasn't as bad as some had it, so I tried not to make too much of it. I had a loving family, and although my mother often came up short financially, she did the best she could."

Hobson's domestic situation made her feel insecure, and she was so embarrassed by the family's many homes that she never invited her friends to visit. "I would always go to my friends' houses," she says. "And if the phone was cut off while we were visiting, I would tell them the next day the phone company made a mistake. In college, I finally stopped hiding the truth and told my friends my real situation. They were shocked."

Hobson struggled in the first grade and was placed into a remedial class. Viewing education as the great equalizer, she created a vision of how she wanted her life to be. "I decided right away I didn't want to be the kid who couldn't keep up," she says. "That's when I became obsessed with my grades and self-improvement. I discovered children's books in the library that were biographies of famous people, and I vowed to read all of them by the end of the sixth grade. Somehow I knew the names of all the Ivy League schools, and I started telling my mother I was going to go to Yale. I posted a sign on the mirror in my bedroom that said 'A+.' Looking back, I can see that school created structure and security for me. It was the one place in my life that wasn't chaotic."[8]

At the close of the 2020 season, Hobson posted the following on her Instagram feed congratulating Lewis: Congratulations to my little brother, @lewishamilton, on his 7th @f1 championship! You are a marvel. When I'm

---

8. "Mellody Hobson."

faltering, I think of your focus, perseverance and strength. Lewis is explicit about the importance of the relationship with Mellody and her husband of *Star Wars* fame, George Lucas, telling SilverArrows.Net in 2022, "that every time he's around the husband-and-wife pair of Mellody Hobson and George Lucas, he's 'just waiting for George to say something because he's literally Yoda's dad.'"[9] The mutual mentor/mentee relationship between the two led to the exciting opportunity for Lewis to become an owner in the sports world himself. Hobson had assembled a bid to join the ownership group of the NFL's Denver Broncos and brought Hamilton along for the ride. Again, the SilverArrows.Net reports this.

> Lewis Hamilton has joined the ownership group of NFL team Denver Broncos, and says he's excited to "become a part of the Broncos story."
>
> The Walton-Penner Family Ownership Group purchased the Denver Broncos earlier this year in a deal worth an estimated $4.65bn, the largest deal involving a sports team in history.
>
> Now they have announced on social media that Lewis Hamilton has joined the group.
>
> "We're delighted to welcome Sir Lewis Hamilton to our ownership group," said Rob Walton.[10]

The transition from athlete to ownership in that realm is rare indeed, with Lewis joining a select few who have done the same, probably most successfully Magic Johnson and Michael Jordan, who enjoyed financial if not competitive success with the NBA's Charlotte Hornets, but has increased his efforts in motorsports with 23XI racing, in NASCAR.

---

9. "Lewis Hamilton Joins NFL Team Ownership Group, Gives Comments," Silver Arrows.net, August 2, 2022, https://www.silverarrows.net/news/lewis-hamilton-joins-nfl-team-ownership-group-gives-comments/.
10. "Lewis Hamilton Joins NFL Team Ownership Group."

What this means for Lewis is that he is both a businessman and a business, man. All of this being said, it is important to re-emphasize two things: Lewis does not allow his business interests and ambitions to blunt the intensity of his activism. He also uses the power and the access wealth grants him to continue his philanthropic mission, which is grounded in the drive for diversity, access, and opportunity.

————

COMMERCIAL SUCCESS IS ONE THING, AND HAMILTON HAS NO SHORTAGE of money or opportunities to make more. What sets him apart from many others is his larger commitment to social justice that we have seen with his support of Black Lives Matter, but it is his Mission 44 that serves as the vehicle for his efforts in diversity, equity, and inclusion. That effort cannot be separated from his Hamilton Commission and the ninety-four-page report it produced. Governments and businesses are always forming "commissions," and they are generally designed to assemble experts to look into a problem and present recommendations for solving them. The executive summary for the Hamilton Commission lays out the stakes of the effort:

> The Hamilton Commission was launched as a result of Sir Lewis Hamilton's concerns about the lack of ethnic diversity within Formula 1 specifically, and the whole of motorsport industry generally. The primary objective of the Commission was to develop a set of recommendations aimed at improving the representation of Black people in UK motorsport. A broader set of underlying causes, many systemic in nature, had to be considered in order to achieve this aspiration. There are ten recommendations, all based in evidence, that the Commission believes will have a long-lasting and positive impact on the representation of Black people in Formula 1 and the wider motorsport sector and which will support the development of

more inclusive cultures which will benefit all people working
in the sector.[11]

The ten recommendations are divided into three broad categories:
Support and Empowerment, Accountability and Measurement, and
Inspiration and Engagement. The first category, Support and Empower-
ment, had five substantive recommendations:

1. We recommend that Formula 1 teams and other motorsport businesses broaden access to motorsport by expanding the apprenticeships provision to include higher apprenticeships and degree
   apprenticeships as an alternate pathway into the sector, as well as
   availability to paid work experience schemes.
2. We recommend that a new exclusions innovation fund be established, developing programmes that address the factors that contribute to the high proportion of students from Black backgrounds being
   excluded from schools.
3. We support the piloting of new approaches to increase the number
   of Black teachers in STEM subjects that lead to careers in engineering, namely mathematics, physics, design and technology, and
   computing.
4. We recommend the creation of targeted support programmes for
   Black students in post-16 education to enable greater progression
   into Higher Education courses and work-based training opportunities linked to the motorsport sector.
5. We support the creation of scholarship programmes to enable Black
   graduates from degrees in engineering and allied subjects to progress
   into specialist motorsport roles.

Lewis is unapologetically concerned about what has to be done to help

---

11. The Hamilton Commission, https://www.hamiltoncommission.org/.

Black people. The frank manner in which he has collected evidence to explain the harm and limitations that sought to limit his prospects is striking, even groundbreaking. Lewis has survived and thrived in a system designed to beat him into submission. He defeated it, or better yet confounded it and manipulated it for his purposes, but he is not content with that. Lewis is not an "I pulled myself up by my bootstraps, why can't you do the same" type of person. He is asking two important questions. First, why am I hanging by my bootstraps in the first place, and second, what can I do to make sure no one else ever finds themselves in a similar position?

The next category of recommendations involves Accountability and Measurement. These recommendations are critically important. What these recommendations do not allow is institutions to hire a few people of color, women, and other underrepresented persons and leave it at that while those hires languish in positions with little if any authority and no possibility of advancement. The recommendations are designed to reorder and reform an entire system that leaves certain people behind as early as primary school.

1. We ask that Formula 1 teams (and other Motorsport organizations) take the lead in implementing a Diversity and Inclusion Charter for motorsports to commit the sector to improve diversity and inclusion across all organizations.
2. We support the promotion of the National Education Union Anti-Racism Charter for schools, and we call on teachers' unions and other leadership bodies in education to work with us to ensure widespread adoption of the Charter.
3. We call on the Department of Education and other bodies holding education data to enable easier public access to disaggregated data on student and staff characteristics at subject level.

Lewis is interested in results. The underlying ethos here is that the sport, from the drivers to employees executing basic tasks, is empirically better when there is more diversity throughout. Not better only in the sense that the results on the track will be demonstrably better, but better in the sense that it is a moral scandal to exclude people from opportunities because of who they are or, for that matter, who they aren't. A foundational assumption of those who oppose diversity and inclusion is that unqualified Black people will take jobs from qualified white people. Lewis's argument is that if not for the Herculean efforts of his father and the support of McLaren, a less qualified white driver would have had his spot. Lewis, the seven-time world champion, has not taken a job from a more qualified person. He believes that given the right system of education and nurturing of talent, the sport will diversify itself and at the same time deliver a better product. The fact that it will enjoy broader fan appeal will also allow kids from every walk of life to dream.

Finally, Lewis would not feel the process was complete without taking stock of Inspiration and Engagement.

1. We recommend the development of best practice guidance for STEM inspiration and outreach activities to enable inclusive engagement with Black students in schools, and with those who influence them.
2. We recommend the additional STEM activity support be provided to supplementary schools that are led by Black community groups across the UK.

The Hamilton Commission puts to rest any argument that Lewis's support for Black Lives Matter was monolithic or a display of so-called virtue signaling. The lack of diversity in motorsports is something Lewis can do something about, and he has identified partners and meticulously assembled a way forward. It is important to note that he does not shy away from demonstrating the linkage between Black Lives Matter and this effort, something many would have worked hard to build a firewall against. The Hamilton Commission Report has a section entitled "The Black Lives Matter Movement and the Lewis Hamilton Effect" that takes this up directly.

> Examples of racism have been evident in motorsport since the outset of Lewis Hamilton's career, most notably during an incident targeting his family at the 2008 Spanish Grand Prix in Barcelona. In response, the FIA threatened to remove the Spanish motor racing authority's two Grand Prix and launched Race Against Racism, a campaign to "drive home the message that racism will not be tolerated at any level of the sport." Lewis Hamilton remains the only Black driver in Formula 1.
>
> In 2020, Lewis Hamilton became increasingly vocal about the need to tackle racism and the lack of diversity in motorsport. Taking the knee ahead of Formula 1 races became a commonplace practice during 2020, with several drivers including Daniel Ricciardo and Sebastian Vettel publicly voicing support for the practice.[12]

Lewis's commission report wants readers to understand that racism is the common thread between the lack of diversity in motorsports and police violence. The report then wants readers to react and address the structures, systems, and mindsets that cause these devastating disparities.

———

LEWIS WAS NOT CONTENT TO HAVE THE NINETY-PLUS PAGES OF THE report take up space on shelves and wait for institutions to act. In 2019, "after reviewing the end of season photo"[13] Hamilton established the

12. The Hamilton Commission, https://www.hamiltoncommission.org/.
13. The Hamilton Commission, https://www.hamiltoncommission.org/ Accessed 10 July 2024.

Hamilton Commission to look into the lack of diversity in Formula One to understand why and what was to be done about it. Mission 44 is the operational institution that came out of the 2021 recommendations of the Hamilton Commission that were published in the 2021 Hamilton Report. The institution "is a charitable foundation that exists to build a fairer, more inclusive future for young people around the world. We invest in solutions that empower young people to overcome social injustice and succeed," according to the website and Victoria McEvoy, a senior associate. The social justice component is focused "on reaching people under the age of 24 who face disadvantage or discrimination, including but not limited to young people from low-income backgrounds, young people from Gypsy, Roma and Traveller communities, and young people of colour."[14] This work is being done in the UK, Brazil, and the United States, again emphasizing the global reach of the Lewis Hamilton brand. The grant-making aspect of Mission 44 is dedicated to funding "to discover, support and scale up solutions that improve outcomes for young people under the age of 24, including but not limited to, young people of colour and those from low-income backgrounds. We're here to get behind solutions with the potential to change the system. Our grantmaking decisions are informed by research and our Youth Advisory Board is involved at every step."[15] This initiative breaks down the barrier to capital investment in tech start-ups by providing first-money-in grants that set these innovators up to access the larger market. The 2023 annual report highlights some of that year's accomplishments:

- 11 million pounds raised in donations;
- 5 research projects commissioned;
- 15 new Youth Advisors and Board Members recruited;
- 3.5 million pounds awarded in grants;
- 15 employees and 7 trustees;

14. Mission 44, https://mission44.org/
15. Mission 44, https://mission44.org/ Accessed September 14, 2024.

- 33 percent of partners are people of color;
- 120 stakeholders attended the Reimagining the Future Event; and
- 18 new partnerships established[16]

Mission 44 is dedicated to equipping under-resourced children with everything they need to be successful, and Lewis is doing all of this while his focus is firmly on his eighth world title.

16. The Hamilton Commission, "Accelerating Change: Improving Representation of Black People in UK Motorsport," Mission44.org, July 2021, https://mission44.org/the-hamilton-commission/.

CHAPTER 20

THE 2021 SEASON

THE YEAR 2020 THREATENED TO UPEND THE WORLD AS WE UNDER-
stand it. As we slowly came out of the depths of the pandemic and the
disorder associated with mass protest of police violence, 2021 was poised
to be a year in transition. It was a heady period for Lewis Hamilton and
Formula One. The season offered the possibility of a driver in his prime
with the opportunity to capture an unprecedented eighth world title,
which would also be his fifth in a row. Lewis and Mercedes were prepared for the challenge. It was clear that the competition would come
from 2020's third-place finisher, the Dutchman Max Verstappen.

Verstappen was a driver who was impossible to ignore. He joined F1 as
the youngest driver in the history of the sport at the time with ambitions
to snatch the record for youngest world champion from Sebastien Vettel. Verstappen is of Dutch and Belgian heritage and began his journey
into motorsport at a very early age. His father, Jos Verstappen, drove in
Formula One between 1994 and 2003 with 106 race starts, no wins, 2
podium finishes, and a total of 17 world championship points. Jos separated from his wife, Sophie Kumpen, herself a kart racer, when Max was
very young. Max lived with his father while his sister remained with his
mother.

In light of the scrutiny that attends the relationship of Anthony

Hamilton with his son and the scrutiny of his personal life and finances, it is important to remark that Jos Verstappen is an incredibly controversial figure.

Jos and his father, Frans, were convicted in 1998 for assaulting a person at a karting track. The victim had a fractured skull, and the two Verstappens were given five-year suspended sentences and reached an out-of-court settlement with the victim. Our era takes violence against women seriously, and Jos Verstappen has been forced to defend himself against various charges on at least three occasions. During his separation from Sophie, Max's mother, Jos was charged and found not guilty of assaulting her but guilty for sending electronic threats and violating a no-contact restraining order. This resulted in yet another suspended prison sentence. Three years later, it was reported in the *Telegraph* that he had beaten his then ex-girlfriend. No charges were filed. A year later he was arrested for attempted murder, allegedly having run his girlfriend off the road. He spent a week or so in jail but was released when the charges were dropped. There is a pattern here that is never brought up surrounding Jos Verstappen, who is a fixture at race weekends.

Despite this turmoil, Max arrived in Formula One with Toro Rosso not even old enough to have a regular driver's license but supremely talented, blindingly fast, and reckless enough to earn the nickname, "Crash-stappen" because of his over-the-line tactics. Max matured to the point of being ready to compete for a championship. The frenzy of attention around the possibility of Hamilton's eighth championship, as well as the popularity of the Netflix series, created an electric environment.

The seventy-second edition of the FIA Formula One World Championship was scheduled for a full twenty-two rounds with the return of spectators. The unexpected death of Charlie Whiting, the long-term racing director, would have catastrophic implications for the season. His successor was Michael Masi, a man who should have been fired during the 2020 season. Masi created a profoundly dangerous circumstance by allowing cars onto the track for a qualifying session when there was a crane on the track at the Turkish Grand Prix.[1] This reckless disregard for procedures and the rules, and also allowing team principals to literally call him up during the race to lobby for their interpretation of rules, created a lawless environment with controversial or outright wrong decisions in Azerbaijan, Belgium, Saudi Arabia, and Abu Dhabi. There is an argument to be made that what turned out to be as an exciting season as one could hope for was in no small part the result of the dynamic incompetence of the race director, Michael Masi.

One of the policies that caused the most problems was that Masi allowed team principals to have direct access to him during the race. This led to a bizarre form of lobbying for results that would frequently devolve into shouting matches over the radio that were often broadcast on television. With all of that going on, the 2021 season was a riveting competition between Lewis and Max, who were first or second in fourteen of the twenty-two races. The season came down to six races: Azerbaijan, Silverstone, Spa, Monza, São Paolo, and Abu Dhabi. Two of these were referenced in the introduction, both of which featured the two antagonists coming together and upping the competition in negative ways—the crash at Silverstone that sent Max's car into the wall and the mess in Italy that put the Dutchman's car on Lewis's head. It was widely reported that after the contact that sent Max into the wall at Silverstone, Lewis was the victim of a deluge of racist attacks that even prompted Facebook to take down a great deal of commentary from its platform.

The Week UK went directly at this ugliness with an article by Mike Starling titled, "F1 British Grand Prix: Racism Overshadows the Racing," writing:

> …while the headlines today should have been all about the racing, the focus has shifted away from the track after it emerged that Hamilton was racially abused online following his victory.

---

1. Connor McDonagh, "Five High-Profile Mistakes Michael Masi Made as F1 Race Director," Crash.net, July 16, 2022, https://www.crash.net/f1/feature/1007954/1/five-highprofile-mistakes-michael-masi-made-f1-race-director.

There were racist messages including "monkey emojis" and other slurs in the replies to a Mercedes post on Instagram celebrating Hamilton's win at Silverstone, Sky Sports reports.

Formula 1, the sport's governing body the FIA and the Mercedes team issued a joint statement condemning the online racist abuse. "These people have no place in our sport and we urge that those responsible should be held accountable for their actions," the statement said. "Formula 1, the FIA, the drivers and the teams are working to build a more diverse and inclusive sport, and such unacceptable instances of online abuse must be highlighted and eliminated."[2]

This is all well and good, but no amount of outrage from the FIA and the teams would do much to address racism on the part of the public. The crash at Silverstone upped the vitriol surrounding the competition between the two and was the negative context for the dangerous crash at Monza that ended the race for both drivers. But the other four races are interesting for different reasons in what they reveal about the drivers, the officials, the fans, and ultimately our society. Silverstone and Monza reveal that neither driver was willing to give ground. Verstappen was making it clear to the seven-time world champion that he would not be cowed by that fact. Hamilton was sending the message that he was also not willing to be content with those titles. He wanted the eighth as badly as the first. Setting that to the side, it is the enduring image of Verstappen walking away from the scene of his car resting on the head of Hamilton without so much as asking if his rival was alive or dead that speaks to the difference in character or perhaps maturity between the two. After the spectacle of Max careening into the wall at Silverstone, Lewis bothered to ask after his health, and sources close to Hamilton say he also went to great lengths to contact him in the hospital. Character matters, and Lewis would need that and more before the 2021 season ended.

---

2. Mike Starling, "F1 British Grand Prix: Racism Overshadows the Racing," *The Week UK*, July 19, 2021, https://theweek.com/sport/formula-1/953541/f1-british-grand -prix-racism-overshadows-the-racing.

Recall that, in 2024, Hamilton was asked what race he would alter the results of, and of the three he offered, Abu Dhabi from the 2021 season is one. Abu Dhabi was decisive, but it is what happened in round six in Azerbaijan that defines the season.

————

FORMULA I AZERBAIJAN GRAND PRIX 2021
BAKU CITY CIRCUIT
BAKU, AZERBAIJAN
JUNE 6, 2021

LEWIS HAD WON ROUNDS ONE, THREE, AND FOUR, FINISHING AN unhelpful seventh in Monaco, where Max took the victory. Max won rounds two and five and the two arrived in Baku separated by four points: Verstappen 105, Hamilton 101. After setting the fastest lap in the race, Max ran into trouble on lap forty-three when he suffered a tire failure that sent him into the wall and out of the race. At the restart, Hamilton made a setup error with his braking and took himself out of the race when he was unable to complete an overtake of the other Red Bull driver, Sergio Pérez, at turn one. If we assume that the dominance of Hamilton had continued and he had pulled off the overtake of Pérez with one lap left, he would have left Baku leading the championship by twenty-one points rather than remaining four points behind Verstappen. This would have changed everything. Lewis knows this, and he knows it was his error that cost him what would have been an insurmountable lead in the competition. Instead, he would ask a genie to change the result of Abu Dhabi, a positive character trait. He is willing to live with his own mistakes and let them stand, fully accountable and self-reflective.

By the time the series arrived at Silverstone, Hamilton was thirty-two points behind Verstappen, who had racked up three straight wins with Lewis finishing second in the first two and fourth in the third in Austria.

After Verstappen's crash, the two left Great Britain separated by only eight points, with Max leading 185 to 177.

———

2021 Belgian Grand Prix
Circuit de Spa-Francorchamps
Stavelot, Belgium
August 29, 2021

This race, planned for forty-four laps, ended after one racing lap. Max Verstappen had qualified on the pole with Lewis in third position. The rain had created such difficult conditions that Sergio Pérez crashed on his way to the grid and was allowed to join the "running" after a lengthy delay. The race was finally started after three hours of delays and several botched starts; the race got underway from the pit lane behind the safety car for three laps, which made it an official race and awarded the drivers half points. The race should have been delayed until the next day or a time when there could actually be a competition. Lewis had come to Spa leading Verstappen by eight points. After Masi's bizarre decision-making, the series left with Lewis's lead cut to three points, 202.5 to 199.5.

———

2021 São Paulo Grand Prix
Interlagos Circuit
São Paulo, Brazil
November 14, 2021

Max enjoyed a comfortable nineteen-point lead when the championship made its way to Brazil, having scored victories at his home grand prix in the Netherlands, the US Grand Prix, and Mexico City, while Lewis had a second-place finish in the Netherlands, a retirement in Italy (the crash), a win in Russia, an anemic fifth in Turkey, and on the second stair in the US and Mexico. With only four races left, if Lewis did not turn things around, the championship was lost.

Lewis understood the stakes and produced perhaps the greatest single drive in the history of Formula One racing. Lewis qualified first with Max behind him. He was referred to the race officials because there was a problem with his drag reduction system (DRS) and was only allowed to participate in the sprint race at the discretion of the race managers. Lewis gave a hint of what was to come on Sunday, recovering to fifth place in sprint race qualifying but then receiving yet another penalty for replacing his engine for the race, starting Sunday in a potentially devastating tenth place.

On lap one, Lewis moved from tenth to seventh through the chaos of the opening moments of the race. By lap three he was in fifth place, moving halfway up the grid in less than 5 percent of the seventy-one-lap event. On lap eleven, the Mercedes pit wall ordered Valtteri to make way for the charging Hamilton, who was now in fourth place. Lewis was in third by lap seventeen and stalking the Red Bull of Sergio Pérez for the second step on the podium. The two traded positions during lap eighteen, and Lewis made the move permanent on lap nineteen.

The only car left was Verstappen, and the question in everyone's mind was whether the two could have an encounter that would leave both cars in the race. There was every incentive for Max to defend aggressively, within reason. On lap forty-eight, Lewis made a move on Verstappen, and Verstappen ran him off the course to the point that both cars were multiple car lengths from the raceway. The Red Bull team principal, Christian Horner, immediately and preemptively called up Michael Masi, the race director, to demand that no action be taken, saying that this is all about "letting them race"—which means that racing means running competitors off the track, leaving them to decide to crash or give way. It took Lewis eleven laps to overtake Max, finally realizing that he was never going to be able to make it happen on a curve because the Red Bull driver had been given the leeway by the stewards to run off the racing line to protect himself from being passed, so he did it on the straightaway, where it would have been obvious if Max turned into him. Lewis's miraculous drive left Verstappen ten seconds adrift, narrowing the gap to fourteen points, 318.5 to 332.5.

The post-race press conference set the stage for the epic finale to the season like no other. The Brazilian former F1 driver turned stock car driver, Felipe Massa, asked the opening questions:

Q: Lewis, it's very difficult to do the questions for you. You are not the driver of the day but the driver of the weekend. Yesterday what you did was just incredible. I saw your face after the race yesterday and today what you give, fighting and overtaking, and also for the people, really for me you were the driver of the weekend. Did you feel anything different because the people were supporting you 100% from yesterday?

LEWIS HAMILTON: I appreciate that, dude. I think I feel what it was like for you here with all the support in 2007 with your amazing country. I'm so grateful for the incredible support I've had this weekend. I've not had it since like Silverstone was when I had my own...a good group of support, but since then it's been really difficult. So to hear these throughout the weekend has been really humbling. I've been saying "obrigado, Brazil." I'm so, so grateful, as I said. What a race. The team did an amazing job, Valtteri did a great job today to get as many points as possible. I was pushing, you know how it is, just pushing as hard as I could. From last on the grid and then another five place penalty I think it was the hardest weekend I've had. But my dad...reminded me of 2004 when I was in Formula 3 in Bahrain, I started last and I finished 10th and then I finished first. So, this one's for my dad.

Q: Can you tell us about the overtaking and can you tell us about the next race? Is it extra help for you to fight for the championship and nothing to lose?

LH: Coming into this weekend I never, ever thought that we would be able to close the gap like we have today. These things that just kept going against us, but I think it shows for everyone, just never give up. Whatever you are facing you have just got to keep pushing, keep tumbling away and never, never stop fighting. And that's really how I've approached this weekend. Inspiration from all round. It feels like the first because I don't think I've had a win for a long time.[3]

Lewis has a long memory. He had lost the championship on this course in 2007 to Kimi Räikkönen and the next year had snatched the title from Felipe Massa at his home grand prix in the final corner. Even more so, Anthony's voice has returned to remind him of his drive to recapture his relationship with McLaren before he had even made it to Formula One. In Qatar and Saudi Arabia, Lewis notched two more victories, holding Max behind him and arriving in the final round tied, 369.5 to 369.5.

——————

2021 ABU DHABI GRAND PRIX
YAS MARINA CIRCUIT
ABU DHABI, UNITED ARAB EMIRATES
DECEMBER 12, 2021

PART OF OUR CULTURE'S PREOCCUPATION WITH SPORTS IS THE CLARITY. You win or you lose. Championships are the final word on the long journey of a season. The 2021 Formula One World Championship found itself in the midst of a tortuous and defining moment in the desert. Lewis and Max were tied. The season could not end in one, however. Max had more wins than Hamilton, so to the extent that they both finished without

3. "FIA Post-Race Press Conference—Sao Paulo," FIA, November 14, 2021, https://www.formula1.com/en/latest/article/fia-post-race-press-conference-sao-paulo-2021.Chc64SCMRTLVuxSHOAwvh.

scoring any points for one reason or another—both finishing lower than tenth, retirement, etc.—Max would be declared champion by virtue of having more first-place finishes than Lewis. For Hamilton, it was all or nothing. He had to finish ahead of Verstappen. Clarity. To make things even more clear, Masi warned the teams that any attempt to scuttle the race by a driver could/would result in sanctions. This was an implicit warning to Verstappen, who was the only driver who could benefit if both he and Hamilton failed to finish the grand prix.

But sports as we understand them are both too big and too small at the same time: too big for the right thing to be more important than winning and too small (ethically) to care about that position.

Max qualified on the pole with Lewis beside him. Their respective teammates were fourth and sixth, too far away to play a part in the critical run to the first corner. The race got off to a wild start. Lewis snatched the lead from Max. At turn nine, Verstappen attempted an overtake, once again running Hamilton off the course, who rejoined ahead again. Verstappen and his team took to the radio demanding that he give the position back, but the stewards determined that there was no more action necessary. For the moment, Masi was "letting them race."

Max pitted on lap fourteen and Lewis one lap later, leading by 27.5 seconds. Lewis was behind Max's teammate, who was leading the grand prix, not having come into the pits. Pérez's only job was to hold Hamilton up so that Verstappen could close the gap, and he did so for several laps. The gap closed to 1.5 seconds.

Things stayed like this until the final laps of the race. Lewis was now up by twelve seconds or more and looked to be headed toward his eighth world title with five laps remaining when disaster struck. It arrived in the form of a meaningless battle on the track between Nicholas Latifi and Mick Schumacher, the son of the legendary Michael Schumacher, for last place. Neither one of these drivers should have been in F1. Latifi's dad owned an international food company and bought his son a seat. Mick was simply not ready. Nicholas went into the wall with five laps left, causing the deployment of the safety car. Lewis stayed out and Max dove into the pit to get new soft tires. This unfolded like the Zapruder film: a slow-motion disaster.

By the time Max joined the safety car procession, there were seven lapped cars (trailing a full lap behind the leaders) between him and Lewis. First, Masi announced that lapped cars would not be allowed to overtake. What is supposed to happen is that once the debris is cleared, lapped cars are then able to step out of line and get past the safety car and the leader in order to get out of the way of the front-runners. With seven cars, that could take the better part of an entire lap. Then, the safety car is to make another entire circuit of the course before leaving with the race back on.

During lap fifty-seven of the fifty-eight-lap race with the safety out and the lapped cars still in the way, the Red Bull principal phoned a friend, calling Masi on the radio.

HORNER: Why aren't we getting these lapped cars out of the way?

MASI: . . . Because, Christian, just give me a second, OK? My main big one is to get the incident clear.[4]

The sports commentators wondered what was going on, noting that the safety car could come in this lap. Keep in mind what this means. There was only one lap left in the race. Calling the safety car in "this lap" means that first the lapped cars have to clear the safety car, then the entire procession is required to go one more full lap before racing can start, which means that the race finishes under the safety car, and Hamilton would win the race and his eighth title. Keep in mind that in Belgium, Masi had run a "race" three laps behind a safety car before awarding half-championship points that proved critical here. Instead, Masi ordered the lapped cars to clear the safety car, putting Max right

4. Jonathan Noble, "FIA Says Wolff, Horner Radios to Masi 'Neither Necessary Nor Helpful,'" Motorsport, March 22, 2022, https://us.motorsport.com/f1/news/the-abu -dhabi-radio-conversations-that-the-fia-felt-hindered-masi/9136719/.

behind Lewis with new tires. That shouldn't matter because there is still another (the final) lap to go holding place.

Masi made a different decision. He called the safety car in without the mandatory extra lap, leaving Hamilton a sitting duck on worn tires. Max passed him immediately and stormed the three miles around the raceway to take his first championship. The Red Bull team was jubilant. The Mercedes boss radioed a terse message to Masi: "Michael, this isn't right."

During all this, Lewis remained relatively quiet. He asked about the number of laps remaining and the status of lapped cars. The rest of the time he kept exhorting the safety car to go faster. What wasn't originally broadcast was Lewis's brief response when he realized that the rules had been thrown away in order to erase the advantage he had meticulously built over fifty-plus laps of flawless driving. "This has been manipulated, man."[5]

Lewis was as gracious as ever in the aftermath of this fiasco:

Q: Lewis, it's been an amazing season to watch for everyone, for the fans of Formula 1, whether you're a Max fan or a Lewis fan, it's been one of those seasons that's gone down to the wire, to the last lap of the race. It didn't go your way but you must be proud of what you have done this year?

LEWIS HAMILTON: Yeah, well firstly a big congratulations to Max and to his team. I think we did an amazing job this year. My team, everyone back at the factory, all the men and women we have, and here, have worked so hard this whole year. It has been the most difficult of seasons. I'm so proud of them, so grateful to be part of the journey with them. We gave it everything. This last part of the season we gave it absolutely everything and we never gave up and that's the most important thing.

5. "This Has Been Manipulated Man. Lewis Hamilton in Last Lap with Max Verstappen," posted December 27, 2022, by Your favorite channel, YouTube, https://youtu.be/K3wHJ6Xgbog?si=Ljb3lvMyZzL7e0U9.

Q: You obviously started a little bit on the back foot at the start of the year, but as you said you guys worked together and had a very strong end to the season. It didn't quite go your way, but I think we've seen the best Lewis Hamilton I've ever seen and you seem very confident in your ability to come back next year and fight for that crown again?

LH: Of course, I've been feeling good, feeling great in the car these last couple of months particularly at the end. If I'm honest, we are still in the pandemic and I just really wish to stay safe and have a good Christmas with all their families and we will see about next year.[6]

What sticks out is at that moment, Lewis was doubtful as to whether he would return for the 2022 season. One can imagine why he would feel that way. Mercedes filed an appeal against Verstappen's win but ultimately dropped it at Lewis's behest. He did not want to win a championship that way. In a perfect world, Max would have felt the same. He knows the safety car rules as well as anyone and knew they were altered to give him an advantage.

There is a world in some other 'verse where Max Verstappen does the right thing. The "sporting" thing. This isn't that world, because here sports are worth too much and too little at the same time. Too valuable to do the right thing and at the same time worth too little to do the right thing. There is a world where, despite the opportunity to drive past Lewis like he had pulled into a parking spot and in doing so snatching away Lewis's eighth world championship and winning his first, Max pulls in behind and follows Lewis across the finish line in the second place he deserved, not the first he didn't. This isn't that world, because winning means more than doing the right thing and that is a serious problem.

---

6. "FIA Post-Race Press Conference—Abu Dhabi," Formula1.com, December 27, 2022, https://www.formula1.com/en/latest/article/fia-post-race-press-conference-abu-dhabi-2021.6ZVMcPf5a762uWc1eVdFzU.

Masi was fired. A report filed by the FIA found that "human error" had marred the results of the race, but no corrective action was in the offing. In 2024, Lewis gave insight into the entire incident to *GQ* magazine in conversation with Daniel Riley.

> Were you robbed? I ask him.
>
> "Was I robbed? Obviously. I mean, you know the story. But I think what was really beautiful in that moment, which I take away from it, was my dad was with me. And we'd gone through this huge roller coaster of life together, ups and downs. And the day that it hurt the most, he was there, and the way he raised me was to always stand up, keep your head high. And I obviously went to congratulate Max, and not visualize the impact that that would have, but also I was really conscious of, like, there's a mini-me watching. This is the defining moment of my life. And I think it really was. I *felt* it. I didn't know how it was going to be perceived. I hadn't, like, visualized it. But I was definitely conscious of these next 50 metres that I walk is where I fall to the ground and die—or I rise up."
>
> I ask him if he fixates on that race.
>
> "If I see a clip of it, I still feel it," he says. "But I'm at peace with it."[7]

George Lucas crystalized all of this in the wake of this wreckage. He tweeted, Heroes are bigger than champions.

7. Daniel Riley, "Changing Lanes," *GQ*, April/May 2024, 52.

CHAPTER 21

ARISE

Three short days after the devastating events in Abu Dhabi, Lewis was summoned to Windsor Castle to be knighted by then Prince Charles. Lewis was silent after leaving the post-race press conference, but the world was abuzz with the unorthodox finish to the season. It was an unmitigated disaster for Hamilton, the fans, and the entire sport. Competition is built on a foundation of trust that a sport's officials will not put their fingers on the scale. Formula One could no longer make that claim. Lewis had willed himself to the championship. It is hard to imagine the spiritual toll it must have taken. Lewis's close friend Samuel L. Jackson tweeted his thoughts:

> I know all too well what it's like to have to defend yourself in public and sit back and watch your friends and family be silent. I can't do that. We shouldn't let Lewis Hamilton fight this alone. Life is

short. Tomorrow isn't promised and more time is not guaranteed for any of us. We shouldn't console him with 'next year.' For a full season we watched Lewis compete with Max for this title fairly and aggressively. Max is an incredible driver. He deserved all his wins this season. But he did not win this championship. Lewis, our brother, was robbed. For 57.5 laps he dominated. Sometimes he even led by 16 secs according to Red Bull's own status cards. F1 has been on a campaign to bring in a wider and diverse audience, but somehow continues to railroad its only black driver in the sport by making arbitrary last minute rules that consistently contradicts the previous ones. These rule changes seem to specifically affect Lewis the most. F1, [the] FIA may not do the right thing…And in that case they deserve lose us fans in the process. While this is entertainment overall and pales in comparison to many other issues we face: we shouldn't ignore that this man is part of our legacy as a people and this is his life's work he is being robbed of.[1]

Jackson, in another tweet, acknowledged the virtuosity of Verstappen's performance but found it hard to believe that anyone could objectively believe he had beaten Lewis in Abu Dhabi.

Lewis and his mother, Carmen Larbalestier, attended the solemn ceremony. The press release for the knighting said that it was to commemorate Lewis tying Michael Schumacher with his seventh title the year before. It must have added insult to injury to appear there knowing in his heart of hearts that he had actually "won" his eighth title.

Prince Charles met Lewis before that ceremony. In 2022, Hamilton joined the *Jimmy Kimmel Live!* show and recalled the time they met when he was thirteen and the fact that the prince recalled the occasion at the ceremony.

1. "Samuel L. Jackson: 'Lewis, Our Brother, Was Robbed,'" SilverArrows.net, December 21, 2021, https://www.silverarrows.net/news/samuel-l-jackson-lewis-our-brother-was-robbed/.

"I met him when I was thirteen. So when I went to McLaren—when I was thirteen years old, I was signed at thirteen years old—I went to the factory and he came to open the factory up.

"And so I was sitting in my go-kart where they have all the cars. And I sat there and he came and he knelt down and asked me what I wanted to do, what my dreams were, and told him one day I wanted to be Formula One world champion.

"I'm at the palace, and you have to take these certain steps to the prince. Very, very formal.

"You take three steps, turn ninety degrees, take another four steps, and then turn left. Bow two steps and then take the knee.

"And I took the knee and he puts the sword on your shoulders. I was very nervous cuz you feel like the sword might be very sharp or something.

"But when I got back up he's like, 'you've come a long way'"[2]

Lewis *had* come a long way. There is no debating that. It is hard to imagine a child, particularly in Britain, who has not fantasized about being a knight. Lewis has, by any metric, achieved everything he set out to do and established himself as the greatest driver the Brits had ever seen. He had received pushback from his countrymen when he received the MBE, the Most Excellent Order of the British Empire, from Queen Elizabeth in 2009 in recognition of his first championship, and the knighting made him the fourth British driver to receive the honor, joining Sir Jackie Stewart, Stirling Moss, and Jack Brabham. The pushback came because of his relocation first to Switzerland and then to Monaco, but after the MBE, Lewis made it clear that he loved his country, not really mentioning the need for radical and legal forms of tax avoidance. Whatever the case, he was entitled to be called "Sir" after the Prince of Wales tapped his shoulders with the sword and ordered him to "arise."

2. Jimmy Kimmel Live, "Sir Lewis Hamilton on Becoming a Knight!" Facebook, October 26, 2022, https://www.facebook.com/watch/?v=657347292612242.

The notion of rising had been a part of Lewis's motivational lexicon for many years. Maya Angelou's iconic poem "Still I Rise" had inspired him to have those words on his helmet and tattooed on the nape of his neck. Lewis endured difficult times, and none could have been more difficult than these, so the words from Angelou could not have been more poignant. They read in part:

> You may write me down in history
> With your bitter, twisted lies,
> You may trod me in the very dirt
> But still, like dust, I'll rise.
>
> Does my sassiness upset you?
> Why are you beset with gloom?
> 'Cause I walk like I've got oil wells
> Pumping in my living room.
>
> Just like moons and like suns,
> With the certainty of tides,
> Just like hopes springing high,
> Still I'll rise.[3]

LEWIS POSED FOR PICTURES WITH HIS MOTHER AFTER THE KNIGHTING ceremony. Then he disappeared. His social media presence went dormant, and he did not appear in public. Questions surfaced as to whether he would return to the sport. Even Toto Wolff, the Mercedes team principal, was not sure what would become of the team's relationship with Hamilton. There were good reasons to walk away. He had been robbed in the most blatant fashion, and it was clear that the FIA had no intention of doing anything about it. Lewis knew better than anyone in the sport

3. Maya Angelou, "Still I Rise," Poetry Foundation, https://www.poetryfoundation.org/poems/46446/still-i-rise.

what had to be done physically, mentally, and spiritually to win a title, and that assumes the rules of the sport are followed. How does an athlete gird himself for a competition when the rules are fluid?

Verstappen's win was not the result of a missed call by an official. This was an instant where the official decided, over an extended period of time, to alter the rules of the game in order to at least achieve what he deemed to be a more exciting finish, if not to ensure that Verstappen won. Hamilton and the strategists at Mercedes made the decision to remain on the track and keep track position because the rules dictated that it was the correct decision. It is analogous to the waning seconds of a game seven of an NBA final where a team is down by two points and makes a three-point shot as time runs out, but the officials call it a one-point shot "just because," and after the fact, the league admits to "human error" but does nothing about it.

Lewis's silence indicated that perhaps this was the last straw. After all he had dealt with during his career, the one thing he felt he could rely upon was that there were rules that were followed once the race started. There always have been and always will be bad calls, but this was something different, and Hamilton, according to sources close to these events, was ready to walk away with his seven titles and get on with his life. Sir Lewis had decisions to make.

After the fact, we have some details about what was going on. Mellody Hobson and George Lucas played an important role in Lewis's processing of the loss. The couple were in Abu Dhabi for the final round and pointedly didn't let Lewis know they were there until after the race. Hobson reached out to the driver and invited him to spend Christmas at their Caribbean residence, an invitation Lewis was assured was not optional. The plan was to avoid conversation about what had happened in the last race, but that is not how things played out. James Burns reported the details on the Jedi News website. Hobson framed the devastation that Lewis felt right after the race:

"He's really stunned," she remembers. "Stunned. Like shock.

He's asking the same question over and over again: 'What happened?' I grabbed him by both shoulders. I was like, 'You did
everything right.' I kept saying that to him. I said, 'It wasn't
you. You did everything right.' And he just literally said, like
four or five times: 'What happened?'"

Hamilton apologized for her coming all that way just to see
him lose. "That's why we came," she told him. "In case you
lost. We didn't come in case you won."[4]

The trip for Christmas proved to be cathartic.

Everyone there was instructed not to bring up what had happened, but many mornings he and Hobson found the other
awake at dawn. "And that's when we spent a lot of time sort of
going in and debriefing," she says. "And I just kept telling him
things like: We make no decisions in times of great anguish
or pain. You have to just sit with this, and it's going to be hard
and uncomfortable. But there's nothing to be done at this
moment. So do nothing."

Hobson told him that she would support him if he didn't go
back but also shared her belief that "this is what you do, and
you're not done."

On the fifth of February 2022, fifty-four days after the final race,
Lewis posted a picture of himself at the Grand Canyon with a short and
simple message, I've been gone. Now I'm back, on Twitter and Instagram.
The question would be, back to what?

4. Burns, "Lewis Hamilton and His Close Friendship."

CHAPTER 22

THE DOWN YEARS REDUX

2022 Austrian Grand Prix
Red Bull Ring
Spielberg, Styria, Austria
July 10, 2022

The world championship win under these controversial circumstances did not dampen the enthusiasm of Verstappen fans. That is fine; however, when the Championship Series made its way to Austria for Red Bull's home race, things got ugly. If you were led to believe that bigotry around Formula One was limited to incidents like the racism during testing in Spain in 2008 or the racist language from Nelson Piquet Sr., you would be wrong.

At the Red Bull ring in Austria sexist, racist, and homophobic abuse was reported.

An increasing number of reports were made on Sunday

morning, citing aggressive misogyny towards female fans, with some spectators saying they felt scared by the atmosphere. Others referred to homophobic slurs and the use of the N-word. Many of the reports referenced the stands where Max Verstappen fans were gathered en masse.

Mercedes and Hamilton were particularly distressed at the experience of one fan who contacted them. Her words were published on Twitter. She described: "five Dutch Max fans lifted up my dress and when I confronted them they said that no Hamilton fan deserves any respect at all." Mercedes contacted the woman in question and brought her to their garage to ensure her safety for the race.[1]

These incidents were universally condemned, and the two rivals from the previous year's championship both made statements in an attempt to stamp out a problem that was both dangerous and could get out of control. Lewis was categorical in his statement, writing:

I arrived with a really positive mindset this morning and then I heard of some of the things that had been said. It was a shock and I was really sad...Someone sitting in a crowd supporting someone and receiving abuse. It's crazy to think we are still experiencing those things in 2022, we have to do more. It highlights it's an issue all over and it comes down to education and ignorance. People should come here and feel included and follow who ever it is you want to follow. It should not matter about your gender, your sexuality, the colour of your skin.[2]

Verstappen expressed anger at the incident while at the same time

1. Giles Richards, "Lewis Hamilton Condemns Reports of Sexist and Racist Harassment of F1 Fans," *The Guardian*, July 10, 2022, https://www.theguardian.com/sport/2022/jul/10/lewis-hamilton-condemns-reports-of-sexist-and-racist-harassment-of-f1-fans.
2. Richards, "Lewis Hamilton Condemns Reports."

expressing "alcohol as potentially playing a role in the abuse, with clear evidence of excessive drinking taking place at the circuit across the weekend."[3] The fact of drinking was demonstrably true, but one has to wonder why intoxication doesn't seem to lead to inclusive rather than bigoted behavior. The FIA warned fans that anyone implicated in this behavior would find themselves banned from races for life.

As Hamilton states, the questions of education and ignorance are certainly at play, but the underlying cause seemed to be the notion that Verstappen had rescued the sport from the clutches of Lewis. This was not an issue of team rivalry or even national identity, which itself can be expressed as hatred but is often moderated. The racist nature of the attacks at the team and the global move to the hard right, especially in Europe, had found its way into Formula One. A month later, the incidents changed, but the motivation remained the same. At the grand prix in Budapest, fans were sighted burning Lewis Hamilton merchandise. Verstappen was asked about it after his victory and said, "Yeah, those videos, or video, of burning merch, I think that's disgusting."[4]

This is the "competition-plus" aspect of Lewis's journey in motorsports that has been a common theme since his days in RC racing. In addition to picking up the pieces from the 2021 season, he was also coping with a resurgence of bigotry around the races that echoes the worst parts of the 2008 season. There was more to deal with as well.

The 2022 season was one of dramatic change. Michael Masi was fired unceremoniously and replaced by two officials. That arrangement lasted until the last four rounds of the season when only one race director was certified, to the general disappointment of the drivers. The biggest change had to do with new aerodynamic requirements that were designed to introduce more overtaking in the sport. The cars were to

3. Richards, "Lewis Hamilton Condemns Reports."

4. Luke Smith, "Verstappen Condemns 'Disgusting' Burning of Mercedes Merchandise by Fans," Motorsport, August 5, 2022, https://us.motorsport.com/f1/news/verstappen-condemns-disgusting-burning-of-mercedes-merchandise-by-fans/10348872/.

be able to follow more closely behind their rivals for longer periods of time when before, staying too close to another car tended to cause over-heating and dramatic tire degradation. Mercedes-Benz, the manufac-turer that had mastered the previous era, dominated the constructors' race and delivered seven (eight, but who is counting?) championships to Lewis, decided to go in a completely different direction than other engineering concepts. To say they got it wrong would be like calling a Category 4 hurricane a summer breeze.

The car was universally deemed to be undrivable, particularly if the intention was to go fast. The car was plagued with what people in the field called "porpoising," which means that at top speed on straightaways, the car bounced like a forty-year-old used car with the original shock absorb-ers. Drivers began to complain of literally being injured from driving the car, and it was simply unmanageable. The Mercedes design was never able to get a hold on this, and for the first time in his career, Lewis did not win a race and never grabbed a pole position. He finished a dejected sixth in the championship, behind the fourth-place finish of his new team-mate, fellow Brit and talented driver George Russell.

Lewis had obviously endured difficult times before. That is why, when McLaren couldn't deliver a competitive car, he packed his bags for Mer-cedes, but even during those times he still won races. During the 2022 season he finished second five times and third four. The problem with that result is that in the last three races of the season, Lewis finished sec-ond, which made the group-think at Mercedes Benz believe the car had come around. They overruled Lewis's demand to rethink the design. They stuck with it, and 2023 was not much better. In many ways it was worse because the team should have known better.

In 2023, Hamilton's highest finishes were three second-place positions matched by three in third. Lewis did infinitely better in qualifying, scor-ing one pole as opposed to zero in 2022, and all the while, by the way, Max was racking up wins and three (in reality two, but who's counting) world championships. The Red Bull team had thoroughly beaten back Mercedes in the team race. Some pundits began to say that Lewis had lost a step, his career was over, and it was time to go away. That is difficult to take seriously when at the same time it was manifestly clear that Mercedes had botched the development of the car. Worse, they were quick to tell Lewis he didn't know what he was talking about.

Netflix's *Drive to Survive* had become the show of record for F1, the real info as it comes to what is going on behind the scenes. Season six, episode six is called "Leap of Faith." The gist of the episode is that Lewis and Mercedes were negotiating his new contract at the time, a process made more difficult because of the record the team and driver had earned; made more difficult in the sense that the business of driver contracts, especially in the latter years of a career, are fraught with competing interests.

Episode six is a poignant episode. There is a revealing scene with Lewis. Driver input is an imperative for getting the car right, because the engineers haven't driven the car and almost universally couldn't drive it fast if they could even get in it. Engineers have no idea what is going on outside of the data they receive from the wind-tunnel and simulators. These simulators are the technologically astounding product of applied math and physics. But the real world adds dimensions that are not part of these models, no matter how hard they try to replicate them. When a driver gets in the car and tests it, or better yet races the car, they need to be listened to—particularly if they happen to be the winningest driver in the history of the sport. Someone, somewhere in the upper reaches of the Mercedes Formula One establishment decided that Lewis didn't know what he was talking about, and what is unsaid but implicit in the driver's confession on Netflix is that he should shut up and drive the damn car.

Later in the episode, Hamilton meets with Toto and the scene is fraught with "it's not you, it's me," "let's start seeing other people" vibes before the two long-term partners fall back on what is easiest and stay together. The boss took accountability, putting it all on the table, and acknowledges that Lewis was not happy with him and his response to the driver's concerns about the development of the car. Now, Wolff says, it is time to "cut their losses and say that the concept of the car is never going to work...." Lewis doesn't say, "I told you so" but it is in the room, and as a practical matter, what would be the point?

Mercedes had wasted two seasons on an innovative concept that just happened to be worthless. There are new design regulations scheduled for 2026, and Toto lays out what he believes to be his closing gambit, telling Lewis that Mercedes does not intend to wait for 2026 to revise the car and will change direction immediately.

LEWIS: Frick, me neither. You can be here for, like 20 more years, 30 more years. I can't.

TOTO: Well, who says that?

LEWIS: This is precious years for me. [Awkward pause] I don't know.

Lewis has wasted a tremendous amount of time in a game where older reaches a tipping point, where the experience side of the ledger gives way to the diminished side of the ledger. "This is precious years for me." What Toto doesn't take into account and Lewis's nonverbal cues seem to be saying is that there is something going on here beyond the algorithms and bright ideas from aerodynamicists. There is a deep psychic wound that he suffered in 2021. The wound has scabbed over and seems to have healed, but the scabs only mask the real harm: the wounds to his spirit.

Lewis is a visionary. Lewis sees what he wants and moves toward it. In this same episode he says that he "can't really remember winning if I'm really honest. Uh, it's been, like, a minute, so I don't remember what that feeling is." If he can't create the conditions for recalling what it means to win, then he can't project it into the future. This goes all the way back to the intensity of his focus on *Blue Peter* with the remote-control car race that he refused to lose. It is what drove him through the field in São Paulo in 2021, which set up the race in Abu Dhabi and what should have been his eighth championship. But it all came to naught.

Then it gets worse. Lewis picks himself up and pulls his racing boots back on. He goes back into the ring to prove that Max only beat him because he got screwed. But Mercedes put him on the back of a horse destined for the glue factory while Max rode Secretariat.

Instead of 2022 being the equivalent of Ali's resolving the question with Joe Frazier at the Thrilla in Manila, 2022 looked a lot like "The Last Hurrah," when Larry Holmes ended Ali's career in a fight that should never have taken place.

Formula One is a sport of cycles. A team is up, then they are down and then up again. The question for Lewis at the time was whether he and Mercedes could find one more wave to ride so he could leave Formula One better than he found it, with more championships to his name than anyone else.

So he took a leap of faith and signed a two-year contract to stay with the manufacturer that he had been with since he was thirteen years old and try to end his career with Toto and the Silver Arrows. It was not to be.

CHAPTER 23

IT'S NOT YOU, IT'S ME...

MARANELLO, ITALY
PRESS RELEASE
FEBRUARY 1, 2024

THE MESSAGE UNDER THE ICONIC PRANCING HORSE AGAINST A RED FIELD was short and, to some ears, sweet: "Scuderia Ferrari is pleased to announce that Lewis Hamilton will be joining the team in 2025, on a multi-year contract." At 12:24 EST that same day, *Fortune* magazine reported that "[s]even time Formula One world champion Lewis Hamilton will make a shock switch from Mercedes to Ferrari for the 2025 season, and the market appears to like it. Ferrari's stock price rose more than 12% on Thursday following reports of the move, which would swell its market capitalization by $10 billion."[1] He's a businessman and a busi-

---

1. Sasha Rogelberg, "Ferrari Stock Rockets, Adding $10 Billion on Solid Earnings—and the News That F1 GOAT Lewis Hamilton Is Joining Its Top Racing Team," *Fortune*, February 1, 2024, https://fortune.com/europe/2024/02/01/why-is-ferrari-stock-rising-lewis-hamilton-formula-one-earnings/.

ness, man. What were the contract terms that led Lewis to head for Italy instead of finishing out his career with Mercedes?

Lewis had signed a two-year deal with the Silver Arrows, a contract that ended before the 2026 season and the new regulations. The contract with Mercedes was simply too short, and the technical difficulties and disrespect of Hamilton's input that plagued the relationship also did not help. Perhaps more important, it was unclear what the relationship beyond driving would be with Mercedes. Despite Toto's assurances, it was not contractually agreed that Lewis could be associated with the brand for twenty or thirty more years. At the end of 2025 Lewis was going to have to negotiate something new with Mercedes or somewhere else, and the quality of that agreement was solely dependent upon his performance in 2024 and 2025. He could not be sure that the team would give him the car that he needed to win an eighth championship. Finally, Mercedes was also uninterested in supporting Lewis's outside ventures. All of that opened the door for what is generally regarded as the most iconic brand in motor racing, Ferrari.

There is romance in the move to the surreal mystique of Ferrari that traces its lineage back to the culture of Italian design and art. In 2016, the artist Christo installed a work called "The Floating Piers" at Lake Iseo in Brescia, Italy, his first project after the death of his partner and collaborator Jeanne-Claude. When Christo was asked about leaving the United States, he referenced the constitutions of the two nation states. In one, the Second Amendment permits the possession of arms, and the other's constitution states in Article 9 that, "The Republic promotes the development of culture and of scientific and technical research. It safeguards natural landscape and the historical and artistic heritage of the Nation."[2] Enzo Ferrari's cars are art, and the canvas that they most urgently paint on is Formula One. Lewis joining the greatest brand in racing gives him the opportunity to create something special, and the people at Ferrari are into it, even before the bump in stock prices that proves them right.

---

2. "Constitution of the Italian Republic," European Union Agency for Fundamental Rights, https://fra.europa.eu/en/law-reference/constitution-italian-republic-23.

The financial terms are staggering. The French sports site Sportune reports that the contract is not just focused on the time he drives with Ferrari but many years beyond, something the folks at Mercedes were not willing to consider.

> This was the disappointment of Hamilton's current contract with Mercedes. However, the debate was long in the board of directors of the German manufacturer, but the quality of ambassador until 2035, proposed by the seven-time world champion, was refused. This rejection resonated with John Elkann, who for his part proposed developing Lewis Hamilton's empire. An agreement which could reach 400 million euros.
>
> The Ferrari boss's first proposal was spread over two seasons and 92 million euros (46 million euros per season). It was then early 2023. Hamilton politely declined, indicating that he did not want just one driver contract, but several deals to ensure the future of his foundation, Mission 44. The current deal would be for 80 million euros for 2025, plus an option for 2026. With around 20 million euros of this amount, delivered in the form of bonuses for the benefit of the pilot's foundation.
>
> The other part of the agreement with Ferrari concerns the after. John Elkann proposes to create a joint investment fund with around 250 million euros, via the Exor family business, in order to invest in Lewis Hamilton's projects and transform him into an ambassador for his own brand.[3]

John Elkann, the executive referenced here, was known to have a close personal relationship with Lewis. Perhaps more important, he was a long-term associate of Frédéric Vasseur, team principal of Scuderia

---

3. Marc Limacher, "Lewis Hamilton et Ferrari Vers un Accord à 410 Millions d'Euros?" Sportune, February 1, 2024, https://sportune.20minutes.fr/lewis-hamilton-et -ferrari-vers-un-accord-a-410-millions-deuros.

Ferrari. This is the same Frédéric Vasseur from the pre–F1 years of Lewis's career who was the manager of Formula Three Euroseries Championship team ASM. Ferrari had pulled themselves back into contention and boasted two young drivers who had proven they could win races, Charles Leclerc and Carlos Sainz. Sainz had to go to make room for Hamilton. Vasseur explained the rationale:

> "The input of Lewis or another driver is not just about qualification lap time and so on," said the 55-year-old.
>
> "It's the finality of the job. What we all collectively can see Saturday or Sunday, at the end of the day, the job of the driver is much wider.
>
> "It's starting sometimes six or eight months before the season, to be able to work on the next project, to bring his own experience, his own view on what we can do, or how we could do it and so on and so on.
>
> "We have time to discuss this with Lewis and, for me, into the building process of the team—you want to have a long-term view and for the next cycle.
>
> "I think we are going in the right direction. But for sure Lewis will add value."[4]

The risk-reward calculus for Ferrari is fairly straightforward and speaks to the reason that Mercedes-Benz was not in a position as a brand to make Lewis the kind of deal that works for the team in Maranello. Mercedes-Benz as an entity has been involved with Formula One since 1954 in one incarnation or the other. Ferrari was there at the beginning in 1950, and the series and the brand have become interrelated. You can go to the Mercedes-Benz manufacturer website and search until the cows come home for any evidence of Formula One. "Racing" is the first

---

4. Kevin McKenna, "Ferrari Boss Explains KEY Reason Behind Hamilton Signing," GP Fans, May 17, 2024, https://www.gpfans.com/en/f1-news/1020638/ferrari-boss-frederic-vasseur-explains-key-reason-behind-lewis-hamilton-signing/.

available tab at Ferrari.com. There are very few owners of Ferraris or those who dream of owning one who aren't aware of the Formula One connection, and Mercedes has, perhaps successfully, depending upon your perspective, effectively separated the racing from their luxury automobile business. That being understood, the request by Lewis for a long-term relationship with Mercedes was a big ask for a company whose clientele don't necessarily know who Lewis Hamilton is while he is racing and really likely couldn't care less when he has retired. This is a different matter for Ferrari, a company for whom its luxury car business is dependent upon its racing identity.

What that means for the Ferrari boardroom is that being the final stop in the racing career of someone many believe to be the greatest of all time is a long-term marketing tool—even more so to the extent that he has won an eighth world championship. When a Ferrari driver wins a grand prix, bells toll all over the Italian peninsula, and everyone is a proud member of the "Tifosi." The word derives from the Latin term "typhus" as in fever and describes, in the abstract, a fanatical supporter of a sports team but has come to define fans of Ferrari.

Every driver who has ever so much as strapped themselves into a kart let alone actually made it to the level of professional open-wheeled racing wants to drive for Ferrari. Sebastian Vettel, former Ferrari driver, perhaps said it best: "Everybody is a Ferrari fan, even if they're not; they are a Ferrari fan. Even if you go to the Mercedes guys and they say, 'Oh yeah, Mercedes is the greatest brand in the world,' they are Ferrari fans."[5]

That is all very important to Lewis, whose father confirmed in the aftermath of the move that this was always in the back of their minds. He wrote on Twitter: Part of my dream, part of his dream. It's one of those things; when you're a young kid, you always dream of racing for Ferrari. We love all of the past teams, McLaren and Mercedes but it's the ultimate dream to be in a red car.

5. @4_f1clips, Tiktok, https://www.tiktok.com/@4_f1clips/video/71677280728069 27622?lang=en 19 November 2022.

How will the Tifosi receive Lewis's insistence upon the continuation of the Mission 44 project? If Mercedes was of concern to the driver, then the reality at Ferrari presents an even greater challenge. Some might say, what do they have to lose? Ferrari has not won a championship since Felipe Massa eked out a one-point victory over Lewis in 2007, and its last constructors' title was 2008. Lewis hit a dry patch but not one that has stricken the Scuderia. Italy, at least in its limited experience, has not been kind to athletes of color in the past. Soccer star Mario Balotelli's career was plagued with controversy, much of it related to the sport's struggles with racism and his mercurial behavior. Lewis is not Balotelli.

This will be the final test of Lewis's grand experiment. To the extent that he diversifies Scuderia Ferrari and brings a world title back to Maranello, fair-minded observers will have a data point that proves diversity just doesn't look good, it wins. Ferrari has made a commitment to be in the Lewis Hamilton business for the next fifteen to twenty years, and the question for the driver is whether the Italian sunshine will help him remember what it feels like to win again.

And what of Mercedes and this final season? At the outset, when the shock wore off, Toto Wolff presented an upbeat message and committed the team to a kind of "farewell tour" that would include a triumphant trip back to the top of the sport to send him to Maranello in style. The results have not lived up to that ambition, and he presented this complex circumstance in an interview in February 2024:

> "We have a year to go, we have 2024 together," Wolff said. "We want to make it the most successful we can.
>
> "Is it realistic that we are competing for a world championship against Max in a Red Bull? You know I'm a probability person, and the odds are against us. But nevertheless, we will give it our best shot."
>
> Wolff did, however, clarify that once Hamilton has left, the Brit securing an eighth title will no longer be his priority.

"When we talked about giving it all for an eighth, that is Lewis in a Mercedes. Lewis in a different car is obviously a totally different story.

"We will be giving it everything we have to win drivers' and constructors' championships in the years to come in the same way as we want to win it in 2024, but maybe with another driver.

"But it doesn't take anything away from historic legacy that will always exist. This journey together will be in the history books, as much as the next journey of a Mercedes driver will hopefully also be there.

"The friend side in me that says he should have an eighth because that was taken away from him. So if he wins that in 2024, that would be a great thing. Going forward, competing on track, I'd rather us win."[6]

The reality of their relationship has been much less ideal. Lewis has been on record asserting that he doesn't expect to out-qualify his teammate George Russell this season.[7] At the 2024 Canadian Grand Prix, Lewis was at the top of the timing sheets until the third round of qualifying, making it appear that he might break his losing streak at the same racecourse where he won his first. In Q3, the car went away from him mysteriously, and it was later revealed that the warmers on his tires prior to that round were set two to three degrees Celsius below where they should have been. He was never able to get his tires to the temperature they had been throughout practice and qualifying, leaving him a dismal

6. "Lewis Hamilton: Toto Wolff Says Mercedes Driver's 2025 Move to Ferrari Was 'Not a Surprise' and He Holds 'No Grudge,'" Sky Sports, February 3, 2024, https://www .skysports.com/f1/news/12433/13062142/lewis-hamilton-toto-wolff-says-mercedes -drivers-2025-move-to-ferrari-was-not-a-surprise-and-he-holds-no-grudge.
7. "Hamilton Not Expecting to Out-Qualify Russell for Rest of 2024 as He Explains 'Frustrating' Saturday Struggles in Monaco," Formula1.com, May 26, 2024, https:// www.formula1.com/en/latest/article/hamilton-not-expecting-to-out-qualify -russell-for-rest-of-2024-as-he.3J8lul5XzzRhTk5saMSpyq.

seventh with George Russell on the pole. This was .2 of a second or so back, a differential fully accountable to tire temperature. Russell ultimately finished third, losing two places, with Lewis in fourth, gaining three. The feeling is that the relationship is broken, and both Mercedes and Hamilton cannot wait until 2025.

CHAPTER 24

AND STILL I RISE

Met Gala
Metropolitan Museum of Art
New York, NY
May 6, 2024

We will end where we started. This isn't a finish line; it is another lap. In 2024, the theme of the Met Gala was "Garden of Time," and Lewis was in attendance. He was, of course, stopped on the red carpet by model Ashley Graham and model/actress Gwendoline Christie, who were interviewing guests for *Vogue* magazine. Lewis explained his Burberry look that was styled by Eric McNeal and the fashion house's Daniel Lee. It was meant to pay homage to Wales's first Black gardener, John Ystumllym. "John" was kidnapped as a child from West Africa and sometime in the mid 1700s, he was transported to Wales, where he trained as a horticulturist. Hamilton explained the inspiration:

> "What I love about the Met, and what Anna [Wintour] does with the Met, is that I'm able to really deep dive into

the theme. I did a lot of research and I came across this eighteenth-century gardener who, through slavery times, came across from Africa to Wales and became the first black gardener in Wales.

"Through adversity, he really triumphed, so that's where the inspiration really came from."[1]

Lewis wore a thorn-inspired necklace that was meant, in his words, to recall the pain of slavery and its aftermath. Inside of the jacket, he had a copy of a poem by Alex Wharton that commemorated the life and example of John Ystumllym. It reads in part:

The Gardener

. . . I am the Gardener.
I clear things up, make good.
Plant seeds, watch them grow.
Mist and light, Moss and bark.
I know where wind moves.
Why birds sing. My thoughts drift—
wrap and climb like clematis.
Nothing separates me from
this land, but the cries of
my mother. A dream or
nightmare. A mixture of both.[2]

Lewis is signaling a great deal here. The message is in many ways a response to his awkward and revealing conversation with Toto Wolff during the "Leap of Faith" episode on Netflix. Toto tells Lewis that there

1. "Lewis Hamilton on His Black History–Inspired Met Look," posted May 6, 2024, by Vogue, YouTube, https://youtu.be/Nq4Y47xNVkQ?si=PfXdFdbWkD6obozT.
2. "Discover Alex Wharton's Poem 'The Gardener,' Inspired by the Life of John Ystumllyn," posted October 24, 2022, by caddwales, YouTube, https://youtu.be /NomyyXgCvgQ?si=p2IuEMhls_57a8U4.

is no reason he cannot be associated with Mercedes for decades to come, saying that he "is one of the people who leads this team forward." That is all well and good, but it does not appear to be what Lewis has planned for his life.

Gwendoline Christie also brings up racing at the Met when she notes that Lewis had just come from the Miami Grand Prix and was there that night to "represent racing." He first responds with a benign "not really," thinks about it, and then lands on a firm "no."

What Toto did not understand about Lewis is that the chances of us seeing him in an advisory role for a team, or hanging around to do podium interviews, or being the type of disgruntled ex-driver who garners attention by clowning the younger drivers are something less than zero. Similarly, Christie didn't seem to understand that Lewis represents so much more than racing. But Lewis knows that for him, Formula One is a garden. Like John Ystumllym, he has planted seeds that are being carefully cultivated. The poem he carried with him to the Met to commemorate the possibility in the problem of slavery is the key to understanding what motivates this athlete. "I am the Gardener. I clear things up, make good. Plant seeds, watch them grow."

The seed that Hamilton has planted in the world of Formula One has borne truly staggering fruit. As of the writing of this book, Hamilton continues to rewrite the record book. After a truly dismal start to the 2024 season, Lewis was victorious at his home race, Silverstone, breaking several records in doing so. He added "Winningest Driver at the Same Grand Prix" with nine victories at Silverstone. That win was seventeen years and twenty-seven days after his first win in Canada in 2007, making it the longest time between first and "last" wins—"last" being in quotes because he will likely win more races. At 39 years and 182 days he is the oldest winner in the twenty-first century and also the first driver to win a race beyond their three hundredth start. Lewis holds the record for the most wins, 104, and on June 21, 2024, his third-place finish in Hungary awarded him his two hundredth podium in Formula One, extending the record he has held since 2020. He holds the record for the most consecutive wins at the same grand prix, five in Spain from 2017 to 2021, which is one of a series of other "mosts." They include most wins in a debut season (4), most wins with the same team (83), most wins at most different circuits (31), most wins from pole position (61); which makes sense since he also holds the record for the most pole positions, 104. Hamilton holds the record for the most seasons with a win (16), most consecutive seasons with a win (15), most wins in a calendar month (4), and most career points, 4,749.5. This could go on; he is still racing, and his longevity will continue to put these records far beyond the reach of other drivers, but Formula One is only one aspect of this amazing life.

Sir Lewis Hamilton is bigger than racing. Its rules and the things that matter to it are too small to contain his radically optimistic and inclusive ambition. Sir Lewis wants to challenge the world to be better. George Lucas was correct and deserves the final word. *Heroes are greater than champions.*

ACKNOWLEDGMENTS

THIS BOOK BENEFITED FROM THE SUPPORT OF THE DAVID C. FREDERICK Honors College at the University of Pittsburgh. Dean Nicola Foote and Brett Say, the director of the Honors Research Program, were kind enough to provide me with the invaluable research assistance of the intrepid Abby Feather.

This project would never have gotten off of the ground without the perpetual support of Pat Cruz, my agent Faith Childs, and Carrie Bloxson. Obviously, books can't be published without publishers. The visionary leadership at Legacy Lit—Krishan Trotman, Tara Kennedy, Amina Iro, Maya Lewis, and Mahito Indi Henderson—have made this dream real. Also, the world-class editing of Andy Rogers cannot be erased. Thank you. Closer to home, Manya Whitaker offered encouragement when I didn't believe this would ever happen.